Caminante, son tus huellas
el camino y nada más.
Caminante, no hay camino;
se hace camino al andar.
Al andar, se hace el camino...

Antonio Machado

Traveller, your footprints
are the only road, nothing else.
Traveller, there is no path;
you make your own path as you walk.
As you walk, you make your own road...

Linda Dangoor

FROM THE TIGRIS TO THE THAMES

Flavours of a Journey

A COOKBOOK

This book is dedicated to my mother for teaching me
the love of food and cooking and more.
To my father whose love of Ibiza and everything
Spanish was infectious.
To my husband for being my chief taster and my soulmate.
And to my family, extended family and friends
for their love and support.
And finally to London which is my home today.

Linda Dangoor

FROM THE TIGRIS TO THE THAMES

Flavours of a Journey

A COOKBOOK

Green Bean Books

Contents

"Every story tells a story that has already been told"

Umberto Eco

Storytelling is part of what it means to be human, enchanting us, taking us into another world, connecting us to others.

This book is my story.

I WAS BORN IN BAGHDAD IN 1949 into a Babylonian Jewish family where my parents and forebears come from. My early childhood ambition was to be a writer – a writer in Arabic, the language that I loved so much. As a very young person, I wrote short stories and poems on lined paper, then sewed the pages together to form books and designed covers for them using calligraphy for the titles. I practised the beautiful Arabic calligraphy for hours, marvelling at the swirly black marks I made.

Once upon a time... so start all stories.

Iraq was a monarchy until 1958 when a military coup overturned it and it became a republic. That event altered the course of my family's life, and mine, forever. In 1959, we left Baghdad for Beirut, Lebanon, where I swam for the first time in the Mediterranean sea and where my taste buds exploded.

Two years later, we emigrated to the UK. A year or so after our arrival in London, the Iraqi government dictated that if we did not return, our citizenship would be withdrawn, and the entirety of our rights and property seized. We did not return.

Thereafter, without a passport, we could only travel by means of a travel document: a '*laissez-passer*'. In effect, we became stateless. We were invisible. Leaving our country to live among strangers felt like a dismantling of our identity.

Four thousand five hundred kilometres span the distance between Beirut and London with about the same separation in culture and climate.

I was 12 years old. It was my first taste of exile. In Baghdad, home was the centre of my world. It was who we were – who I was. And in that first year in London, I was faced with a new language, a new set of rules, and a new world. Over time, we spoke less and less Arabic at home. My parents encouraged my brothers and I to only speak in English to each other, so as to integrate more rapidly. Over the years, I stopped writing short stories in Arabic. I stopped drawing my calligraphy.

It dawned on me then that exile was more than just moving from one country to another, it was also about loss; one of which was home and community and the other was language.

And is not language the equivalent of home and belonging, just as food is? In which language now to express my thoughts? In which language now to dream?

My mother suggested I study art at school. That opened my life to expression in the visual language of drawing and painting. It led me to art school, where I studied painting and graphic design at the Central School in London. I subsequently worked as a designer, first in London and then in Paris where I lived for many years.

I returned to London in 1994. It was yet another beginning. Modern British cuisine. Husband. There, by happenstance, I met a potter who introduced me to clay. Touching this malleable, sensual material was a revelation. A love at first touch. I immersed myself in the world of clay. In the beginning, I made dishes and bowls. Containers that spoke of nourishment and plenitude – asking to be filled with food.

And of course, food had always played an important part in my life. The love of it has pushed me to explore, more and more, the cuisines of different countries and cultures. It led me to write my first cookbook, *Flavours of Babylon*, in which I share and celebrate the flavours and recipes of my Baghdadi heritage.

My love of food is the thread sewn into the pages of this book.

Introduction

"...the past is a country from which we have all emigrated..."

Salman Rushdie – *Imaginary Homelands*

In our modern world, many of us are now part of not just one, but many cultures and groups. We are where we have trod and more. So it is, that since my family's exile from our Iraqi homeland in the late 1950s, I have inhabited and sojourned in many countries and the word 'home' has taken on another, somewhat fragmented, meaning. Is Home where I was born; or where I have put down roots? Is Home a dish or perhaps a flavour? As Salman Rushdie so aptly put it, our "identity is at once plural and partial"*. And this plurality, this mingling between cultures, has enriched my own identity – and also the food that I cook today.

We are where we have trod and more.

Each journey that I took to a new country brought with it the hope of a new beginning and the possibility of putting down roots. During those years, I encountered new languages and new traditions and, like a rolling stone, collected stories and new flavours along the way. Thus, *From the Tigris to the Thames* is not a formal cookbook. It does not focus on a specific cuisine as

* Salman Rushdie, *Imaginary Homelands*

my other book, *Flavours of Babylon*. Rather, it is a tapestry, part memoir and part cookbook, where I interweave recipes with personal reflections on the idea of home and belonging.

Our identity is at once plural and partial.

It comprises six chapters. The first five trace the move from Baghdad to Beirut; then from Beirut to London; and from London and Ibiza to Paris. These chapters include recipes which are, in the main, from countries that hug the Mediterranean basin where the Arab conquests and the Jewish diaspora left their culinary marks.

The book culminates in chapter six, in *The Return Home*, my ultimate journey from Paris to London, where I invite you to my kitchen to share with you the dishes that I cook for our family and our friends: predominantly salads, fish and vegetable dishes; some chicken and meat dishes, as well as sauces, dips and desserts.

This book is a tapestry, part memoir and part cookbook.

We humans have always used food to define who we are, to which community or group we belong, and wherein our rituals and traditions are inextricably entwined. Today, more than ever, food continues to define us: we are vegetarians, vegans, pescatarians, carnivores, omnivores – each requiring specific meals, be it wheat-free, gluten-free, dairy-free, nut-free, or fat-free – and so it goes on. Consequently, cooking for my family and friends has gradually become a more complicated affair, inspiring me to create varied menus to accommodate everyone. And this diversity is reflected in this book, which I hope will find favour (and flavour) in your kitchen.

Baghdad

Chapter One

Home

Baghdad 1949–1959

Let me tell you a little about my childhood home.

It stood very close to the Tigris river with only a narrow road separating it from the water's edge. Seen from afar, it resembled a large grey cube.

Its outer walls of raw unpainted concrete did not boast of any remarkable features, except for a decorative relief running along the roof's edge, two thin columns which framed the wooden entrance door, and the simple balustrades that surrounded the balconies and the flat roof.

At the back of this sober building, however, there nestled an enchanting walled garden, where as children we spent magical afternoons playing while the adults looked on from the terrace above. During the hot afternoons, the fragrant sighs of jasmine and orange blossom would drift from tree to tree, infusing the garden with their delicate perfume, and, flowing upwards, they enveloped the balconies and terraces too.

Before my parents married, the house was already populated by many family members: my father, his parents, his three brothers, two sisters, sister-in-law and uncle. As was the custom, my mother came to live in that house when she married my father. A few years after I was born, I acquired two brothers and three cousins – all boys. Our tradition of living with various family members meant that our home was always buzzing. You could say we were a tribe; a society in miniature.

There was a certain comfort and security in that traditional way of living. We felt protected and supported. It helped us children become social beings and taught some of us what it meant to share with others. Of course, it also promoted favouritism and fierce competition at times. For the adults, in hindsight, it might have been a different story. Living as a mini society under the same roof could have engendered some friction, but we were not aware of it.

To us kids our home was paradise.

Living with a gang of boys, I sometimes wished I had a sister, a soulmate, because I felt so outnumbered, and because, regardless of their merit, boys enjoyed more of a status in our culture than girls. I felt this injustice keenly. Even at that tender age, I knew girls were equal to boys and could do as well. So I became one of the boys. All of us attended the same school, and although we made many friends whom we saw at school or on the occasion of a festival or a birthday party, we did not actively seek their company as we had each other.

Afsa

WHENEVER A CHILD WAS BORN (six were born in a matter of nine years in our house) the women got together to make an *afsa*, an Iraqi amulet, which was traditionally placed on a newborn's cot for protection against misfortune and the evil eye. There was one for the mother as well which she would pin on her jacket or on her pillow.

Depending on the family, some of them were made of gold with precious stones; others were simpler with a small blue or turquoise stone. A small *afsa* that includes a garlic clove – again for protection – was included in the *shassha*: a parcel filled with nuts, popcorn and sweets, given as a present to family and friends on the arrival of a baby girl. Today, this is also done for the birth of a baby boy.

The evil eye has been and still is considered the curse of a malevolent gaze associated with envy. This is a very old belief or superstition that many cultures around the world share, even today, and is particularly widespread around the Mediterranean region and North Africa. Amulets and talismans are still crafted today as a protection.

These come in different designs and in different materials: garlic; salt; horseshoes; *Hamza* hands and eyes, are all designed to ward off the ill intentions of the envious or the Devil himself.

The colour blue is believed to protect the wearer from misfortune, and there is a belief that too many compliments can provoke the opposite. Thus, even compliments are not welcomed by those who see them as disguised sentiments of envy. For many, being humble and low key has been a way of avoiding the evil eye.

Summers were always unbearably hot.

Our skin tingled and itched, even indoors. On occasion, even the earth became parched, cracked and arid while the hot wind ushered in waves of fine sand that covered everything it touched, making the landscape monochrome and ghost-like.

To escape the heat at night, all of us slept on the roof of our house. Water to slake our thirst was furnished in a long-necked, fat-bellied, unglazed earthenware pot, which kept the water amazingly cool and which was accompanied by five earthenware goblets. I still remember the refreshing smell of the damp earthenware and the rough feel of the unglazed cup against my lips as I drank.

During these summer months, fishermen would bring in their catch every night (usually *shabbut* or *biz*, oily river fish, similar to carp) and would barbecue them over a brushwood fire on the banks of the river. These fires could be seen dotted all along the shores, delineating the river's meandering route and illuminating the night with a soft glow.

The fishermen butterflied the fish, brushed them with oil and seasoned them with herbs and spices. Then, each fish was impaled on wooden stakes, planted in the ground and grilled at an angle over the open fire. This way of cooking the fish is Iraq's iconic dish called *samak masgouf*, or simply *masgouf*. The fish was then sold to the many passers-by.

And while we lay in bed, gazing at the stars, we would slowly drift into the arms of Morpheus, lulled by the smoky aromas from the *masgouf* rising up to our roof from the river below.

The fisherman butterflied the fish, brushed them with oil and seasoned them with herbs and spices.

Masgouf
Aromatic Barbecued Fish

Masgouf used to be one of the popular dishes for parties and celebrations. Alas, it is very difficult to reproduce its taste without the aromatic brushwood fire. A way round this is to barbecue an oily fish such as carp, trout or sea bream (ideally in a clamshell grill with a handle) seasoned beforehand with herbs and a spicy marinade. Pan-frying, grilling or baking are acceptable alternatives.

The fish must be at room temperature.

SERVES 4

2 whole sea bream 450g/1lb each, gutted and butterflied or

4 sea bream or haddock fillets, 185g/6½oz each

3 small shallots, thinly sliced

a handful of cherry tomatoes

fresh parsley, roughly chopped, to garnish

FOR THE MARINADE

1 tablespoon each, curry powder and tomato purée

1 teaspoon salt

1 teaspoon ground turmeric

1 teaspoon Aleppo pepper

½ teaspoon bouillon powder

4 plump garlic cloves, pressed

juice of ½ lemon

7–8 tablespoons olive oil

- Preheat the oven to 180°C Fan (200°C/400°F/Gas Mark 6), or prepare your barbecue.
- Put all the marinade ingredients in a jar and shake to blend.
- Place the fish in a roasting tray or a large ovenproof dish. Pour the marinade all over the fish, and massage gently.
- Scatter the shallots and tomatoes around the fish and bake for about 15–20 minutes (depending on the thickness of your fish) until the fish is cooked through.
- Turn off the oven, leaving the fish to rest in the oven for about 5 minutes.
- Remove from the oven and baste the fish with the marinade in the tray, then garnish with the parsley.

→ Serve with rice or boiled potatoes.

Note: if you wish to barbecue the fish, marinate as above, keeping some of the marinade for basting. Place the fish in a clamshell grill or straight onto an oiled grill and baste every so often during cooking.

At dawn, like clockwork,

we were awakened by the boisterous alarm of the rooster. The sun began its ascent, bathing the rooftops with a warm orange hue. These were moments of complete stillness. From afar, a soft rippling sound of water could be heard – a man in his *balam* (small boat) was rowing. Our swimming lesson in the Tigris was soon to begin. And thereafter, breakfast: *qeimar* (clotted cream) and date syrup, eggs and *amba* (page 25), fried aubergines and hot *khubez*.

The Tigris river flowed directly in front of our house. Every day, slow barges and small boats bobbed along on it; women washed clothes in it, and men their heads of lettuce. An energetic river the Tigris – I used to watch it at length sitting on the balcony. That river was where I learned to swim with my brothers and cousins. It was where my husband learned to swim, where most of my school friends learned to swim. It was there too that we picnicked in the summer on the *jezra* – those sandy islands that would pop up when the water level was low. And because of its fast current, our swimming instructor would run from our starting point to catch us up at the finishing line, as the current perilously pushed us along.

The river's name in Arabic has its roots in the old Persian language, meaning fast, pointed or speedy. The Babylonians and Akkadians called it Idiqlat, which eventually gave rise to the Arabic name Dijla. In ancient times and until the beginning of the last century, *kuffas* or coracles – circular boats made of bundles of reeds and waterproofed with bitumen – were extensively used on the Tigris for transporting people, goods and animals.

Emerging from the Taurus mountains of Turkey, the Tigris flows into Iraq in parallel with its sister river, the Euphrates, crossing the whole country from north to south, and thence, into the Persian Gulf. A very important transport route in ancient times where, because of the rich sediment and silt deposits, the river was a vital lifeline for the agricultural settlements dotted along its banks.

The Tigris was a big part of our life.

It spoke of stability to me. Like a parent or a guardian watching over us, it was Permanence, in a land which would eventually see so many changes and experience so many upheavals.

But nostalgia has no place here, for I know full well that, were I to go back today, I would feel a disconnect, an un-belonging. In the same way as Adam and Eve, who, once out of the Garden of Eden, could no longer return because they had been changed. We too have been uprooted and deeply transformed. So what I carry within me are sensory connections, early imprints of familiar sounds, of language, of flavours, of perfumes. This is the soil in which my roots are planted.

I can still hear the voices of the older boys,

money in hand, scrambling over each other at the counter of our school's tuck shop, clamouring for *amba* (page 25) and half a samoon (Iraqi bread). This combination of bread stuffed with pickled mango made a cheap and tasty sandwich for lunch, and is still very popular to this day. We had one commercial brand of bottled *amba* in Baghdad called 'Ship'. This is the original product which, in my opinion, has not been bettered. You can now buy it in London in Iraqi grocery stores.

Amba has an Indian origin and is one of the few hot spicy condiments we use in our Iraqi food. The name comes from the Indian Marathi word meaning mango, which in turn came from the Sanskrit word, *amra*. It is believed that, in the early 19th century, it was the Iraqi Jews (living and working in Bombay – as it was then called) who, inspired by the local pickles and chutneys, created the relish as a product for export.

Bottles of *amba* were exported to Iraq via the port of Basra and, since then, it has become the national Iraqi 'ketchup'. Simply made with sour mangoes, vinegar and spices, it differed from the Indian pickles because it did not include oil or ghee and, by using unripe, sour green mangoes, it made the flavour sharper and lighter, very much to the liking of the Baghdadi palate.

Since its first journey from India to Iraq, *amba* has made another journey. This time all the way to Israel, brought by the Babylonian Jewish refugees who arrived there in the 1950s. The condiment spoke their language, kept them rooted and, with it, they retained their identity in that new and foreign land.

Today, *amba* has become very popular in Israeli and Palestinian restaurants alike, in the same way as *zaatar*, humous and tahina, but it remains resolutely Iraqi.

Amba
Pickled Green Mango Condiment

Although this condiment is readily available to buy, why not try your hand at making *amba* at home? Initially, I used apple cider vinegar and ripe green mangoes: both of which are sweet – contrary to the required tartness of this condiment. You need to use unripe green mangoes and white vinegar.

MAKES
about 1 litre/35fl oz/4¼ cups

2 large green unripe mangoes, peeled, stoned and sliced

½ teaspoon each, cumin and mustard seeds

120ml/4fl oz/½ cup white vinegar, or as needed

1 tablespoon curry powder

½ teaspoon each, cayenne pepper and ground turmeric

¾ tablespoon each, salt and ground fenugreek

250ml/8fl oz/1 cup water, or as needed

- Dry-fry (roast) the mustard and cumin seeds in a frying pan on medium heat and, as soon as they begin to pop, add the vinegar, curry powder, mango pieces, turmeric, fenugreek, cayenne pepper, salt and water, and bring to the boil. Then simmer for 5 minutes, stirring and roughly crushing some of the mango pieces with a fork.
- Transfer the mixture into the sterilised jar. The mango has to be covered completely. If not, add a little more vinegar.
- Close the jar and leave to pickle in a cool, dry place for a week or two before consuming.

Note: this pickle will keep for many months. Remember to use a clean, dry spoon or fork each time you scoop some out.

"Nana, how much flour?" I asked my grandmother.
"Not much, a cup or two. And add the water."
"How much water?"
"As much as the flour can take.
And then mix and knead the dough."
"For how long should I knead it?"
"When your arms begin to ache, the dough is ready."

Many recipes were often explained in this way. It was only by watching and recording every step, during the making, that I could finally end up with a precise recipe.

Bread accompanied all our meals, as did rice. The general Arabic name for bread is khoubez. In Iraq, we had many types. The most popular and typical are samoon, a white bread shaped like an elongated diamond or boat with two pointed ends, and khoubez, a large round wholewheat flatbread traditionally baked in a *tannour* (clay or stone oven) with many air bubbles on its surface which appear during baking. This was my favourite. Without a *tannour* or stone oven, it is difficult to achieve the same texture and quality. The recipe below is for pocket flatbreads. They make great sandwiches, filled with anything you desire.

Khoubez
Flatbread

MAKES
8 flatbreads

½ teaspoon honey

120ml/4fl oz/½ cup warm water

180g/6¼oz/1¼ cups strong white bread flour, plus extra for dusting

¼ teaspoon salt

1 teaspoon fast-action dried yeast

2 tablespoons olive oil

- Mix the honey with the warm water.
- Sift the flour into a mixing bowl. Add the salt on one side of the bowl and the yeast on the other side. Make a well in the middle and add some of the water. Stir with a spoon until you have a shaggy dough with some of the flour still unincorporated. Then, stir in the rest of the water and the olive oil.
- Knead well in the bowl for a good 10 minutes until you achieve a smooth, elastic dough. Cover the bowl and set aside in a warm place for about an hour or two until the dough doubles in size.
- Punch the dough, then tip it onto a lightly floured worktop and divide into 8 pieces. Roll each piece into a ball and smooth down the sides of each one, making sure there are no cracks, otherwise the bread will not puff up. Cover again and leave to rest for 15 minutes.
- Take one ball at a time and slowly roll it out flat, turning it after every roll to achieve a circle.
- Lightly oil a frying pan and heat the pan to very hot. Place the rolled-out circular dough onto it, lower the heat to medium, then after 20 seconds, turn the dough over. Keep turning and patting it down with a spatula until it puffs up and is slightly golden on both sides.
- Place the bread on a plate and cover it with a tea towel. Before cooking the next one, wipe the pan clean to remove any debris and then lightly oil it again. Repeat as above.

→ Serve warm. You can also sprinkle some of them with *zaatar* and olive oil.

These soft bagel-like rings, are known in Arabic as *ka'ak*.

They are very popular in Iraq, Turkey and the Levant, each country and each family making them in a slightly different way. Some are made sweet, akin to biscuits, with sesame seeds sprinkled on top; others more bread-like, seasoned with spices. In our Baghdadi family, fennel was the star flavour. A mixture of seeds and spices were ground beforehand from which a tablespoon or two were incorporated into the dough. This spice mixture had the advantage of keeping for a month or two in the fridge, ready to be used for many subsequent bakes. My friend Samira Balas took time one day to show me how she makes her *ka'ak*. Below is a combination of her recipe and one given to me by Amanda Ellis, with whom I have often baked these bracelets.

The uncommon spices in the ingredients list can be found in most Middle Eastern shops.

Ka'ak
Soft Wheat Bracelets

MAKES
about 18–20 rings

FOR THE SPICES

100g/3½oz ground fennel seeds

½ tablespoon ground nigella seeds

½ teaspoon ground *mahlab**

½ teaspoon ground fenugreek seeds

¼ teaspoon ground cardamom (optional)

FOR THE DOUGH

¼ teaspoon granulated sugar

300ml/10fl oz/1¼ cups warm water

350g/12oz/2½ cups strong white bread flour

150g/5½oz/1 cup strong brown bread flour

1 teaspoon fast-action dried yeast

½ teaspoon baking powder

1½ teaspoons salt

2½ tablespoons of the mixed spices

4 tablespoons light olive oil

1 egg, beaten, for the glaze

- First grind a batch of spices which can last for many subsequent bakes. Store them in a glass jar in the fridge.
- Mix the sugar with the warm water.
- In a large bowl, sift both flours and mix in the dried yeast, baking powder, salt and the measured mixed spices. Mix in the warm water. Then, add the oil and mix until the dough comes together. Knead the dough on your lightly floured worktop for at least 10 minutes, until it is pliable and smooth.
- Place the dough in a lightly oiled bowl. Cover it with a damp tea towel or cling film and leave to prove in a warm place for about 3–4 hours until it doubles in size.
- Then punch it to release all the air and cover. Leave to prove again until it doubles in size.
- Preheat the oven to 200°C Fan (220°C/425°F/Gas Mark 7).
- Line two oven trays with baking parchment.
- Once risen, punch the dough again and knead it for a few seconds and then shape it into a thick roll. Divide the roll into 50g/2oz pieces, covering them with a tea towel as you work. Gently roll out each piece into a long sausage and cover again as you work.
- Take one sausage at a time and gently roll it out again into a longer sausage. Then shape each sausage into a ring and press the two ends together. Place the ring on the lined oven tray and cover as you work.
- Lightly brush the top of each ring with the beaten egg to glaze. Bake for about 9–11 minutes or until lightly golden. Transfer to a wire rack. The *ka'ak* should be soft and not crisp.

→ Serve warm.

Note: you can sprinkle some sesame seeds on the tops after the egg wash, if you like. Store in the fridge or freezer and warm them before serving.

*An aromatic spice with a slightly bitter almond flavour. Used in small quantities, it sharpens sweet foods and cakes.

Most days, our home tasted of rice. Rice and spice, cardamom and cumin, and rosewater too.

Our kitchen, situated at the back of the house, was quite dark, with a deep red terracotta tiled flooring. It had only one small window, positioned so high up the wall that I could only see the sky through it. There was a door at the other end, with a net curtain to let in fresh air and keep the flies out. It opened onto the outside courtyard where a mulberry tree grew and where the *tannour* resided. Only wafer-thin unleavened bread (*jaradouq*) for Passover was baked in our *tannour*. All the other cooking was done indoors on the gas hob. We did not have a modern electric oven in the kitchen. Instead, a hermetically-sealed metal box specifically made to be placed on top of the hob, acted as an oven. *Makhbouz* (sweet and savoury pastries) and cakes were baked in it.

In one corner of the kitchen sat a large, majestic mortar and pestle. Made of solid brass, it was a permanent fixture and an important implement in any Middle Eastern kitchen. Many a morning you could hear the rhythmic hammering and pounding of the heavy pestle coming down on some dried limes, crushing them to be included in a stew or in the stuffing for *arouk*.*
At other times, it was engaged in pulverising rice into a flour for making *kubba* paste (made of rice and minced meat to cover the meatballs) in preparation for a sweet and sour dish.

In the early 20th century, the Jewish quarter in Baghdad was a collection of narrow streets, always crowded, with houses built so close together that – so the story goes – you could overhear your neighbours' conversations. My aunt Eileen depicts a colourful and sonorous picture of walking to school with her sister through these narrow lanes, to the rhythmic pounding of the mortar and pestle echoing all around like church bells.

* Arouk is similar to a burger in shape. It is made out of a rice and fish (or meat) paste which is filled with a citrusy fish or meat stuffing. The arouk is first boiled and then fried.

One just knew it was Friday. Every Jewish household was preparing the *kubba* paste.

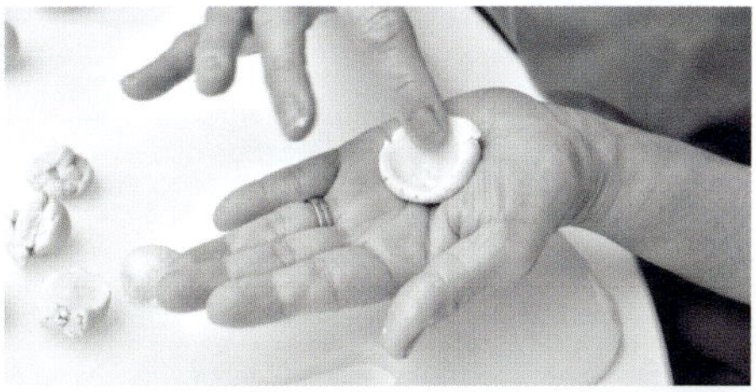

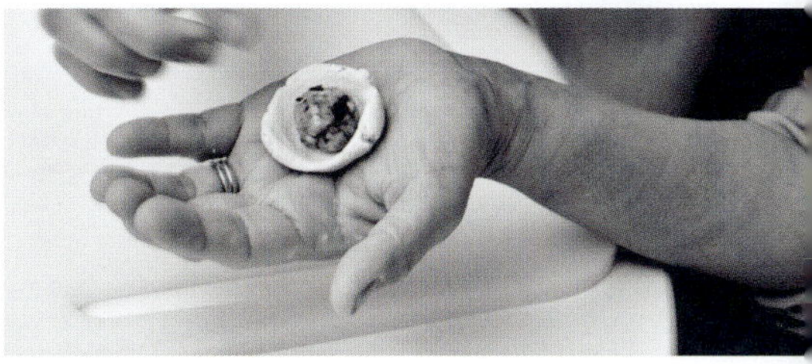

For as long as I can remember, *kubba* was our traditional Friday lunch. We had either *kubba bamia* (*kubba* with okra, page 32) *kubba shwandar* (with beetroots) or *kubba hulwa* (with courgettes).

In my time, we no longer lived in that neighbourhood. Nonetheless, I still heard this repeated pounding emanating from our kitchen every Friday morning just as we were getting ready to go to school. My paternal grandmother, Nana, was the only one who made the *kubbas.* No one else was permitted to give her a hand. She made small *kubbas* covered in paper-thin shells. "Small kubbas are nicer to the eye and mouth" she used to say, "... some people make them far too large." My grandmother had what the French call a *doigté;* a skilful agility of the fingers to perform intricate tasks. At the time, it was said that a woman's worth was judged on how thinly she made her *kubba* shells – the thinner the better.

Kubba Bamia
Okra Kubba

MAKES
about 40 small kubba balls. You will need 450g/1lb of minced meat in all.

400g/14oz frozen or fresh okra (if using fresh, wash and cut off the tough stems without slicing the okra pod itself)

2 tablespoons finely chopped fresh mint, to garnish

FOR THE SHELL
125g/4½oz minced lamb or beef

250g/9oz/1 cup fine ground rice

½ teaspoon salt

a pinch of freshly ground black pepper

FOR THE FILLING
325g/11½oz minced lamb or beef

1 teaspoon fine matza meal or fine dried breadcrumbs

4 tablespoons finely chopped fresh parsley

½ teaspoon salt

a pinch of freshly ground black pepper

FOR THE SAUCE
1 large onion, finely chopped

2 tablespoons olive oil

400g/14oz tin chopped tomatoes

1 tablespoon tomato purée

2–3 garlic cloves, finely chopped

500ml/18fl oz/generous 2 cups water or vegetable stock

1 teaspoon salt

a pinch of freshly ground black pepper

2–3 tablespoons pomegranate molasses

3 tablespoons granulated sugar

juice of 2½ lemons

- Place all the ingredients for the shell in a bowl or a food processor with 2–3 tablespoons of water and knead or blitz into a smooth pliable paste.
- Set a bowl of water near you. Wet your hands and then roll them into balls about the size of a small walnut and arrange them on a tray.
- Mix all the filling ingredients together in a separate bowl.

TO MAKE THE KUBBAS
- Wet your hands again and lightly flatten each paste ball as thinly as you can. Then place a teaspoon of the filling in the centre of each.
- Gently gather up the sides of the paste to cover the filling completely and roll each into a ball. Arrange on a tray and set aside.

THE SAUCE
- Sauté the onion in the olive oil until soft and golden, about 15–20 minutes (use a pan wide enough to cook the *kubbas* without overcrowding them).
- Stir in the tomatoes, cover and simmer on a low heat for about 25 minutes, stirring occasionally. Add the tomato purée, garlic, the water or stock, the salt and black pepper. Bring to the boil and continue cooking for 5 minutes.
- Next, gently drop the *kubba* balls, one at a time, into the sauce. The liquid should cover them completely. If not, add some more hot water. Pop the lid on and cook on a medium heat for about 20 minutes or so.
- Gently nestle the okra in between the balls. Bring back to the boil and simmer for about 20–25 minutes.

- Mix the pomegranate molasses, sugar and lemon juice together and add to the pan. Do not use a spoon to mix, just gently shake the pan from time to time and simmer for another 10 minutes.
- Taste and adjust the seasoning and the sweet and sour flavour. It should be sweet with a sour edge. The sauce should be thicker at the end, almost honey-like. If not, cook for another 5 minutes.

→ Garnish with the chopped mint. Serve with plain basmati rice.

Variation: a quicker way is to make the okra dish with meatballs only, leaving out the shell. Just make the balls with the meat filling and proceed as above. The flavour is great too.

The rhythm of our festivals structured our year and the weekly routine of the Sabbath grounded us.

With so many of us in the house for whom to cater, it was more practical for the adults to take their meals downstairs in the dining room, while us kids ate separately upstairs. This was the daily norm for us, with the exception of Saturdays and special feast days and festivals, when we joined the adults in the dining room. Every Thursday we had *kitchrie*, a vegetarian dish of rice, red lentils and fried eggs, and every Friday we had rice and fried fish for dinner. The preferred meat was lamb, which we ate on most days.

As no cooking nor any kind of work is permitted on Saturdays, all the preparation for the Sabbath meal was done the day before.

Traditional *t'beet* with a whole chicken.

An ingenious method of slow cooking was devised whereby a whole chicken, stuffed with rice and spices, buried almost completely in rice, was cooked in a large pot overnight for over 12 hours. The slow cooking gave the dish a much richer and deeper flavour. A dozen eggs were placed on the lid of the pot to cook in its heat and steam. The eggs would be covered with another lid, which in turn was covered with numerous towels to keep the heat from escaping (very much like a tea cosy). The pot was left to cook slowly on charcoal embers until the next morning. This method provided hot brown *t'beet* eggs for breakfast and a hot chicken meal for lunch.

This chicken dish is to the Sabbath what turkey is to Christmas, but with one exception – we had it every Saturday, 52 times a year.

T'beet Express with Brown Eggs
Chicken Buried in Aromatic Rice

I used to cook *t'beet* in the traditional way, by stuffing a whole chicken and slow-cooking it overnight. People are now reluctant to make this dish because it is quite time-consuming.

The recipe below is very easy and quick to prepare. It calls for chicken pieces rather than a whole chicken.

The spices are the most important ingredient, cardamom and cinnamon being the star spices that give *t'beet* its traditional taste. I grind the cardamom and cumin for a more intense flavour. I sometimes add a few eggs on top of the rice to get the brown *t'beet* eggs, but that is optional.

FOR THE CHICKEN

600g/1lb 5oz/3 cups basmati rice

4 tablespoons olive oil

4 chicken drumsticks

4 chicken thighs

1 onion, finely chopped

1 plump garlic clove, roughly chopped

2 tomatoes, finely chopped

2 tablespoons tomato purée

750ml/26fl oz/3½ cups boiling water

4 eggs (optional)

FOR THE SPICES

1 teaspoon ground cumin

1½ heaped tablespoons ground cinnamon

1½ tablespoons ground cardamom

1½ tablespoons baharat or mixed spice

½ teaspoon ground ginger

½ teaspoon paprika

1 teaspoon salt

¼ teaspoon freshly ground black pepper

¼ teaspoon Aleppo pepper (optional)

a good pinch of ground cloves

SERVES 4–6

METHOD

- Rinse the rice several times until the water runs clear and then leave to soak while browning the chicken.
- In a large, non-stick, oven-safe pan with a tight-fitting lid, heat the olive oil on medium heat, add the chicken pieces, season with salt and pepper and lightly brown them on both sides.
- Transfer to a plate and set aside.
- Preheat the oven to 200°C Fan (220°C/425°F/Gas Mark 7).
- In the same pan, add the onion and sauté until softened. Stir in the garlic, then the tomatoes and tomato paste and continue cooking for 5 minutes, stirring occasionally. Then return the chicken pieces, mix in the spices and cook for another minute.
- Drain the rice and scatter over the chicken. Pour the boiling water over them and place the eggs (if using), on top. Bring to the boil, cover and transfer to the preheated oven.
- Bake for 30 minutes. Then lower the heat to 160°C Fan (180°C/350°F/Gas Mark 4) and bake for an hour.

→ Serve in the oven pot or carefully arrange the chicken and rice in a serving dish with the eggs and crispy *hakaka* on top.

Note: if you are not ready to serve, lower the heat to 100°C Fan (110°C/225°F/Gas Mark ¼) and keep baking for another 2–3 hours (this will get the eggs really brown) and serve whenever you are ready. The dish won't burn.

To create our sweet and sour sauces,

we used pomegranate molasses and date syrup, as well as quinces and lemons, dried limes and Seville oranges, with or without tomatoes. This combination of fruits in savoury dishes is a Persian influence which dates back to medieval times, if not earlier. Today, tomatoes are ubiquitously used to make a sauce, but before tomatoes spread to Europe and beyond, different fruits were pressed or added whole to enrich the simmering stews. The Babylonian Jews have retained this sweet and sour tradition in most of their stews and stuffed vegetables.

When in season from the middle of autumn, quinces were made into jam and enjoyed with cheese. Of course, quinces were also included in savoury dishes. Paired with lamb, the recipe opposite was Maman's, my maternal grandmother's speciality which she made in the winter for special occasions. The combination of the sweet and slightly tart quince with the savoury lamb makes for a flavoursome marriage.

Hums b'Sfargal

Sweet and Sour Lamb and Quince Stew

SERVES 4 OR MORE

2–3 quinces, washed, cored and cubed

3 tablespoons olive oil

2 onions, grated or roughly chopped

3 garlic cloves, pressed

600g/1lb 5oz lamb shank or shoulder, de-boned and cubed

2 tablespoons tomato purée

about 800ml/28fl oz/3¼ cups water

3 tablespoons lemon juice

1 tablespoon granulated sugar

2 tablespoons pomegranate molasses (optional)

a handful of chopped fresh parsley, to garnish

FOR THE SYRUP

400g/14oz/2 cups granulated sugar

250ml/8fl oz/1 cup water

3 green cardamom pods, lightly crushed (optional)

FOR THE SPICES

1½ teaspoons ground cinnamon

1 teaspoon ground cardamom

1 tablespoon Aleppo pepper

½ teaspoon freshly ground black pepper

1½ teaspoons salt

Note: this dish is best cooked a few hours or a day in advance to allow the flavours to intensify.

- Mix the syrup ingredients together in a saucepan and heat gently. Do not allow it to boil.
- Once the sugar has melted, add the quince pieces, pop the lid on and simmer gently for about 30 minutes. (You want the quince to soften but not fall apart.) Set aside.
- In a large, heavy-based pan or ovenproof casserole, heat the olive oil and sauté the onions until soft and golden. This will take about 15–20 minutes. Add the garlic and cook for another minute.
- Mix all the dry spices together and tip them in the pan. Stir-fry for a scant minute. Add a few drops of water to loosen the mixture. Turn up the heat, add the lamb and brown on all sides, stirring occasionally. Mix the tomato purée with 5 tablespoons of the water and stir it into the lamb mixture. Then, cover and simmer for about 15 minutes.
- Raise the heat to high and stir the lamb mixture until it's sizzling. Very gradually, pour in the remaining water in stages and scrape the bottom of the pan to loosen the lovely brown bits at the bottom. Then bring to the boil for a minute or so. Pop the lid on and simmer gently for 1 hour. (Be careful not to burn the bottom and keep an eye on the water level, adding a dash more water every so often if needed.)
- After an hour of braising, stir in 2 tablespoons of the quince syrup and then nestle the quince pieces in between the lamb. (You can keep the rest of the syrup in the fridge to poach some other fruit.)
- Mix in the lemon juice, sugar and pomegranate molasses. Cover the pot and simmer for another 30–40 minutes or until the lamb is very tender and soft and the sauce is thick and honey-like.
- Taste and adjust the seasoning to your liking. If the stew is too thick, loosen it with a little water. If it's too sweet, you can add some more lemon juice. Let the stew rest for at least 20 minutes before serving.

→ Garnish with some chopped parsley and serve with plain basmati rice or couscous.

The name *louzina* originates from the Middle Persian, *louzinaj,* *

a paste made with sugar and *loz* (almonds). *Louzina* (a Jewish-Iraqi confection and speciality, made with quinces and decorated with ground almonds) is probably the precursor to the Spanish *membrillo* which has a softer texture. Those who make *louzina* are always very appreciative when offered some because they know how much work and elbow grease goes into making them. I have to admit, it is time-consuming. It needs much stirring to achieve the right texture, but the end result is worth the trouble. The use of a food processor shortens the work.

Nana, my paternal grandmother, was the one who toiled to make our much-loved *louzina*, which she infused with cardamom and rosewater, cut them into diamond shapes, like *baklawa,* and topped them with ground almonds.

Most households made it at home then, and a few still do.

* Rodinson, Arberry and Perry. *Medieval Arab Cookery.*

Louzina
Diamond-shaped Quince Sweets

MAKES ABOUT 30 SWEETS

7–8 quinces (about 2.5–3kg/5lb 8oz–6lb 8oz)

granulated sugar (see method – you need 70% of the weight of fruit in sugar)

500ml/18fl oz/generous 2 cups water

4 tablespoons rosewater

3 teaspoons ground cardamom

½ teaspoon lemon juice

350g/12oz/3½ cups blanched and ground almonds

- Wash, peel and quarter the quinces, removing the pips and the hard core, then dice them into small cubes.
- Weigh the fruit. You need 70% of its weight in sugar. If you have a sweet tooth, you can increase to 75–80% of sugar. The traditional ratio, which I find too sweet, is 100% of sugar to the weight of fruit, making it extremely sweet.
- Steam the quince for about 50 minutes or until very soft, testing with a fork from time to time.
- Tip the sugar into a heavy-based pan with half the water and bring to the boil. Then simmer until the sugar has melted.
- Add the rest of the water, the steamed quince, the rosewater and 1 teaspoon of the ground cardamom. Mix well, cover the pan and bring to the boil. Then cook on a gentle heat for 25 minutes, stirring occasionally.
- Place the quince mixture in a food processor and blend into a smooth purée.
- Transfer the purée to a heavy-based pan and bring to the boil. Then, cook on medium heat for an hour or more, stirring frequently, until the purée starts to thicken. Be careful because it splutters as it cooks. The purée will thicken and the colour will deepen yet further.
- You will know that the quince paste is ready when you have to stir with more vigour and it does not stick to the sides or the bottom of the pan. To make sure, take a teaspoon of the paste, let it cool down completely and then roll it into a ball. If it holds its shape and doesn't stick to your fingers, it is ready.
- Take the pan off the heat and stir in the lemon juice until well combined, then stir from time to time until it cools down considerably.
- Transfer the paste onto a rectangular tray and smooth it out evenly into a rough rectangle to about 2cm/¾in thickness.
- Mix the ground almonds with the remaining 2 teaspoons of ground cardamom. Sprinkle and press half the mixture into the paste. You will need the rest for the topping.

Continued overleaf

- Refrigerate until the following day.
- The chilled paste will have hardened. Cut it into small diamond shapes, using a ruler to achieve uniform shapes.
- Turn the pieces over and gently press the rest of the almond and cardamom mixture into them. Then, leave them out for a few hours to dry before storing them in a container, covering each layer with a sheet of baking parchment.

→ Store the *louzina* in the fridge – they will keep for several weeks. Serve at room temperature. You can also freeze them for several months.

WE WERE SIX: my three cousins, my two brothers and I, fighting over thin pieces of glistening white lamb fat, ensconced on long skewers in between the lamb pieces. There was never enough for everyone. I still remember the smoky taste of the slightly burnt edges of the fat and the lushness of it in my mouth.

In Iraq, we had a special breed of sheep called the fat-tailed sheep. Unlike British sheep and lambs, whose fat spreads all over their bodies, the Iraqi breed stored most, if not all, of their fat in their large and very heavy tails. We had a specific name for this fat; we called it *leeyeh* in Arabic (not used to designate any other fat) which shows you how special it was. An early mention of this fat as *alya*, in Hebrew, can be found in the Bible in Exodus and Leviticus, when describing a sacrificial offering.

I couldn't think of eating it today. But, in those days, animals were reared differently. They foraged all day in open pastures, so consequently, had a delicious and distinctive flavour.

During my grandmothers' and mother's time, date syrup, *silan*, was made at home.

Every year an artisan, specialising in making the syrup, would arrive pushing his huge press to extract the juice of perhaps a hundred kilos of fresh dates. The machine had a wooden or metal platform at the bottom and another one at the top, both of which were attached to a lever for pulling it up and down. Sandwiched in between were about 15 or more shelves called *khassafa* in Arabic. These were flat mats made of interwoven cane strands, similar to a basket weave, which acted as a sort of strainer. A quantity of dates were spread out on all the mats and compressed together by pulling down the heavy wooden top, thus yielding a stream of dark sticky syrup (my grandmother would call them 'rivers').

The syrup would last throughout the year and was used in many ways: at breakfast mixed with tahina (sesame paste) as a spread on bread; with *qeimar* (the thick buffalo cream similar to clotted cream) or in cooking our sweet and sour dishes. Its flavour is earthy, rich and less sweet than honey; a little amount goes a long way. It works very well with chicken or turkey.

Jars of Basra date syrup are available in Middle Eastern shops in London.

Silan Chicken

Chicken in a Date Syrup Marinade

SERVES 4

8 Medjool dates, halved and stoned

4 chicken thighs, skin-on, bone-in

4 chicken drumsticks, skin-on, bone-in

FOR THE MARINADE

85ml/3fl oz/⅓ cup date syrup

2 tablespoons balsamic vinegar

1 teaspoon grated lemon zest

3 tablespoons lemon juice

60ml/2fl oz/¼ cup water or chicken stock

6 tablespoons olive oil

3 plump garlic cloves, finely chopped

¼ teaspoon ground cumin

a good pinch of cayenne or Aleppo pepper

1 teaspoon salt, or to taste

- Mix all the marinade ingredients together.
- Place the dates, chicken thighs and drumsticks in a wide pot. Pour the marinade over them and massage well into the chicken using your hands. Leave to marinate at room temperature for 30 minutes.
- Cover the pot and cook on medium-low heat for 40 minutes, basting frequently, or until the chicken is thoroughly cooked. (Add more water if the sauce dries out.)

→ Serve with plain rice or sweet potato mash.

Pomegranates arrive in the autumn, in time for Rosh Hashana,

our Jewish New Year, gracing the dinner table (among other symbolic foods) with their abundant seeds, symbolising fertility and charitable deeds for the year ahead. We also used pomegranates and their juice to enhance many a savoury dish. One example is *Fasenjun*, a Persian dish adopted by the Iraqis many moons ago and considered an Iraqi dish today. It was traditionally cooked with duck, now chicken is favoured instead. Some cooks shred the chicken quite finely, making it indistinguishable from the sauce after long cooking.

Here, I have left some of the pieces more or less intact. As for the pomegranate fruit and molasses, you can find these in Middle Eastern shops and some supermarkets. If you prefer to buy the seeds already picked out of the fruit, you will find them packaged in some supermarkets along with other peeled and chopped fruits. This dish is best cooked a day in advance.

Fasenjun
Chicken in a Pomegranate and Walnut Sauce

SERVES 4

250g/9oz/2½ cups walnut halves

60ml/2fl oz/¼ cup olive oil

4 chicken thighs, skinned and boned

4 chicken drumsticks, bone-in and skinned

2 onions, grated or very finely chopped

3 tablespoons tomato purée

½ teaspoon ground cinnamon

2 teaspoons salt, or to taste

a good pinch of freshly ground black pepper

600ml/20fl oz/2½ cups water or chicken stock

4 tablespoons pomegranate juice

3 tablespoons pomegranate molasses

2 tablespoons lemon juice (about ½ lemon)

3–4 tablespoons granulated sugar or honey

FOR THE GARNISH

fresh pomegranate seeds

chopped fresh parsley

- Lightly toast the walnuts in a frying pan on medium heat until lightly coloured, about 8 minutes, being careful not to let them burn, then allow to cool. Once cooled, grind 200g/7oz/2 cups of them to a medium-fine texture and set aside.
- Roughly chop the rest of the walnuts and set aside.
- Heat the olive oil on medium heat in a pan (wide enough to hold all the chicken pieces in a single layer) and lightly brown the chicken on all sides. Take out the chicken and set aside.
- In the same pan, sweat the onions on medium-low heat until very soft and just coloured, about 15–20 minutes.
- Stir in the tomato purée, cinnamon, salt and black pepper and cook for a minute or two.
- Add the water or stock and mix.
- Stir in the ground walnuts and cook on medium heat for 30 minutes, stirring frequently.

- Return the chicken pieces to the pan, baste with the walnut sauce and cook, half-covered, for another 40–45 minutes, stirring occasionally. Add a little more water if the sauce thickens too much.
- Stir in the roughly chopped walnuts, the pomegranate juice, pomegranate molasses, lemon juice and sugar or honey and simmer, half-covered, for another 25 minutes.
- Taste and adjust the sweet and sour flavour to your liking.

→ The dish is now ready to serve. Garnish with a sprinkling of pomegranate seeds and chopped parsley. Serve with plain rice or saffron rice.

Note: for a deeper flavour refrigerate overnight before reheating with ½ cup of extra pomegranate juice and serving the next day. The sauce will thicken and become dark brown and honey-like.

Shaa'reeya Rice
Vermicelli Rice

SERVES 4–6

500g/1lb 2oz/generous 2½ cups white basmati rice

4 tablespoons olive oil

100g/3½oz dried vermicelli

½ tablespoon salt

650ml/22fl oz/2¾ cups water or vegetable stock

- Rinse the rice until the water runs clear, then soak in cold water for at least 30 minutes, up to a few hours, or overnight.
- In a heavy-based, non-stick pot, heat the olive oil, then add the raw vermicelli and toast on medium heat for 5 minutes or until the strands start to turn a light golden brown. Remember to stir frequently as they burn easily.
- Drain the rice and add it to the pot of vermicelli with the salt and the water or stock. Stir and then bring to the boil.
- Reduce the heat to as low as possible. Cover tightly and cook for about 20–25 minutes until all the liquid has been absorbed.
- Turn off the heat and let the rice rest for about 5–10 minutes.

→ Fluff up the rice with a fork and serve.

Note: if you wish to achieve hakaka (toasted crust of cooked rice), continue cooking on a very low heat for another 40–50 minutes. Once rested, turn the pot upside down onto a serving dish and present the rice as a cake.

Our *Eid el Sukka*, the Festival of Succoth,

was originally an agricultural festival celebrating the gathering of the harvest at the beginning of autumn. Another layer of meaning was added to this ancient festival to commemorate the 40 years of travel the children of Israel spent roaming the desert on their way to the Promised Land living in booths or *sukkahs*.

Every year, such a *sukkah* was constructed on the terrace facing our garden. It was a temporary trellis-like structure, a 'lean-to', enclosed on three sides, its back being the wall of our house. Its roof, covered with palm branches, was adorned with hanging seasonal fruits: bunches of grapes, fresh dates and pomegranates. Meals were eaten inside the *sukkah* throughout the eight-day festival.

On the sixth day, the tradition was for the men to pray all night until the next day. The women of our household stayed up too, not praying but spending the night making *shaa'reeya*, a rice-shaped pasta which would be cooked with rice the following day. They sat on low stools around an enormous tray generously dusted with flour. Balls of dough were placed around the edge of the tray from which the women pulled tiny amounts, rolling them, one at a time, between thumb and forefinger, then shaping them into rice-like grains. These were then thrown into the flour so as not to stick together. They would be sifted later to remove the excess flour, ready to be cooked the next day with the rice. Very much like the Italian *orzo* and the Greek *kritharaki* in shape and size, the *shaa'reeya* was first fried, then mixed and cooked with rice. Today, we use vermicelli.

This tradition of women cooking and preparing food together is an ancient one the world over. There is something moving about them sitting together, usually in a circle, singing, chanting and telling stories while their nimble, experienced hands prepared and cooked food, all the while forging and deepening relationships and friendships.

We Iraqis call rice *timman*,

whereas most Arabic speaking nations call it by its literary name *ruz*. Back then, we ate rice with every meal. My father used to say that a meal is not a meal without a dish of rice. The most prized variety in Iraq was the *Ambar* rice, an aromatic and slightly golden long-grain speciality which was cultivated for home-use and not so much for export. My husband's family used to grow *Ambar* in Shamiyeh, a province south of Baghdad. The silt from the overflow of the Euphrates river was propitious for its growth and gave it a wonderful aroma. Today, basmati rice makes a good substitute.

Our aluminium cooking pots were massive – or at least that's how they seemed to me as a child. Huge amounts of rice and stews were cooked in those pots every day. And every day you could hear the grating noise of metal upon metal that the cook made with the *kifkeer* (a special rice spatula) while he prized out the coveted *hakaka* – that toasted, slow cooked rice stuck at the bottom of the pot – which we loved, and still love, to eat.

Today, using a good non-stick pan makes this operation relatively easy. When the rice is ready to serve, the pot is inverted and a toasted cake-like form, moulded to the shape of the pot, is slipped out and carefully placed on a large serving plate, exposing the golden *hakaka*. As children, and now as adults, we still take great pleasure in breaking the *hakaka* to reveal the soft and fluffy rice inside.

But in my childhood days it was an arduous job to scrape out the crispy crust intact. Every young woman was given a *kifkeer* as part of her wedding dowry – an essential implement in her future kitchen arsenal. Having small holes, the spatula also acted as a sieve, useful for serving meat or vegetable stews without including too much sauce.

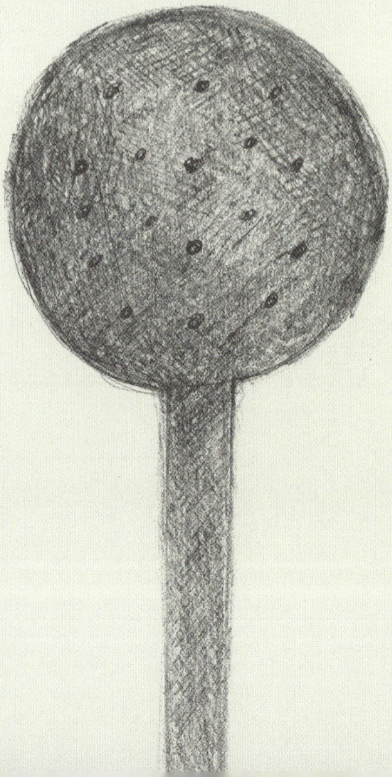

SALTED

The Jewish Festival of *Shavuot* was known in Iraq as '*eid al-ziyara*',

which is Arabic for the Pilgrimage Festival. Iraqi Jews traditionally performed a pilgrimage to the holy shrines of the prophets to receive blessings. Many women who couldn't conceive went there to pray in the hope of doing so one day, and the sick visited in the hope of being healed. People came to these shrines in droves, staying overnight with families nearby as there were no hotels there at the time. Some even stayed for a week or two.

Shavuot is a spring festival connected to the ancient grain season: it was the time for the wheat harvest and the milking season, when the cows were fat and their milk plentiful, having been well-fed during spring. And that is the most likely reason why we eat pastries made of wheat and dairy products during *Shavuot*. But many opinions abound on the matter; one theory propounds that because milk and dairy products are white, they symbolised purity, therefore a fitting ingredient on that feast day.

In ancient times, the grain harvest lasted seven weeks, beginning with the barley season during Passover and ending with the wheat harvest at *Shavuot*. Hence the name *Shavuot*, meaning weeks in Hebrew.

Kahi
Sweet Pastries

Kahi is a simple Iraqi pastry, very popular with all Iraqis. For *Shavuot*, the Babylonian Jews traditionally make *kahi* for this feast in the spring. The dough is made of wheat flour and water, rolled extremely thinly, cut into squares, then spread with butter and finished with a sprinkling of sugar. It is folded many times to the size of your palm or smaller, each fold spread with butter. It is then fried in butter, sprinkled with sugar and eaten with or without *silan* (date syrup) or clotted cream. Today, though, I would recommend baking rather than frying them.

As a child, I used to look forward to these pastries, which, if you think about it, are nothing more than sweetened puff pastry nibbles, enjoyed with a *stikan* of hot *chai* (a glass of black tea).

MAKES 16

40g/1½oz/3 tablespoons unsalted butter

4 filo pastry sheets, cut into quarters

icing sugar, for dusting

I recommend wearing gloves before you start and have some kitchen paper nearby to wipe your fingers.

- Preheat the oven to 200°C Fan (220°C/425°F/Gas Mark 7).
- Line an oven tray with baking parchment.
- In a small pot, melt the butter on a very low heat, stirring from time to time. You do not want the butter to brown or burn.
- Once melted, remove from the heat, dip a pastry brush into it and lightly brush the filo squares or rectangles all over.
- Fold each piece of filo in half and brush again with the melted butter. Do this twice more.
- With a fork, prick each piece in a few places (this is to stop them from puffing up too much) and arrange them on the lined oven tray.
- Bake for 5 minutes. You want the pastry to have a golden colour.
- Take out of the oven and allow to cool a little before sprinkling with icing sugar.

→ You can add a dollop of clotted cream and a drizzle of *silan* (date syrup) or your favourite jam on top. Enjoy with a cup of tea or coffee.

Note: as an alternative, shop-bought puff pastry works well too. You need to roll the pastry very thinly and then proceed as above.

Rosewater, my Edible Heritage. All the grandmothers of my childhood smelled of rosewater.

Rosewater is my Edible Heritage*, among many other foods. My palate immediately recognises it as something that is mine – like family. Without even having to think about it, its heady fragrance and flavour informs me of who I am and where I came from. It smells and spells grandmothers, aunties and community. And this deliciously fragrant pudding does exactly that for me. You can use almond milk instead of cow's milk, if you prefer. I sometimes use dried rose petals for decoration – and these can be found in most Middle Eastern shops.

* Edible Heritage is a phrase coined by A. A. Gill in his article 'Turtle' (2004).

Saffron-infused Mahallabia
Rosewater and Saffron Milk Pudding

SERVES 6

1 litre/35fl oz/4¼ cups milk

6 tablespoons cornflour

10–15 saffron strands

3–4 tablespoons rosewater

5–6 tablespoons granulated sugar

4 tablespoons single cream (optional)

1 teaspoon vanilla extract

2 heaped tablespoons, flaked almonds

2 heaped tablespoons, ground almonds

½ teaspoon ground cardamom

FOR THE GARNISH

1 teaspoon ground cardamom

2–3 tablespoons date syrup

3–4 tablespoons mixed almonds and pistachios, roughly ground

a few almond slivers

1 tablespoon dried rose petals or pomegranate seeds (optional)

- Stir a little cold milk into the cornflour until you have a smooth slurry. Be sure to eliminate all the lumps. Set aside.
- Crush the saffron with a little of the sugar in a mortar and pestle, and then mix in the rosewater and set aside.
- Place a saucepan on a medium heat. Add the rest of the milk to the pan along with the remaining sugar, cream (if using), vanilla extract, flaked and ground almonds and ground cardamom. Mix well and stir from time to time.
- Once the mixture becomes moderately hot, mix in the infused saffron, and rosewater. Add the cornflour mixture and stir vigorously. To avoid lumps, you can use a whisk.
- Keep stirring until the mixture thickens to an almost custard-like consistency. Be careful not to let the mixture stick to the bottom of the pan.
- It will thicken further once cooled down, so do not worry if it is slightly watery.
- Pour the mixture into a serving bowl or individual serving dishes.
- Decorate with a sprinkling of ground cardamom, a good drizzle of date syrup and the mixed ground almonds and pistachios. Scatter some almond slivers and dried rose petals (if using) on top and leave to cool.
- When completely cool, cover and place in the fridge for a few hours before serving.

→ Serve chilled.

Shakar Lamah/Ghraybeh
Shortbread Biscuits

Shakar Lamah or *Ghraybeh,* as we Iraqis call them, are very popular biscuits in the Middle East. These delicate biscuits are similar to shortbread. Traditionally, they are made with ghee or butter, sugar and flour, with a pistachio each for the decoration. I also add some ground cardamom and a hint of vanilla extract or rosewater.

I have made these with butter and ghee. The ones made with ghee were a little lighter and more crumbly. When using butter in the food processor, the trick is to melt it first before mixing it into the flour. If making the dough by hand, just use softened butter.

MAKES ABOUT 30 BISCUITS

100g/3½oz/scant ½ cup unsalted butter (softened) or ghee

140g/5oz/generous 1 cup plain flour, sifted

70g/2½oz/½ cup icing sugar (do not use granulated or caster sugar)

½ tablespoon ground cardamom

½ teaspoon vanilla extract

1 teaspoon rosewater (optional)

whole or halved (shelled) pistachios, to decorate

- Preheat the oven to 150°C Fan (170°C/340°F/Gas Mark 3½).
- Line an oven tray with baking parchment.

MAKING THE DOUGH IN A FOOD PROCESSOR

- If using butter, cut it into small pieces and melt it in a pan on a very low heat. Keep stirring to avoid burning it. When melted, set aside and cover to keep it warm and prevent it solidifying. If using hardened ghee, melt it in the same way as butter. If your ghee is soft and oily, you can use it straight away.
- Put the flour and icing sugar in the small bowl of a food processor and pulse a few times to mix properly. Add the melted butter or ghee and all the other ingredients (except the pistachios) and blend until you get a soft, crumbly dough consistency, about 2 minutes.
- You might need to use a spatula to scrape down the sides of the bowl. Test by pinching a small amount of the mixture between your fingers. If it holds together, then it is ready.
- Form the dough into a ball, wrap in cling film and refrigerate for 15 minutes.

MAKING THE DOUGH BY HAND

- Beat the softened butter or ghee in a bowl until fluffy.
- Add the icing sugar and mix until combined and creamy. Mix in the cardamom, vanilla extract and rosewater (if using).
- Add the sifted flour and mix with a spatula and then with your

hands. Incorporate all the flour until you get a soft, crumbly dough consistency. Test by pinching a small amount of the mixture between your fingers. If it holds together, then it is ready.

- Form the dough into a ball, wrap in cling film and refrigerate for 15 minutes.

SHAPING AND BAKING THE DOUGH

- Divide the dough into 15g/½oz pieces (about 30) and form into small balls – do this by rolling each ball in the warmth of your palms.
- Arrange the biscuits on the lined oven tray.
- Push a pistachio into the middle of each biscuit.
- Bake for 9–12 minutes. You want the biscuits to stay soft and crumbly in your mouth, so keep an eye on them and do not let them brown. The longer you bake them the crispier and harder they become.
- Take out of the oven, then place the oven tray on your worktop and leave the biscuits to cool.
- They must cool down *completely* before removing and handling them.

→ Store in an airtight container for up to 3 days at room temperature or refrigerate for up to a week.

Note: depending on your butter or ghee, some of these cookies might lose their shape and become flat.

Coffee cup readings were, and still are, a playful tradition in our family,

as with other families of the Middle East. It was a fun thing to do after lunch or in the afternoons. My paternal grandmother though, took the practice very seriously. One day, when the adults had finished drinking their Turkish coffees in the usual tiny cups, and once the thick coffee sediments had settled to the bottom, my father's cup, was rested on its saucer, upside down, to dry out a little. When it was ready for a reading, my grandmother picked it up and very gently turned it the right way up. Peering intently into the cup, turning it this way and that, she said to her son, "I see a clear sky... you will receive a letter... good news." A letter was always something to look forward to in those days and, consequently, it became one of the standard predictions. She continued, "I see movement, a voyage, a short one... no, a long one... I see you leaving us soon."

One summer morning in 1958,

we were abruptly awakened by an alarming cacophony. From the roof of our house, where the whole family had been sleeping, we turned towards the river, to the King's palace – *the house next to it was already in flames!* Black smoke and an acrid smell of burning permeated the air. People were running and screaming in the street below; the staccato din of artillery and the crash and clash of metal obliterated the tranquillity of our morning.

From the radio broadcasts, we learned that the King was dead and Iraq had been declared a republic.

Everything changed. Fear entered the equation. The year that followed was turbulent. Strict curfews were implemented. The airport was closed to the outside world. The military were everywhere and their behaviour unpredictable. We had to be seen to be supporting the new regime. Photos of the new leaders replaced those of King Faisal II on all the walls. My parents told us not to speak French between ourselves, only Arabic. French was deemed foreign and it brought attention to oneself.

Then, one summer's day, an oil refinery was attacked and a colossal fire ensued. The fire was like a giant dragon, so huge its many tongues seemed to be touching the heavens. Although the refinery was far from the houses, we could feel the burning heat emanating from it. The night sky was ablaze with light, and stayed illuminated for days before the fire was finally quelled. It was frightening. I remember thinking of going to the river to sit in the water until it was safe to come back home.

I didn't know at the time that I was leaving my home and homeland ... for good.

Towards the end of that year, the airport was re-opened for travel. Visas were issued to those who wished to take a holiday. A journey was planned and our suitcases were packed. We were to leave as soon as possible, depending on when we got those exit visas. I didn't know at the time that I was leaving my home and homeland, my school and my friends, my garden and my extended family, for good. For the child that I was, the enormity of this event was not easily understood. Leaving seemed exciting. We were going away on a holiday, or so I thought. It was the beginning of something new.

Our journey began one August day in 1959. From the back window of the car taking us to the airport, I caught a glimpse of my grandparents waving, my grandmother wiping her tears with a handkerchief, and Gershone, the cook, pouring a bucketful of water over the road behind the car as we sped away. This was a tradition to wish us a safe journey and a very quick return home.

We never returned.

Beirut

Chapter Two

The Sea and Small Plates

Beirut 1959–1961

The airport taxi to Beirut took a route that hugged the Mediterranean. "*The sea! The sea! It's so blue.*" I exclaimed, as we entered the city.

I HAD NEVER SEEN A SEA BEFORE. Stretched out in front of us was a vast expanse of blueness, a tapestry of shimmering turquoise, glittering and winking at me – so unlike our muddy Tigris river. I was 10 years old when we set up home in Beirut. It was mid-August and very hot. The choice of school and other administrative decisions were attended to by my father. He was to start travelling often, going to and fro, from Beirut to Baghdad, to sort out his business concerns there – leaving us for months on end alone with our mother. My parents tried hard to keep up an appearance of normalcy so as not to worry us. But I could glean the effect this move had on them. A change was taking place within our lives, the consequences of which we could not yet foresee. Nevertheless, when my brothers and I started school, life for us kids seemed more or less normal again, and a routine soon ensued.

The landlady, who lived on the floor below us, was most helpful. She informed my mother about the various must-see places, recommending traders and restaurants and whatever else my mother needed to know.

Every morning, buffalo milk was delivered to us straight from a farm that belonged to our Maronite cook, Marie. Still warm, with a pungent odour, it was immediately put on the hob to pasteurise it by boiling. It was then left to cool before placing it in the fridge, where the fatty cream would float up to the top and set in one layer. This is what we Iraqis call *qeimar*: a glorious cream, richer than clotted cream, so thick you could slice it with a knife.

We used the bread to scoop up the creamy labneh...

The following morning, my mother would lift the cream from the pot and serve it for breakfast with a drizzle of *silan* (date syrup). This was accompanied by a small plate of *zaatar* mixed with olive oil; a plate of *labneh* with a well of golden olive oil at its centre; bitter green olives, their flesh cracked slightly open; and a pile of fresh flatbreads. We used the bread to scoop up the creamy *labneh* or the sweet *qeimar*.

Olives, or I should say an olive, was always eaten wrapped in a small piece of bread too, a practice I continue to this day. Using bread as a scoop always seemed to enhance the flavour of the food – perhaps eating with one's hands, instead of cutlery, has something to do with it.

We sometimes accompanied my mother and Marie, to the food market, returning with a sumptuous array of ripe fruits and vegetables. This was something new and exciting because the women of our tribe never went food shopping in Baghdad, it being the prerogative of the men.

From time to time, Marie used to bake us *manakeesh* (page 70) for breakfast: warm round breads with a topping of *zaatar* and olive oil, which she sliced into long pieces, to dunk into soft boiled eggs – a real treat. Occasionally, she would spoil us by making a delicious finger dessert called *znoud el sit,* literally meaning the upper arms of a lady! The name used to make us kids giggle as we watched Marie's substantial upper arms wobble while she prepared the dish. We loved eating these cigar-shaped delicacies: thin pastry stuffed with sweetened cream and rolled like a cigar, then deep-fried, drenched immediately in syrup and garnished with chopped pistachios. What's not to like?

The women of our tribe never went food shopping in Baghdad, it being the prerogative of the men.

Zaatar Manakeesh
Bread topped with zaatar

MAKES 12

½ teaspoon fast-action dried yeast

½ teaspoon caster sugar

250ml/8fl oz/1 cup warm water (the water must not be hot, otherwise it will kill the yeast)

360g/12½oz/2½ cups strong white bread flour, plus extra for dusting

½ teaspoon salt

80ml/2½fl oz/⅓ cup olive oil plus 3 tablespoons

35g/1¼oz *zaatar*

Note: you can also make a delicious open sandwich by adding very thin slices of tomato or cucumber on top of each cooked manakeesh. A spread of cottage cheese or ricotta works well too. And to enjoy a soft-boiled egg, slice the manakeesh into long strips (soldiers) for dipping into the yolk.

- Mix the yeast with the sugar and half the warm water in a small bowl and set aside.
- In a large bowl, sift the flour and salt together. Add the olive oil and the yeast mixture and mix well. Add the rest of the warm water and continue mixing. Once you get a ragged dough, use your hands to knead it in the bowl, incorporating all the dry flour.
- Turn the dough onto your lightly floured work surface and knead it for 10–15 minutes until smooth but not sticky.
- Lightly oil the same bowl, put the dough back in and cover with a damp cloth, leaving it to prove in a warm place for an hour or so.
- Once the dough has doubled in size, plop it onto your lightly floured work surface and roll it into a thick sausage, then cut it in half.
- Divide each half into six even pieces, making 12 pieces in all. Take each piece and roll it into a ball. Place the balls on a tray, cover with a damp cloth and leave to rest in a warm place for about 15–20 minutes.

- Preheat the oven to 160°C Fan (180°C/350°F/Gas Mark 4).
- Prepare four balls at a time by flattening each ball into a circle with your hands. Make sure the edges are higher and fatter than the middle, a bit like a pizza so as to contain the filling.
- Now with your fingers, press down on the middle of each bread to prevent it from puffing up.
- Combine the remaining 3 tablespoons of olive oil and the *zaatar* in a small bowl. Brush some of the mixture on top of each dough circle, leaving a clear margin all around.
- Place four flatbreads on an oven tray. Repeat with the remaining eight flatbreads, in batches of four. Bake for around 8 minutes or until the edges have a slight colour.
- Remove from the oven and transfer the breads onto a wire rack, then let them cool. (I usually cover them loosely with foil to keep the moisture in and the bread soft.)

→ Serve immediately.

It was in Lebanon that my taste buds were awakened by new flavours and new dishes. And it was in Zahle that I had my first restaurant experience. I had never been to a restaurant in Baghdad.

Nestled high up in the mountains, about an hour's drive from the hustle and heat of Beirut, Zahle – known as the bread basket of Lebanon – was a place where one could enjoy a temperate climate in the summer and a great culinary experience all year round.

Arriving one August day, we found the town buzzing with restaurants offering their *mezze* delights of small dishes, their regional wines, and their famous local liquor, *arak,* an aniseed drink speciality of Zahle. The fruity scent of sweetened tobacco smoke, exhaled by very contented customers sucking at their *narguiles* (hookah pipes) wafted through the narrow streets – discernible even through the redolent aromas from the various kitchens. All the restaurants offered this famous floor-standing hookah pipe, now ubiquitous in certain parts of London.

By lunchtime, the place became very animated with people chatting and eating – parents, children, grandparents and their friends. An exuberant atmosphere pervaded. Our cousins' family who, like us, had moved to Lebanon, joined us for lunch. My parents chose a table in a beautiful setting where two live peacocks welcomed us at the entrance. Inside, pine trees granted a much-appreciated shade. A waterfall, which trickled right through the midst of the establishment, made a continuous and gentle gurgling sound, which was soothing and refreshing. No sooner had my parents given their order, than ...

... a succession of small plates emerged one after the other, 15 in all, accompanied by freshly baked pitta bread puffed up like pillows.

Bitter olives, *labneh* encircling a pool of olive oil, their renowned cracked wheat salad *tabbouleh* with heaps of chopped parsley and mint, *fatouche,* a mixed salad with fried pieces of bread; stuffed vine leaves; *makdous,* the stuffed aubergine pickle (page 74) *tourshi,* pickled pink turnips; *kibbeh*, humous and *baba ghanouj* (page 78) *falafel* (page 80) *muhamara,* the red pepper and walnut dip (page 77) and more, all to be washed down with *arak*, by the adults, of course.

These dishes arrived on trays carried by waiters who balanced them high above their heads with great dexterity. Like twirling dervishes, they moved from table to table without spilling or breaking a single dish. It takes practice and a happy disposition to do this work every day.

Like twirling dervishes, they moved from table to table.

The chatter and tinkling of knives and forks melded with the flavours in our mouths. The two peacocks who had welcomed us were now strutting among us, flaunting their magnificently coloured plumage. The atmosphere was suffused with the spirit of *bonhomie.*

And so it was there, in Zahle, at this particular restaurant, that my interest in food and in eating began in earnest. Thus far, I had only experienced home cooking. Not only was eating a meal in a restaurant a treat in itself, but also Lebanese food differed from ours, being on the whole, lighter and daintier, and with its proximity to the sea, adding more fish and seafood dishes to its repertoire.

Makdous
Stuffed Aubergines Pickled in Oil

Makdous is a pickle of oil-cured baby aubergines (these are available in Middle Eastern shops) stuffed with red peppers, walnuts, chilli and garlic. Traditionally eaten at breakfast with flatbreads, they also make tasty sandwiches and a tangy addition to a *mezze* spread.

MAKES 15 PICKLES

you will need a sterilised 1 litre/35fl oz/4¼ cup jar with a lid

15 mini aubergines, washed and stalks removed (be careful not to cut into the flesh)

1 tablespoon lemon juice

salt

FOR THE STUFFING

2 red peppers, cored and deseeded

5–6 plump garlic cloves, peeled

1 fresh red chilli

120g/4¼oz/1¼ cup walnut halves, roughly chopped

olive oil

salt and freshly ground black pepper, to taste

- First, prepare the aubergines.
- Put the aubergines in a pan of cold water with the lemon juice. Cover them with a plate to keep them submerged, as they have a tendency to float up.
- Bring to the boil and then simmer for 10–12 minutes. Do not worry, the plate will not crack. You want the aubergines to be soft but not collapsed, so check by taking one out of the water and piercing it with a fork. If the fork goes in easily, the aubergines are done.
- Transfer them to a colander and set aside until cool enough to handle.
- Make a short vertical slit on the side of each one. Depending on the size of the aubergines, stuff about half a teaspoon of salt into each opening. Then press them shut and place them neatly in a colander with a bowl underneath to collect the juices.
- Cover them with a plate using a tin of beans or similar to weigh down the plate. Leave to drain at room temperature for 24 hours or overnight. It is important that all the water drains out.
- Once drained, transfer the aubergines onto a tray to dry, without overlapping them.
- While the aubergines are drying, make the stuffing.
- Coarsley chop the peppers, garlic and fresh chilli by hand or in a food processor, being careful not to end up with a mush or purée.
- Put the mixture in a muslin or cheesecloth and squeeze out all the juice. You want the peppers to be as dry as possible. (You can keep the juice and use it, in your stews or pasta dishes, mixed with some tomato purée.)

- Mix the pepper mixture and the walnuts together. You will have a dryish mixture. Add to it a pinch of salt and pepper and mix.
- Stuff each aubergine with a scant tablespoon or one heaped teaspoon of the stuffing and close tightly.
- Carefully fill the jar with the aubergines, slit side up, gently pressing them down.
- Cover them completely with olive oil. Tap the jar gently on your worktop to remove any air bubbles or you can use a clean spoon to dislodge them.
- Close the jar and store at room temperature away from light.

→ Leave the aubergines for at least 3 weeks before eating. The longer they pickle the better. They will keep for up to a year without any problem, that is, if not gobbled down before!

Muhamara
Spicy Red Pepper and Walnut Dip

This is a most delicious spread which often graced our *mezze* table. Made with roasted peppers (I use a jar of roasted peppers) walnuts and pomegranate juice, you can use it as a dip or as a spread in sandwiches, instead of butter. You can also spoon it over grilled chicken, fish or beef burgers to enhance their flavour. I have added cashew nuts for sweetness and creaminess.

SERVES ABOUT 6

70g/2½oz/¾ cup walnut halves

30g/1oz/¼ cup raw cashew nuts

30g/1oz fine matza meal or fine dried breadcrumbs

¾ teaspoon salt

2–3 tablespoons Aleppo pepper

1 tablespoon paprika

3 roasted red peppers from a jar, drained (about 250g/9oz)

2 tablespoons olive oil

1 plump garlic clove, crushed

3 tablespoons lemon juice

2 tablespoons pomegranate juice (or use a good balsamic vinegar)

2 teaspoons tomato purée

- In a blender, loosely grind the nuts, the matza meal or breadcrumbs, salt, Aleppo pepper and paprika together until you get a grainy mixture. You will see that some nuts will be finely ground and others will be more coarse and that's what you want.
- Add the drained peppers and the rest of the ingredients and blend again. You should get a nice thick mixture that is not too smooth.

→ Spoon into a serving dish and serve garnished with a few pomegranate seeds, chopped parsley and chopped walnuts.

Mutabal (or Baba Ghanouj)
Charred Aubergine Dip with Harissa

Mutabal or *baba ghanouj* is the staple Middle Eastern dip together with humous. *Mutabal* is sometimes called *baba ghanouj* and vice versa; both dips feature a smoky, charred aubergine purée for a base. The former has tahina, yogurt, garlic and parsley. The latter has no tahina but can include tomatoes, onions, parsley and sometimes pomegranate seeds and walnuts as a garnish. Both are delicious!

I sometimes mix one teaspoon of rose harissa in the dip to spice it up. It isn't traditional, but a delicious change.

SERVES 4

2 large aubergines

FOR THE SAUCE

3 tablespoons tahina

2 tablespoons lemon juice

2 tablespoons water

3 tablespoons olive oil

2 tablespoons natural yogurt (optional)

1 teaspoon rose harissa (optional)

½ teaspoon salt, or to taste

½ teaspoon Aleppo or cayenne pepper, or to taste

FOR THE GARNISH

1 tablespoon fresh parsley or mint, finely chopped

1 generous tablespoon chopped walnuts

- Wash the aubergines and prick them all over with a fork. This will stop them from bursting while being charred or grilled.
- Chargrill the whole aubergines directly over the gas flame of a hob. Keep turning them until the skin turns black on all sides.
- If you don't have a gas hob, you can char the aubergines whole on a barbecue, or under a hot grill. Make sure the skin is really charred.
- Allow the charred aubergines to cool sufficiently, then peel off the skin, and then top and tail them. The flesh should be cooked and very soft.
- Mash the flesh with a fork until smooth. If you prefer a very creamy texture, you can use a food processor or a stick blender.
- Put all the sauce ingredients in a glass jar, close and shake to emulsify.

→ When you are ready to serve, mix the sauce and the aubergine together. Taste and adjust the seasoning. Garnish with the chopped walnuts and parsley or mint.

Falafel
Chickpea Balls

I discovered *falafel* during our first year in Beirut and fell in love with them. This classic Middle Eastern snack is a mixture of ground raw chickpeas, fresh herbs and spices, made into balls and deep-fried. It originated in Egypt, where it is made with dried broad (fava) beans. Do not use the tinned chickpeas because they are cooked, making the *falafel* too wet.

MAKES 20 BALLS

350g/12oz/2 cups dried chickpeas

½ teaspoon bicarbonate of soda

grated zest of 1 lemon

1 tablespoon lemon juice

25g/1oz fresh parsley leaves, coarsely chopped

25g/1oz fresh coriander leaves, coarsely chopped

½ onion, very finely chopped

3–5 garlic cloves, coarsely chopped

1½ teaspoons salt, or to taste

1 teaspoon freshly ground black pepper

1 tablespoon plain flour

½ tablespoon ground cumin

1 teaspoon Aleppo or cayenne pepper

1 teaspoon baking powder

sesame seeds, for coating

vegetable oil or light olive oil, for frying

- Soak the dried chickpeas with the bicarbonate of soda in cold water overnight. The next day, rinse and drain them.
- Using a food processor, tip in the chickpeas, and all the other ingredients (except the sesame seeds and the frying oil). Pulse several times to achieve a sticky paste.
- Transfer the paste into a bowl, cover and place in the fridge for an hour or two, or better still, overnight. The paste will firm up and make it easier to handle.
- Shape the paste into about 20 balls the size of golf balls (if you make them too large, they will burn on the outside before being cooked on the inside) and place them in a single layer on a large dish. You can either use a measuring tablespoon or a small ice-cream scoop to form the balls, or make them by hand, wetting your hands if needs be.
- Spread some sesame seeds on a plate. Roll each ball in them, covering it all over.
- Using a small deep saucepan (so as not to use too much oil). Fill the oil to no more than two-thirds to allow space for the balls. Heat the oil on high heat until it bubbles slightly. Then lower the heat a little and drop a very small amount of the mixture in the oil. If it sizzles immediately, the oil is ready.
- Carefully drop a few balls into the hot oil. You want to fry them in batches to avoid overcrowding. The oil should cover the balls completely. Fry them for about 4–5 minutes or so until the balls are brown all over. Then scoop out and drain on a dish lined with kitchen paper. Repeat with the rest.

→ Serve immediately or when just warm. Remember that, like all fried foods, their crispness will dissipate after a while.

Mujaddara

Brown Rice, Lentils and Caramelised Onions

This lentil and rice dish is ubiquitous throughout the Middle East, with certain variations from country to country. *Mujaddara* traditionally calls for caramelised onions, white rice and brown or green lentils. I use Puy lentils because they hold their shape better, and short-grain brown rice to give the dish a nutty texture. I recommend parboiling it first before incorporating the lentils. The caramelised onions are a very important part of *mujaddara* because they impart a sweet and smoky flavour.

SERVES 6

2 large onions, finely sliced

4 tablespoons olive oil

1½ teaspoons salt

½ teaspoon freshly ground black pepper

1 teaspoon Aleppo pepper (optional)

1 teaspoon cumin seeds

2 garlic cloves, finely chopped

900ml/32fl oz/3¾ cups water

200g/7oz/heaped 1 cup short-grain brown rice

200g/7oz/1 cup dried Puy lentils, rinsed

FOR THE GARNISH

4 tablespoons olive oil

2 large onions, finely sliced

2 tablespoons fresh parsley, roughly chopped

- Fry the onions in the olive oil, on medium heat, until they reach a deep golden colour, about 30–40 minutes. Do not let them burn.
- Add the salt and black pepper, the Aleppo pepper, cumin seeds and garlic and stir-fry for a minute.
- Stir in the water and bring to the boil.
- Add the rice and bring back to the boil. Lower the heat, cover and cook for about 15 minutes or so.
- Add the lentils to the rice. Mix well and bring back to the boil.
- Turn down the heat to low, cover and cook for 25–30 minutes or until both rice and lentils are cooked through. Then turn off the heat and leave to rest for a few minutes.
- Meanwhile, for the garnish, heat the olive oil on medium heat in a wide frying pan and fry the onions until caramelised and brown, about 35–45 minutes. Then drain on kitchen paper.
- Mix some of the caramelised onions into the rice mixture, leaving some for the garnish.

→ Spoon the rice mixture onto a serving platter and garnish with the parsley and the rest of the caramelised onions. Serve with some natural yogurt and a simple tomato salad.

Sfouf
Lebanese Turmeric Cake

I fondly remember this cake which my friend Nadia served whenever I visited. *Sfouf* literally means rows in Arabic on account of the rows of squares or diamond shapes into which the cake is divided. It is a simple, slightly sweet cake made with flour and semolina and has a light, gritty consistency, similar to corn bread. The surprising ingredient of ground turmeric gives it a bright earthy colour. In this recipe, I have included almond flour, which is optional. *Sfouf* can be totally vegan by adding water instead of milk.

SERVES ABOUT 6–8

you will need a 22cm/8½in round cake tin or a 20 × 30cm/8 × 12in rectangular one

1 tablespoon oil or tahina, for oiling the tin

30g/1oz/scant ¼ cup almond flour (optional)

120g/4¼oz/scant 1 cup plain flour

180g/6¼oz fine semolina

1½ teaspoons baking powder

a pinch of salt

2 teaspoons ground turmeric

150g/5½ oz/scant ¾ cup granulated sugar

125ml/4fl oz/½ cup light olive oil

250ml/8fl oz/1 cup milk or water

1 teaspoon vanilla extract

a small handful of flaked almonds, blanched whole almonds or pine nuts, to decorate

- Preheat the oven to 160°C Fan (180°C/350°F/Gas Mark 4).
- Brush the tin all round with the oil or tahina, or line it with baking parchment.
- In a bowl, gently mix all the dry ingredients together using a spoon or a hand whisk.
- Add the oil and incorporate well with the flour.
- Add the milk or water and vanilla extract. Mix to a smooth consistency. If the mixture feels too thick, add an extra spoonful or two of milk or water.
- Pour the mixture into the tin and shake it a few times to get the top to settle level and smooth.
- With the tip of a knife, lightly score the surface into diamonds or squares. Gently push an almond or a pine nut into the top of each segment.
- Bake for 30–35 minutes or until the top is golden (halfway through the baking score the segments again).
- It is important to allow the cake to cool down completely in the tin before cutting through the scored segments or it will crumble.

The small mountain village of Dhour al Shueir was where we escaped the summer heat.

The area was dotted with pine trees. Tall and elegant, they permeated the air with their fresh sprucy scent. We were left very much to ourselves during the day. With no television to distract us or while away the time, it was up to us children to entertain ourselves. Apart from playing backgammon or Monopoly, what we loved most of all was being outdoors, roaming the countryside around where we lived.

We tried climbing the pine trees to pick their cones, alas, with little success as they were so tall. So, more often than not, we had to jump up as high as we could to catch one of the branches and pick one or two. Then we prised out the pine nuts from inside the cones and crushed them with a pebble, picked out their creamy white kernels, and devoured them with glee. Fresh pine nuts have such a distinctive delicate flavour and are used in many Lebanese dishes.

My father's love of fruit took us on weekly buying expeditions to an orchard nearby. Going from one tree to the next, we picked and tasted different fruits, their succulent juices dribbling down our chins.

Once we had made our choice, the fruits were picked directly from the tree by the farmer, whose wife, always pleased to see us, would generously invite us to share some fresh goat's cheese accompanied by juicy slices of chilled watermelon.

We returned home with baskets full of apricots, white-fleshed peaches, green and purple figs (as sweet as honey) juicy plums, melons and watermelons, grapes and sometimes a few *akiduniyas* (loquats) if we happened to catch them before the end of their season.

I have the fondest memories of Lebanon and its people, though, sadly, I have not returned since. I enjoyed my two years at the Maronite Christian school, even though my brothers and I were bullied at first by our classmates for being foreign and Jewish – coming from our sheltered upbringing, this was a big surprise to us kids. They mocked us for not speaking Arabic with a Lebanese accent – and worse – bullied us for having killed the son of god. Their god! At the time, I had no idea to what they were referring. Surely, I thought, god is more powerful than any human being? How could I have killed him...? We fought back and earned their respect and friendship in the end. So, some days were uncomfortable (as the Arabic saying goes: *yom basal wa yom asal*) literally, some days tasted of onions and others of honey, but we never told our parents.

What has stayed with me from those childhood days is the turquoise blue of the Mediterranean sea, the fragrant smell of pine trees on hot summer days and the Lebanese people themselves, fun-loving and joyous.

There was, of course, their food, shared throughout the Levant region, with an emphasis on vegetables, and so seemingly simple, compared to ours, yet still diverse and so delicious. And the language, or should I say their Arabic pronunciation, which is musical, elegant, not guttural like our Iraqi Arabic (although some believe ours is the correct pronunciation). Of course, since that time, Lebanon has, sadly, experienced many trials and tribulations. For us, living there in the early 60s, life was full of optimism and sunny days.

After a couple of years in Lebanon, my parents decided to emigrate to London to be with other family members who were already living there.

London

Chapter Three

Fish and Chips and Mary Quant

London 1961–1979

Rain, rain go away, come again another day.
I found it exotic, at first.
But the rain came back *every* day.

It was drizzling as we disembarked from the plane. London welcomed us with a humid and wet embrace. Everything looked grey and undefined. A thick fog was descending over the city, enveloping everything. It seemed as if we were living in the clouds, piquing my interest in this new land which I would eventually call home.

The following morning, the rain having stopped, I dashed to the small balcony of our flat to see what was outside. I was surprised that no one was at their window in the building opposite us. I looked down to the street below. A surge of sombre-attired women, and men in bowler hats, were hurrying along in the same direction like one undulating black mass. Were they trying to escape from some danger?

A surge of sombre-attired women, and men in bowler hats, were hurrying along in the same direction ...

I called out to my parents: "Look, look at these people running! Something must have happened." Only to be told that they were most likely hurrying to catch the train or bus to go to work. What had alarmed me, though, were their numbers and their pace, so pressing and urgent – so unlike the ambling gait of people in the Middle East.

London in the early 60s was an eye-opener, both food-wise and otherwise. The foggy, cold weather being one, television another and, of course, there was the language and culture, both so new; as were the trusting newspaper salesmen who would leave their small stand of papers unattended, with a tin box on the side into which people dropped their pennies before grabbing the daily news – unheard of in our country! And the bobby on the beat always so friendly and not at all threatening.

While my brothers attended English schools, I went to a French school, which, come to think of it, seems quite odd now. I imagine that my mother's love of everything French must have had something to do with that choice. We had just begun life in a new country where English was the language of the land – and my knowledge of it was quite rudimentary. And, although I did enjoy my school years, being in that French school heightened my sense of deracination. During those teenage years, I was straddling three different cultures in one day: spending most of the week in a French enclave, while the outside world was English, and our family home Iraqi. It was confusing, to say the least.

I also got used to this frequent refrain:
"*Where are you from?*" "Iraq." "*Iran?*" "No, Iraq."
"*Where is that?*" In the Middle East."
"*Lebanon?*" "No, Iraq."

Tired of explaining where Iraq was, I began by saying "Lebanon, I come from Lebanon." Back then, most people had not heard of Iraq. I didn't mind. It was easier to say Lebanon. But it made my life more complicated as I became an actor in my own story. Over the years, I found myself inventing and reinventing myself depending on what language I was speaking or in which country I was living, each time imagining a different identity to slip into, much like a garment.

It was the beginning of the Swinging Sixties when we arrived in London: the pill, women's liberation, drugs, sexual freedom, the Beatles, LSD – all things I could not then comprehend. At school, I was a newcomer and the only girl wearing socks, while most of the girls in my class were already wearing stockings and talking about clothes and boyfriends. And, of course, I didn't have a boyfriend. How could I have had one?

I was a newcomer and the only girl wearing socks …

I was still a child and besides, compared to my girl friends my upbringing was strict, almost Victorian. Clearly, I was out of step with the times. Soon though, I did acquire a boyfriend – an imaginary one, of course – so that I could participate in their gossip. I wanted to be accepted and to be one of the girls. Not much later, though, I did start wearing stockings. These were most uncomfortable to say the least, because only suspenders were the order of the day. What with a bra on top and suspenders controlling my leg movements, I felt in perpetual constriction, but consoled myself with the thought that this was the beginning of womanhood. I was thrilled, however, when tights came on the market.

Quite soon my brothers and I, barely teenagers, began our love affair with everything British: peaches (tinned, of course) and cream, strawberries and cream, Ambrosia milk pudding (tinned), jelly and custard from a packet, all delicious and more. We also loved the squares of orange-coloured cheese slices that came in small packets, neatly separated by sheets of cellophane. Instant mash potato was another favourite and the various instant cake mixes that were advertised on television, informing us that all we had to do was add water to the contents, bake it, and a cake would appear all puffed up and proud. Sadly, by the time we got around to eating it, it had shrunk to half its size, deflated like a soufflé! We didn't mind though.

In those early days, television advertisements captivated and entertained us and had a big influence on our purchases. Last, but not least, was the British soft sliced bread: that white fluffy consistency, so soft and bland, and so enticing spread with butter and jam or lemon curd. Nothing like that had ever entered our mouths before and was so different from our usual flatbreads – ironically, all the rage these days!

Television advertisements captivated and entertained us ...

We also fell in love with the sweets: the fluorescent gobstoppers, the bubble gum balls in their garish colours, liquorice allsorts, Smarties, wine gums, Curly Wurlies, jelly babies – the list goes on.

We'd never had these kinds of sweets before. Ah! But you might be thinking, the confections and desserts of the Middle East are also very sweet and syrupy – and you would be right. However, these were not daily treats but, instead, specialities to be offered to guests or enjoyed on the special occasion of a marriage, an engagement or the like. Now, the corner shop near where we lived sported an endless supply of these technicoloured edible baubles available every minute of the day.

Of course, those 'delicacies' were what caught our foreign eyes because of their utter novelty. And they were generally popular. But that is not to say that the country as a whole chose processed food over homecooked fresh

ingredients. From our perspective, however, as we grappled to engage with the British culture, it appeared to us that these foods and treats were common currency.

As time passed, I gained confidence and began to be interested in boys and fashion. Carnaby Street was the hub for new and creative clothes. It was where all of us went, young teenagers and adults alike. Clothes were sharp, straight cut and colourful. Women wore trousers. Hair was straight and cut strikingly short. I liked Mary Quant's style which was fun and sleek. Her hair too – super straight and short.

Clothes were sharp, straight cut and colourful. Women wore trousers.

She had the Vidal Sassoon cut which I dreamt of having. Mine, alas, was a helmet of thick, frizzy and unruly hair (not at all fashionable at the time). It had to be ironed – yes, ironed – so as to achieve that Mary Quant look which was all the rage. Of course, it did not stay straight for long, only maintaining its Mary Quant sleekness as long as I stayed indoors. It frizzed up again whenever I went outdoors – the rain and humid air cruelly returning it to its natural unruly state.

From time to time, I would visit my friend Christine on Saturdays.

She lived at the top of Portobello Road in Notting Hill Gate. Her father, Geoffrey Van, was a celebrated antiques dealer, selling 16th and 17th century furniture and *objets d'art* in his shops there. I was interested in old objects so, very early one dark Sunday morning, torch in hand, Christine and I decided to go to Brick Lane to buy a few bits and pieces. At the time, Brick Lane was a good market for antiques (as was Bermondsey Market) where, if you were lucky, you could find something that was interesting and out of the ordinary.

We bought a few objects, which we took home to clean and polish. We displayed them the following week on a makeshift table in front of Christine's house in Portobello road. A continuous throng of people passed by, heading to the main shops further down the road, but many stopped at our table. By the end of the day, we had sold almost everything! And that gave us a real thrill. Selling the objects was an endorsement that we had bought well and that we had a good eye. And so started my love of antiques and beautiful objects.

The experience of collecting was an education. Far better than the courses on the history of art that I attended at art school. These objects made history real and palpable for me. Collecting became a passion that I pursued for many years.

We discovered fish and chips early on. It was my father's favourite dish in the 1930s while he studied in London.

I remember the day he took us to the iconic Sea Shell Restaurant: a veritable chippie institution which opened after World War I and relocated some sixty years ago to Lisson Grove. We watched as the fish was first dipped in batter and then dropped into hot oil to cook to a crispy golden wonder. It was such an exciting novelty, standing and eating the hot fish which, at the time, was out of a newspaper, the oil and vinegar dissolving the black ink of its typeface as we ate. I marvelled at the ingenuity of using newspapers as a substitute for plates. Health and safety rules were more relaxed then, but I am sure that the fish and the chips tasted better when served that way!

The origin of fish and chips is an interesting one.

You may be surprised to learn that it was the Marranos (Jews who were forced to convert to Catholicism) fleeing religious persecution in 15th and 16th century Spain and Portugal, who brought this culinary speciality to England. Their fish was coated in flour or batter and deep-fried. They sold it in the streets of London and elsewhere on large trays hung by straps around their necks.

Fried fish was the traditional Sephardi dish, cooked on Fridays and eaten cold on Saturdays, as cooking is not allowed on the Sabbath. We, Iraqi (Babylonian) Jews, also had fried fish on Fridays and so did the Baghdadi Jews of Bombay.

The first time a recipe for fried fish was published in England was in 1747, in *The Art of Cookery Made Plain and Easy* by Hannah Glasse. And another fried fish recipe appeared in 1845 in a book called *Modern Cookery for Private Families* by Eliza Acton.

As for the French fries,

there are competing claims between the French and the Belgians about its invention. Each contend that it is theirs. But the fact that we call them French fries could indicate that we received them from France, perhaps from the protestant refugees, the Huguenots, who were fleeing persecution from Catholic France.

If the two ingredients that make up our fish 'n' chips speciality were brought to England by immigrants, you might ask: "What makes it British?" Well, it is the clever pairing of the two! It is said that a Jewish immigrant called Joseph Malin came up with the idea. He opened a restaurant in the East End of London in around 1860, and on his menu was a dish called 'Fish fried in the Jewish Fashion'. Others claim that it was a Mr Lees from Lancashire who first opened a chippie in 1863. Whoever started it first can claim the invention of a truly British dish recognised the world over.

Fried Fish in Batter

There are many ways to make a batter. You can use ordinary plain flour, self-raising flour or rice flour to which you can add water, beer, milk or vinegar. You can also add an egg, bicarbonate of soda or olive oil to the batter. Breadcrumbs are used by some as a final coat which can be spiced up with chilli flakes or Aleppo pepper, chopped fresh herbs or some crushed nuts and seeds.

SERVES 4

1 tablespoon malt vinegar

250ml/8fl oz/1 cup light beer or lager

about 700ml/24fl oz/3 cups light olive oil, for frying

about 600g–700g/1lb 5oz–1lb 9oz haddock, cod or pollock fillets (skin-on), cut into 4 fillets

1 teaspoon salt, plus extra for seasoning

60g/2¼oz/scant ½ cup rice flour, plus extra for dusting

30g/1oz/scant ¼ cup self-raising flour

30g/1oz/¼ cup cornflour

1 teaspoon paprika

¼ teaspoon bicarbonate of soda

lemon wedges, to serve

- Refrigerate the vinegar and beer or lager until cold.
- Pat your fish fillets dry with kitchen paper (do not skip this important step, otherwise the fried batter will become soggy).
- Season the fish with salt and dust them all over with the extra rice flour. Shake off the excess and set aside.
- In a bowl, mix together the rice flour, the self-raising flour, cornflour, the salt, paprika and bicarbonate of soda.
- Heat the olive oil in a large, heavy-based pot on medium heat.
- Drop a small piece of bread into the oil. If it sizzles and turns golden in a few seconds, the oil is ready. If the oil is not hot enough, your fish will be oily and soggy.
- When you are ready to fry, pour the chilled vinegar and beer or lager into the flour mixture and whisk until you get a smooth, lump-free batter. It should be a little thicker than double cream.
- Dip the fish into the batter, one fillet at a time. Then very slowly ease it into the hot oil and fry for about 3 minutes on each side.
- Place a wire rack next to the cooking pot with baking parchment or a newspaper underneath to catch the drips of oil.
- Once the batter has turned golden brown, transfer the fillet onto the wire rack. Repeat with the rest of the fish.

→ Tradionally served with lemon wedges, mushy peas and chips.

My mother experimented with many different English recipes.

Roast beef was a favourite (with roast potatoes, but no Yorkshire pudding). Welsh rarebit – "It's more than just cheese on toast," she would say – and bread and butter pudding, which she baked once in a while for us on Sundays. And, of course, Peach Melba – that famous dessert, created by Auguste Escoffier, head chef at the Savoy hotel in the late 19th century, specifically for the opera singer Dame Nellie Melba – which my mother prepared for guests during the summer months when fresh peaches and raspberries were available. On the whole though, her cooking was Middle Eastern in flavour, with us sampling the classic afternoon English teas when my parents took us out for a treat, in those early days, to Lyons' Corner House. We loved the various finger sandwiches of soft white bread cut into small squares or triangles – the cucumber ones were my favourite – and the warm scones filled with clotted cream and jam.

During my teens, I was my mother's *sous-chef*. I washed vegetables, helped her chop enormous amounts of fresh mint and parsley for a *tabbouleh* salad, beat the eggs manually to make mayonnaise (for what seemed to me to be an eternity, as we did not have a blender then) and rolled out pastry to make *sambouseks*. I enjoyed helping her, acquiring a good grounding in cooking and a passion for food. But I have to confess, not all our dishes were a success, and certainly not right at the beginning. For one thing, we couldn't buy many Middle Eastern ingredients in those days, and only a handful of Indian and Greek Cypriot shops stocked those so-called exotic products. Our go-to shop was Athena in Moscow Road where we could buy olives and olive oil; feta and halloumi cheese; fresh and wonderfully thin filo pastry as well as some seasonal fruits and vegetables. Notwithstanding our initial difficulties, we soon got the hang of it with whatever products were available and this learning process later involved my brothers as well. As a result, the whole family cooks today.

Ironically, it was in London where I discovered Italian food. The Swinging Sixties saw a plethora of Italian restaurants and sandwich bars. A school friend of mine was from Calabria, Italy. Her parents had a small bar in Soho, where most of her family worked. They served all sorts of salads, sandwiches and, of course, freshly ground coffee, the delicious aroma of which permeated the premises. Italian food was in fashion and was soon to become a big part of English culture in the same way as curry. Lasagne, pizza and spaghetti bolognese became firm favourites. My dish of choice, however, was *vitello al limone*: thin pieces of veal escalopes poached in a rich lemony sauce that Dinos, a restaurant near my school in South Kensington, cooked so well.

Another appetising surprise was Chinese food. I loved the small servings of steamed rice, stir-fried vegetables and delicate soups and, above all, the novelty of eating with chopsticks. For me, however, a flavour that was inseparable from being in London was curry. To celebrate our first year's anniversary in London, our parents took us to an Indian restaurant. The place smelt pleasantly of spices, and soft sitar music could be heard in the background. We tasted different dishes, various pickles (too spicy for me, then) and a wonderful fluffy rice which reminded me of home. My favourite dish at the time was egg curry (page 103).

So it was, that although I grew up with a strong identity as an Iraqi Jew, I began to embrace everything English in an effort to integrate and (I thought naïvely) to become truly English. Slowly, I began to distance myself from my background and from our family traditions, and vacillated, throughout my teens, between these two identities; battling between the original authentic me and the new me – often feeling like a fraud. The question of identity and how I perceived myself in relation to my new country was a preoccupation that lasted many years. Thankfully, these contradictory feelings gradually abated over time.

Egg Curry

SERVES 4

3 tablespoons olive oil

½ teaspoon cumin seeds

2 large onions, halved and thinly sliced

1½ teaspoons mild chilli powder (or to taste)

½ teaspoon ground turmeric

½ teaspoon ground coriander

½ teaspoon paprika

3 garlic cloves, roughly chopped

about 4–5cm/1½–2in piece of fresh root ginger, peeled and roughly chopped

generous 1.2 litres/40fl oz/ 5¼ cups water

2 small tomatoes, roughly chopped

2 small spring onions, green part only, finely sliced

1 tablespoon lemon juice

4 eggs

2 tablespoons chopped fresh coriander leaves

1 green chilli, deseeded and finely chopped

1 red chilli, deseeded and finely chopped

salt and freshly ground black pepper, to taste

- Heat 2 tablespoons of the olive oil in a pan on a medium heat, then stir-fry the cumin seeds for 30 seconds.
- Add the onions and cook, stirring occasionally, until a deep golden colour, about 20–25 minutes.
- Stir in the remaining 1 tablespoon of olive oil, the chilli powder, turmeric, ground coriander and paprika. Cook for a minute and then set aside.
- Using a stick blender (in a bowl) or the small bowl of a food processor, blend the garlic and ginger with 60ml/2fl oz/¼ cup of the water to a smooth paste. Add the cooked onions, season with salt and pepper and add 475ml/16fl oz/2 cups of the water in several stages, blending each time until you get a smooth paste.
- Pour the paste into a large pan and cook on a medium heat for a minute or so, stirring frequently.
- Add the tomatoes, half the spring onions, the lemon juice and a further 475ml/16fl oz/2 cups of the water and bring to the boil. Continue with a gentle boil until most of the water has evaporated and you end up with a rich, thick sauce.
- Mix in the remaining 225ml/8fl oz/1 cup of water and bring to the boil. Reduce it to a thick sauce again.
- Meanwhile, cook the eggs in a separate pan of boiling water for about 7 minutes, then plunge into cold water, peel and cut them in half lengthways.
- When you are ready to serve, place the egg halves in the sauce and cook for a minute on a medium heat.
- Garnish with the chopped coriander, the rest of the spring onions and the green and red chillies.

→ Serve with plain white basmati rice.

3ª MH-1-456
CALO D'EN FUST II

Ibiza

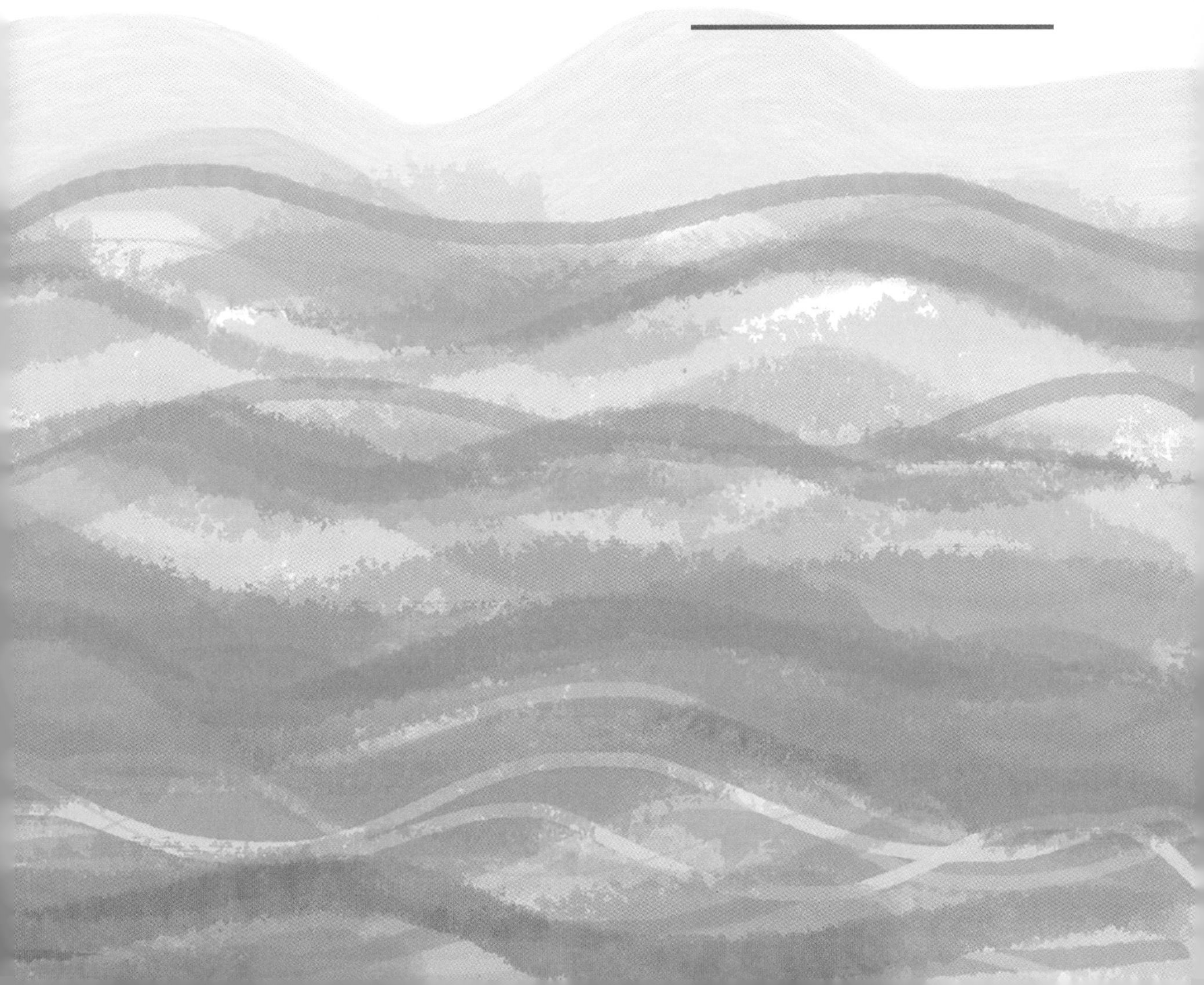

Chapter Four

Sea, Garlic and Anchovies

Ibiza/Spain 1967 onwards

A few years after our arrival in the UK, our parents took us to Spain for a holiday, more precisely to Ibiza. I was still a teenager.

It was the mid-1960s and Ibiza was not yet the must-go-to travel destination it has now become. There was only one taxi for the whole island. There were no traffic lights (those appeared later in the 80s, much to everyone's chagrin) and a couple of the *Ibicenco* farmers we met at that time still lived in 'caves' in the countryside: dwellings set slightly underground. I learned later that, in times gone by, in the mountainous regions of Andalucia in southern Spain, caves provided a safe haven for people from harsh weather and wild animals. Small chapels for worship were also housed in them. Today, these do not exist in Ibiza, but in the region of Granada, these ancient cave homes have been, and still are, inhabited by various communities who choose to live a simple and peaceful life, close to nature and away from the rat race of cities.

My father's work took him first to Madrid and later to Ibiza where, my parents eventually resided for a major part of the year. The weather and rhythm of life suited them as it was similar to the life they had left behind. My brothers and I spent all our summers there, longing in vain for it never to end, or to continue for just a little longer. Yet somehow, back in London, we looked forward to autumn's crisp and cool days, to donning our woollen jumpers and socks and seeing our school friends again.

Ibiza is one of the earliest towns in Europe, founded by the Carthaginians in the 7th century BC. It became an important strategic port and was consequently conquered many times by successive peoples: Romans, Moors, Arabs and Catalans. *Eivissa*, its Catalan name, is also called *La Isla Blanca*, the White Island, on account of its salt ponds and historical sea salt production that goes back 3,000 years. The white salt hills and pools drying in the sun gave it and, its much smaller sister island, Formentera, a beautiful and eerie landscape redolent of reflected white light, so strong that one needed to wear sunglasses in the same way as one does on snowy mountains.

They were like us, I thought...

As island people, I found the *Ibicencos* insular and, on first encounter, very reserved, almost unfriendly. But once you engaged with them and established a relationship, they gave their friendship heartily. I felt an affinity with them. It was something in the way they treated their elders and their children that resonated and endeared them to me. They moved as a family, as a group, in restaurants, on the beaches, in markets, taking their grandparents and their children with them wherever they went. They were like us, I thought.

In the late afternoon or early evening, you could observe familiar scenes of women in their Sunday best walking slowly arm in arm, talking, perhaps whispering the latest bit of gossip in each other's ears and laughing warmly; children and grandchildren running and screeching; parents stopping for a smoke, talking to friends. All this world ambling thus, doing their habitual '*paseo*' before dinner, on the promenade by the sea. It made me think, wistfully, that they were of that place, of that land, not scattered all over the globe as we were. They felt stable and secure.

Watching them drink and talk animatedly over a few tapas dishes was one of my special pleasures. They ate with relish. Sucking on a prawn's head with gusto or enjoying a plate of mussels, slurping gleefully as they prized the reticent mollusc out of its shell – and how they sipped the buttery sauce using those same shells in lieu of spoons. And the delectation of it all could be seen on their faces, on their lips and on their fingers smothered in oil.

Garlic was everywhere, so much so you couldn't smell it any more.

And there was the language too, which felt agreeable in my mouth – as if it had always lived there. From the onset, learning Spanish was vital for me. I wanted to be of that place, to be able to communicate with the *Ibicencos* – they spoke so quickly though, I sometimes had to run after their words to catch them! One loses so much otherwise, so much laughter, so many personal connections. So being able to speak the language, however tentatively, made me feel very much at home in Ibiza and in Spain in general. To my surprise, I found that the Spanish language had absorbed many Arabic words and names. A relic of almost 500 years of Moor and Arab

presence there. And the discovery of these words is still a delight for me, resulting in a feeling of closeness and familiarity that I have towards that language.

I came to know the local baker, cheesemonger and fishmonger by their first names, and also Pepe, the farmer who, knowing my father's predilection for fruit, would bring us his first fruits of the season, the first crops of spring and summer. And there was the fruit and vegetable market at the foot of the old city, which was always very lively. One small stall, close to my heart, belonged to an elderly *Ibicenco* couple, who must have been there for decades, selling different types of olives: small ones crushed slightly open, cured in brine; larger green ones marinated in olive oil and chillies; black wrinkled ones in salt; others in oil with garlic or fennel and artichoke hearts. I never tired of shopping there.

The way they treated their elders and their children resonated and endeared them to me.

And we loved our traditional morning visit to the main square of Ibiza town. There we enjoyed a typical Balearic sweet bread called *ensaimada* (page 110) with a *café con leche* or a refreshing *horchata* – a milky drink made from tiger nuts (page 112) – at one of the oldest establishments in the island, the *Monte Sol Café*. It was situated very close to the ramparts of the exquisite *Dalt Villa,* the old town of Ibiza, which was declared a UNESCO world heritage site in 1999. The café was our favourite place to sit and watch the world go by. It had a faded *Belle Époque* charm, as did its waiters who had been working there since their youth. Sadly, a few years ago, it was bought by property developers and remained closed for many years. A real pity as it marked the end of an era. I hear it has been refurbished and has now reopened.

Ensaimada
Balearic Sweet Bread

Made of strong bread flour, sugar and eggs, this sweet bread can be made by hand or in a stand mixer with a dough hook. Although it is an easy recipe, a lot of kneading and resting is necessary to make the dough very elastic. Proving is crucial at the various stages for a fluffy texture. So allow enough time. I usually start making the dough the night before, when I shape it into coils and then leave it to ferment until the next day, ready to be baked.

This pastry is said to have originated on the Catalan island of Mallorca. Within the name of this sweet bread lies the essential ingredient *saim,* meaning pork lard in Catalan. So *ensaimada* literally means larded – a thinly stretched dough that is larded, rolled and coiled into a spiral, then baked and dusted with sugar. We loved this bread, perhaps because it reminded us of our Iraqi *kahi* (page 54) but of course, we did not know at the time that it contained lard. I would order it for breakfast along with a cup of coffee, or better still, dip it in a thick hot chocolate drink. It was one of my favourite excesses. Although traditionalists still adhere to using lard, today a lot of *ensaimadas* are baked using butter instead to accommodate various tourists or communities who do not eat pork.

During the Spanish Inquisition of the 15th and 16th centuries, the Jewish and Muslim communities were given the 'choice' to either convert to Christianity or leave Spain. Pork being a religiously forbidden food for both Jews and Muslims, became a weapon for the inquisitors to tease out those who converted in name only but were still adhering to their previous religion. Thus eating pork became proof that the *conversos* (the converted) were truly Christians.

MAKES 4 BREADS

400g/14oz/3 cups strong white bread flour

2 teaspoons fast-action dried yeast

120g/4½oz/⅔ cup caster sugar

170–180ml/6fl oz/¾ cup lukewarm water or milk

185g/6½ oz/¾ cup butter, at room temperature

1 large egg or 2 small eggs, lightly beaten

icing sugar, for dusting

Note: you can of course knead the dough by hand, for about 30 minutes, until it is elastic and smooth.

METHOD

- Put the flour, yeast, caster sugar, milk, butter, and egg(s) in a stand mixer. Slowly knead with a dough hook for about 20 minutes, scraping down the sides as needs be. The dough should now be elastic and smooth.
- Now shape the dough into a ball and plop it into a well-oiled bowl. Cover with cling film and leave it to rest and rise in a warm place for at least 2 hours.
- Once the dough has risen, punch it in the bowl to let the air out, then cover and leave it to rise again in a warm place for about 30 minutes. Knead it again for a few seconds and then divide it into four equal pieces. Roll the pieces into balls and place them on a tray. Cover them with cling film and leave to rest on for another 30 minutes.
- Line an oven tray with baking parchment.
- Liberally brush your worktop with some butter. Take one ball and flatten it, then use a rolling pin, roll it into a long rectangle about 4mm/¼in thick. Generously spread it with butter all over. Then very gently stretch the dough by pulling the edges. Lift and put your hand under the dough, then gently stretch again. The dough should become a little transparent.
- Roll the dough from the longer side into a long sausage. Do the same with the rest of the dough. You should have 4 long sausages. Take hold of the ends of each roll and lift to allow the roll to stretch a little further by its own weight. Twist and shape the dough into a tight coil and place on the lined oven tray. Repeat with the other rolls, leaving some space between them for expansion.
- Cover with cling film and leave to prove in a warm place for at least 4 hours or overnight.
- Preheat the oven to 160°C Fan (180°C/350°F/Gas Mark 4).
- Bake for about 12 minutes or until the tops are golden.

→ Remove from the oven and dust with icing sugar. Leave to cool completely, then dust again with icing sugar. Serve the pastries on their own or with honey or jam.

Note: these are best eaten on the day of baking, but can be stored in an airtight container or wrapped in cling film in the fridge for 2–3 days. Gently warm the pastries in the oven before serving.

Horchata de Chufa
Homemade Tiger Nut Drink

My first taste of *horchata* was in Ibiza in a local café called *Los Valencianos*, where it was made from scratch – ensuring the place was always packed. The milky drink is not made from a real nut but from tubers called tiger nuts or *chufa* in Spanish. The milk, similar to that of almonds, is sweeter. The dried nuts are hard and have to be soaked for a good 24 hours to soften them. This gluten-free drink is very popular in Valencia and in other Catalan regions like Ibiza. Served very cold or semi-frozen in tall glasses with a straw, this refreshing drink was a daily must for me in the summer.

SERVES 2–4
(depending on the size of your glasses)

500g/1lb 2oz dried tiger nuts, thoroughly washed and soaked in cold water for 24 hours, then drained

3 tablespoons granulated sugar, or to taste

1 litre/35fl oz/4¼ cups water

1 large piece of cheesecloth or muslin

- Finely blend the tiger nuts and sugar with the water in a blender for at least 5 minutes.
- Once blended, place a large piece of cheesecloth over a bowl and pour the mixture into the centre. If using muslin, which is thinner, fold it a few times first.
- Close in the sides and tie the cloth tightly with a rubber band or string so as to make a sack.
- Squeeze the sack to extract as much of the milk as possible. Do not throw away the leftover pulp. You can use it to make biscuits. Taste and adjust the sweetness of the drink to your liking.

→ Refrigerate for a few hours before serving the *horchata* in long glasses or, on a very hot day, place in the freezer for about 25 minutes to get what the Spanish call a *granizado*, a slightly slushy frozen liquid, like crushed ice. In that case, serve it with a drinking straw.

My love of anchovies was born in Ibiza.

At mealtimes, we would invariably order a few tapas to start: small plates of *pimientos de Padrón,* tortilla with sardines, *gazpacho* or *ajo blanco* (page 119) and of course, those brilliant white fillets of raw anchovies marinated in vinegar, seasoned with garlic and parsley and steeped in olive oil called *boquerones en vinagre* (opposite). We ate them with chunks of bread dipped in their marinade. The Spanish word *boquerones* means big mouth and the fish are so-called on account of their large mouths relative to their tiny size. A distinction is made between anchovies cured in salt, which undergo a lengthy process of maceration, turning their flesh a deeper brown, and that of fresh anchovies, which are marinated in vinegar for a short time until their flesh turns white. The first are called *anchoas* and the latter *boquerones*.

Boqueranes en Vinagre
Anchovies Marinated in Vinegar

Fresh anchovies are rarely readily available at fishmongers and you usually have to order them. They are seasonal in the Mediterranean from May to September. You will be surprised at the delicate flavour of these home-marinated anchovies, compared to the commercial ones. Although you can ask your fishmonger to gut and clean them, it is an easy operation to do so at home.

SERVES 4

about 400g/14oz raw fresh anchovies

250ml/8fl oz/1 cup white wine vinegar

3 plump garlic cloves, finely chopped

2 tablespoons finely chopped fresh parsley

250ml/8fl oz/1 cup olive oil

salt and freshly ground black pepper, to taste

- Snap or cut the head off each anchovy. Slit open the abdominal cavity and remove the viscera, then gently slide out the backbone.
- Rinse well and pat dry.
- Open each anchovy out flat and slice them in half lengthways. Lay them out individually and sprinkle a pinch of salt on each fillet.
- At this point, because the anchovies will be eaten raw, it is strongly recommended to freeze them on a tray for about 5 hours or overnight so as to kill the parasites that populate their flesh.
- Next, defrost the fillets, then submerge them in the vinegar in a dish, cover and leave in the fridge to marinate for 3–4 hours.
- Thereafter, drain off and discard the vinegar, then place the fillets in a serving dish.
- Sprinkle the garlic, parsley, some salt and pepper and the olive oil over the fillets, then cover and leave to marinate in the fridge for a further hour or two.

→ Serve at room temperature and include them in a tomato, potato or white bean salad accompanied with some rustic bread and olives.

Tortilla Espanola
Spanish Omelette

Ubiquitous throughout the whole of Spain, a Spanish omelette is a potato and egg affair. Sometimes onions or a green pepper are added to it. The potatoes are gently poached in olive oil rather than fried or baked and this gives the potatoes a melting texture. A tortilla is always round in shape and is served warm or at room temperature, cut into thick wedges and served as a tapas snack or with a salad for a light meal. The Spanish like their tortilla slightly runny inside, but it is up to you how well cooked you like your eggs. I like to add some parsley and onions to my tortilla.

SERVES 4–6

you will need a 20cm/8in frying pan with a lid

500g/1lb 2oz potatoes, peeled and thinly sliced

1 small onion, cut in half and thinly sliced

olive oil, for frying

8 eggs

a handful of fresh parsley, finely chopped

salt and freshly ground black pepper, to taste

- Dab the potatoes dry with some kitchen paper and place them, with the onion in the frying pan. Pour in enough olive oil to just cover them, then bring to a gentle simmer on medium-low heat. Pop the lid on and cook for about 20 minutes. Do not stir, but shake the pan from time to time.
- In the meantime, beat the eggs in a large bowl. Mix in the parsley and some salt and pepper to taste.
- Test the potatoes and onion with a fork. If cooked, carefully lift them out with a flat spatula so as not to crush them and lay them on a plate lined with kitchen paper to drain. Reserve the oil. Let the potatoes and onions cool down a little before gently folding in the egg mixture.
- In the same pan, heat 2 tablespoons of the reserved oil until hot, then pour in the egg mixture.
- Cover the pan and cook on medium-low heat for about 10 minutes or so until the bottom has set.
- To cook the top, put the pan under a preheated hot grill for a few minutes, until golden brown.

→ Serve warm or at room temperature, accompanied by a leafy tomato salad.

Translated literally, *ajo blanco* means white garlic.

In fact, there is very little garlic in this soup which is made almost entirely of blanched almonds. It is sometimes called *gazpacho blanco* (white *gazpacho*) as opposed to the well-known red one with tomato. Originally, before the discovery of the New World in the 15th century, and probably as far back as Roman times, *gazpacho* was a simple soup typical of southern Spain, consisting of garlic, stale bread and water, with some vinegar and olive oil. This basic soup became more elaborate over time by the addition of almonds and grapes in the case of *ajo blanco,* and later on with tomatoes, peppers and cucumbers in the case of the *gazpacho Andaluz.*

Ajo Blanco
Chilled Almond Soup

Ajo blanco is a very refreshing soup to enjoy cold in the summer months. The quantity of garlic is really up to you. What makes the soup wonderfully creamy are the almonds, while the vinegar gives it an edge. The white grapes, a tradition of Malaga, add a sweet lift that has inspired many other variations, such as using apple and cucumber instead. You can blanch the almonds yourself, but shop-bought are fine.

SERVES 4

180g/6oz/1¼ cups blanched almonds

70g/2½oz stale white bread, crusts off

300ml/10fl oz/1¼ cups water

3 tablespoons apple cider vinegar or sherry vinegar

2 garlic cloves, peeled

½ teaspoon salt

150ml/5fl oz/⅔ cup olive oil

FOR THE GARNISH

about 8 or more seedless white grapes, cut in half lengthways

small slivers of blanched almonds

a few drops of olive oil

Note: to blanch the almonds yourself, soak them in water for a few hours or overnight and then peel off their skin.

- Soak the bread in the water and vinegar for 10 minutes to soften.
- Place the blanched almonds, the garlic, salt and the bread with the soaking water in a food processor and blend to a smooth paste.
- While the machine is running, gradually add the olive oil and blend until smooth and creamy. Taste and adjust the seasoning (add more salt or vinegar) and the consistency, adding a little more water, if it's too thick.
- Pour into a serving bowl(s) then cover and chill in the fridge for 2 hours or more before serving.

→ Garnish with the grapes, a speck of slivered almonds and a few drops of olive oil.

Ensalada de pimientos
Smoky red pepper salad

This is a sweet and smoky salad that is served in restaurants all over Spain. It complements grilled chicken or fish, or enjoy it on its own with some crusty bread. Place the peppers under the grill or directly on a gas hob to char their skin. In Ibiza, boiled potatoes or salted cod pieces are sometimes added.

SERVES 4

4 large red peppers

½ small onion, very finely sliced into half moons

1 small garlic clove, finely chopped

1 teaspoon tiny capers in brine

2 tablespoons olive oil

½ teaspoon lemon juice or apple cider vinegar

a pinch of salt and pepper

1 teaspoon fresh parsley, finely chopped, to garnish

- Wash and dry the peppers. Put them on a gas hob or if grilling, place them in a Pyrex dish or in an oven tray lined with baking parchment (this is to prevent a sticky mess on the tray).
- Grill or char the skins of the peppers on all sides until the skins turn black.
- Then place in a dish or bowl and cover with cling film or a plate. (This allows them to steam in the residual heat and stay soft while cooling.)
- Once sufficiently cool, peel off the skins and deseed the peppers, reserving their juice. Then slice them into thin strands and transfer them to a serving dish with their juice.
- Mix in the onions, garlic and capers. Add the olive oil, lemon juice and salt and pepper and mix well.
- Garnish with the chopped parsley.

→ Serve slightly chilled or at room temperature.

THE FIRST TIME I TASTED *Lubina a la sal* (sea bass cooked in salt) was in a local restaurant in Ibiza town. *A la sal* is the Spanish name for the method of baking fish in a salt crust. A whole fish is totally encased in salt, thus stopping any moisture from evaporating. This allows the fish to cook in its natural juices.

It was a speciality of Theo's, the cook and owner of a port-side restaurant. I still remember how he stood, proudly holding a large tray on which lay an amorphous white lump of salt. Setting the tray on the table, he proceeded to give the salt a few taps and then, like a magician, deftly removed the top layer in one unbroken sheet, revealing the treasure inside. Then came the delicate operation of filleting the fish, without spilling any crumbs of salt on it, and serving the moist fillets unadorned, save for a squeeze of lemon juice, accompanied by a few boiled potatoes and a bowl of *aioli* (page 127) with bread on the side. Only the freshest fish could be served in this way. It unveiled a new delight for me. The accompaniment of the *aioli* dip was perfect.

A whole fish is totally encased in salt...

Baking fish enveloped in salt follows the same principle as baking food wrapped in a pouch or *en papillote.* Somehow the fish comes out tastier in salt. By hermetically sealing it in salt, the flesh bakes and steams in its own juices, leaving it moist yet firm. Done correctly, the fish comes out wonderfully plump and not at all salty.

There are two ways of preparing the salt container: either by mixing salt with a small amount of water, or by adding egg whites to the salt. With the first option, if the salt crust is not packed firmly, it might break up into little pieces when you lift it off the fish. The egg whites, in the second option, bind the salt together, making it airtight and less flaky.

I have tried both options and prefer using the egg whites.

Lubina a la Sal
Sea Bass Baked in Salt

This method is suitable for a whole sea bass or sea bream, gutted, fins and gills removed, with skin and scales on, if possible (the scales protect the flesh further from the salt.) Use kosher or sea salt, not table salt. Baking times depend on the weight of the fish and your oven. To make sure the fish is cooked, tug at the tail. If it comes off easily, the fish is cooked. If it resists, give it a few more minutes in the oven.

SERVES 2

about 800g/1¾lb whole sea bass or sea bream, prepared as above

kosher or sea salt, 2½ times the weight of the fish

2–3 large egg whites

olive oil, for brushing

FOR THE GARNISH

a few slices of lemon

a dollop of *aioli* (page 127)

a sprig or two of fresh coriander or parsley

- Preheat the oven to 180°C Fan (200°C /400°F/Gas Mark 6)
- Weigh the fish and measure out the salt.
- Beat the egg whites in a bowl until frothy, then add the salt and mix well. The consistency should be that of wet sand.
- Spread about a third of the salt mixture over your oven tray in an even layer, just a little larger than the shape of the fish. Press down to make sure it is compact.
- Pat the fish dry, then lightly brush it with olive oil. Place it on top of the salt mixture and then cover it with the rest of the salt mixture, leaving part of the tail exposed. Press the salt down with your hands to compress it. The fish has to be sealed completely with the salt, except for part of the tail.
- Bake for about 30–40 minutes or until the tail comes off easily when pulled.
- Remove from the oven and let the fish rest for about 5 minutes. Then, crack the top layer of salt with the back of a large heavy spoon until it breaks into chunks. Carefully lift all the salt pieces from the top. Brush some of the fine salt off the fish and gently peel off the skin.
- Ease away the flesh from the backbone with a flat spatula or a spoon and a fork, and place each fillet on individual serving plates.

→ Garnish with the lemon slices, *aioli* and coriander or parsley sprigs. Serve with some more *aioli* on the side and some boiled potatoes or cooked vegetables of your choice.

Aioli

Intensely garlicky, this ancient Catalan dip goes back at least 2,000 years. Historically, *aioli* (*aioli* in Catalan, *alioli* in Spanish – meaning garlic and oil) was made with only two ingredients: garlic cloves and olive oil, as its name suggests. The garlic was first pounded into a paste with some salt and thereafter blended with olive oil. In the past, this was a somewhat laborious undertaking. (Remember there were no food processors at the time, so all the beating and vigorous mixing was done by hand using a mortar and pestle or with a whisk.) This did not always succeed as the emulsification was difficult to achieve and stabilise.

Authentic *aioli,* meaning the eggless condiment, is the precursor of the 17th century mayonnaise, or *salsa mahonesa* as the Menorcans like to call it. The contested story goes that, in the mid 1700s, a French cook, residing in Mahon, the Catalan capital of Menorca, added an egg as a binder to facilitate the emulsification. This ingenious addition helped to quickly thicken, emulsify and stabilise the sauce. I say the story is contested, because both the French and the Menorcans claim the sauce as theirs. And, today, people erroneously say *aioli* meaning mayonnaise.

Bowls of *aioli* or mayonnaise and green olives, accompanied by baskets of fresh bread, are always placed at the tables of restaurants and bars in Ibiza. However, nowadays, because the dip contains raw eggs, many restaurants in Spain make it without eggs. I love both versions, the former is very garlicky and the latter (with egg) is less so and is more creamy, like a mayonnaise.

Authentic *Aioli*
Garlic Dip

MAKES 1 SMALL BOWLFUL

7–8 plump garlic cloves

½ teaspoon salt

250–300ml/9–10fl oz/generous 1 cup–1¼ cups olive oil

- I have found using a stick blender is the easiest and least laborious way to make authentic *aioli*.
- Peel the garlic cloves, cut each in half and discard the green germ in the centre.
- Put the garlic with the salt in a narrow beaker with half the olive oil.
- Blend for a minute or two using a stick blender, until melded.
- Add the rest of the oil. Keep the blender firmly at the bottom of the beaker and blend for at least a further minute or two.
- Once you see a white creamy mixture forming at the bottom, then very carefully and slowly raise the blender up and down (as you would when making mayonnaise). This action forces air into the mixture, making it lighter and fluffier. Keep blending until all the oil is incorporated and a thick cream is formed.

→ You can store the *aioli* in a sealed glass jar in the fridge for a week or two as it does not contain eggs.

So, it was in Ibiza that I truly acquired my love of fish.

I REGULARLY VISITED THE FISH MARKET in Ibiza. I would set off at the crack of dawn to buy the best catch from the fishermen as they arrived – so fresh you could even eat it raw! An array of the most colourful fish was on display: bluefin tuna, gilt-head bream, sea bass, red mullet, mackerel, anchovies (both fresh and pickled), prawns, sardines, swordfish, grouper, mussels, hake, razor clams, octopus and more.

I invariably chose the simplest method of cooking my fish: that of grilling or poaching. From a filleted *grouper* or a *John Dory* (also called St Pierre or Peter's fish) to a *dorada* (the Mediterranean gilt-head bream) or a *lubina* (sea bass), I served them with a bowl of *aioli*, boiled potatoes and a tomato and sweet onion salad. Poached or baked, fried or grilled, barbecued or simmered in a *sofrito* sauce, fish is cooked in so many ways in Ibiza.

A typical *Ibicenco* dish that I loved to eat was *Bullit de Peix* – literally translates as boiled fish. That doesn't sound very appetising, but it is. *Bullit de Peix* is a stew of fish simmered in a *sofrito* base of lightly fried onions, tomatoes, red peppers and garlic in olive oil, sometimes flavoured with a pinch of saffron and smothered in a runny *aioli*.

Bullit de Peix
Poached Fish in a Sofrito Sauce

Traditionally, this fish and potato stew was cooked by fishermen on their boats while at sea (typically with monkfish, red scorpion fish, John Dory or any other fish they had to hand). Today it is eaten as a two-part dish: the fish and potatoes, smothered in a runny *aioli* or sauce (page 127), are served first. Thereafter, rice, cooked in the reserved fish broth, is served. For my part, the fish and potato stew suffice. You can use any white fish such as, hake, haddock or halibut.

Saffron imparts a special flavour to the fish. If you don't have that in your store cupboard, use ground turmeric.

Bullit de Peix
Poached Fish in a Sofrito Sauce

SERVES 4–6

450g/1lb/2 cups white rice

10 saffron strands, or ¼ teaspoon ground saffron or ground turmeric

1 tablespoon hot water

2–3 tablespoons cold water

homemade *aioli* (page 127) or good quality shop-bought mayonnaise

3 tablespoons olive oil

1 onion, finely chopped

1 green pepper, deseeded and finely diced

3 garlic cloves, finely chopped

2 large ripe fresh tomatoes or 2 tinned plum tomatoes, finely chopped

3–4 medium potatoes, peeled and thickly sliced

salt and freshly ground black pepper, to taste

1 litre/35fl oz/4¼ cups fish or vegetable stock

800g–1kg/1¾lb–2¼lb white fish fillets, cut into thick pieces

a handful of fresh parsley, finely chopped

METHOD

- Wash the rice and soak it in cold water for about 15 minutes, then drain and set aside.
- Steep the saffron strands (if using) in the hot water and set aside.
- Add the cold water to the *aioli* or mayonnaise to loosen it, mix well and set aside.
- Stir-fry the onions in olive oil on medium heat for a good 5 minutes until softened, stirring frequently.
- Add the green pepper and cook for another 3 minutes, stirring occasionally. Add the garlic and stir-fry for a scant minute.
- Throw in the tomatoes and the steeped or ground saffron or turmeric and stir to mix. Simmer on medium heat for 2–3 minutes.
- Lay the potato slices on top. Add a sprinkling of salt and pepper and pour the stock over to cover. Cook covered on medium heat for 25 minutes or until the potatoes are cooked through.
- Then carefully nestle in the fish pieces, cover the pan and cook on medium heat for about 3 minutes. Then turn off the heat and leave to rest for 10 minutes. The fish will keep cooking.
- The fish is now ready. Carefully lift out all the ingredients with a slotted spoon and arrange them elegantly on a serving plate. Reserve the broth.
- Pour the *aioli* or mayonnaise over the fish. Sprinkle the chopped parsley over to finish, then serve.

THE RICE

- The rice is traditionally served, on its own, after the fish course but you can serve it together if you wish.
- Tip the drained rice into the pot of the remaining broth. The broth should be about two fingers above the level of the rice, so add extra water if needed. Bring to the boil, then lower the heat to a simmer.
- Cook covered for about 15–20 minutes or until the rice is tender.

Paella

The origin of the word paella is thought to be from the old Valencian/ Catalan language meaning pan, which has its roots in the Latin word *patella* also meaning pan. So, the term paella refers to both the dish and the pan in which the dish is cooked.

The first time I tasted a paella was in the 70s. I was a young teenager on a summer holiday with my family. We were enjoying a newly discovered beach on the eastern coast of Ibiza, where, in a temporary structure called a *chiringuito*, a cook was dishing out delicious platters of this iconic Spanish dish. I was hooked from the first mouthful.

Traditionally, paella was a rice dish made with chicken, rabbit, a few snails and some beans, and is believed to have originated in the countryside of Valencia where the farmers cooked their makeshift lunches on a wood fire in the fields. The staple ingredient was rice, to which was added whatever else was to hand. From these humble beginnings, paella developed into a richer platter of rice and seafood. The exuberant versions of paella of southern Spain would contain a handful of shrimps, prawns and mussels, sometimes lobster and octopus, as well as some vegetables. Chicken might also be added.

Another dish, not as ubiquitous as paella, is *fideuà*. Also originating in Valencia, it is a variation of paella with the same ingredients. However, instead of rice it is cooked with a vermicelli pasta. *Cappellini* and spaghetti are also often used. Black rice, produced by the addition of the squid's black ink (*arroz negro* or *arroz con pulp)* is also very popular. And there are also vegetarian variations.

Use the traditional Spanish *Bomba* or *Calaspara* rice if you can. If either of these are hard to come by, Arborio or a short-grain white rice will do, but bear in mind that the amount of liquid might differ. Unlike the rice for a risotto, which must be stirred to create that starchy creaminess with which we associate it, once the paella rice is tipped into the stock, it must not be disturbed. It can be shaken but not stirred, so as not to activate the starch.

The Spanish like their paella rice slightly underdone, very much al dente in fact. If not cooked just right, it can be downright raw – as some restaurants have served it! I prefer my rice well cooked with a crispy *soccarat* layer at the bottom. (See note on page 135.)

The following recipe was generously shared with me by our friend Lorenzo Soriano whose family comes from Valencia. Not only did he share the recipe, but he also demonstrated how to cook it. This he did by lighting a makeshift fire in the courtyard outside his garage, using pieces of dry wood placed on top of a barrel. An iron frame was secured astride the wood where the paella pan would sit. That afternoon was hot and windy so the fire took very quickly.

"This is the true Valencian paella that I am about to cook for you." Lorenzo proudly explained, "It doesn't contain fish or seafood or red peppers. Traditionally, we make it with rice, white butter beans, some green beans, chicken, sometimes rabbit and very small snails."

The one he cooked for us was with small pieces of chicken (no rabbit and no snails), some butter beans and some flat green beans. It was delicious in its simplicity.

History tells us that Queen Isabella of Spain issued a decree in 1492 ordering the expulsion of all Jews from the land. Those who wished to remain were forced to convert to Catholicism. Most of the Jews who did not want to renounce their faith went to Valencia, using it as a transit point from where they embarked on boats taking them to different parts of Europe. However, on arrival in Valencia, certain Jewish families had second thoughts and decided to stay and convert to Christianity. These were known as the *conversos*. Our friend, Lorenzo, comes from one of those families who, six centuries ago, stayed in Valencia and converted.

Over the last 50 years, my brothers and I visited Ibiza whenever we had the chance, until very recently, when my father passed away and my mother decided to sell their home there. I still regard Ibiza, and Spain in general, as my second home.

Lorenzo's Paella Valenciana
The 'true' Paella from Valencia

SERVES 4

(using a 50cm/20in diameter paella pan or a wide, shallow pan)

5 tablespoons olive oil

6 skinless, bone-in chicken thighs

1 garlic clove, smashed

1 teaspoon salt

4–5 tablespoons butter beans, from a tin or jar, drained

4 flat green or Helda beans, each sliced into 3 or 4 pieces

2 tomatoes, roughly chopped

1 litre/35fl oz/4¼ cups water

1 tablespoon ground turmeric

2 teaspoons sweet paprika

200g/7oz/1 cup Bomba rice

1–2 sprigs of fresh rosemary

1 lemon, quartered, to serve

- Using a paella pan or a wide, shallow pan, put the olive oil on a high heat.
- Add the pieces of chicken and the garlic clove. Sprinkle the salt over the chicken and then cook for 15 minutes or until golden brown on all sides, turning occasionally.
- After 5 minutes, discard the garlic (it is only there to give a hint of flavour).
- Stir in the butter beans, the green beans and the tomatoes. Cook for about 2–3 minutes.
- Add the water (you might need to add a little more later on).
- Mix in the turmeric and paprika. Bring to the boil, then simmer on medium heat for 15–20 minutes. Taste and adjust the flavour. The sauce might need a little more salt once you incorporate the rice.
- Drizzle the Bomba rice, a little at a time, into the pan. With a spoon, gently push the rice under the sauce. Do not stir.
- Throw in the rosemary sprigs. Give the pan a good shake. (The rice must not be stirred, no matter how much you are itching to see how it is doing. You can, however, shake the pan every so often.) Let it simmer gently for 16–18 minutes.
- Once the water has been absorbed, taste and see if the rice is cooked. If it is too al dente for you, add 2–3 more tablespoons of hot water and cook for 2–3 more minutes.
- Take off the heat, cover with foil or a plate and let it rest for 15 minutes before serving. The whole thing needs time to settle.

→ Serve with lemon quarters to squeeze on top of the rice.

Note: once the rice has been cooked, if you like, you can cover the pan and continue simmering on a medium-low heat to achieve the much-desired toasted layer of rice at the bottom called soccarat (the same as our hakaka – page 266) which the Spanish love. Be careful not to burn the rice though.

CAFÉ de la PAIX
LES FRUITS DE MER
du Café de la Paix
LE KIOSQUE
PLACE DE L'OPÉRA

Paris

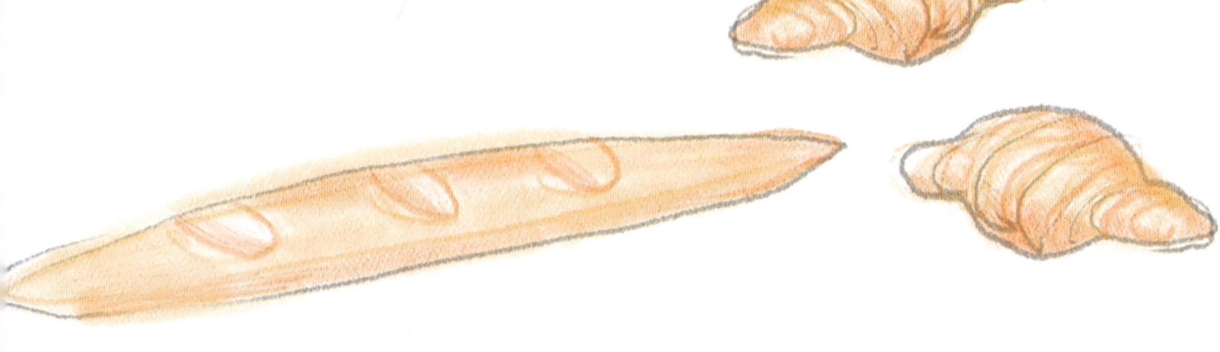

Chapter Five

Of Wine and Rosewater

Paris 1979–1993

"Dis-moi ce que tu manges, je te dirai ce que tu es."

"Tell me what you eat, I shall tell you what you are."

Anthelme Brillat-Savarin

It was love that made me move from London to Paris. That romance did not last long, but my love affair with France and everything French endured. Paris, I thought, is a city for women. Always written about in the feminine, she is the epitome of a beautiful one. Having moved from the sad, three-day-week of 70s London, Paris could not have been anything *but* exciting and I resolved to live and work in that city – which I did for the best part of fourteen years, delighting in everything Gallic. Paris was vibrant then, and happily, my work was well received.

I had arrived during the nouvelle cuisine era and found the food exciting. A fresher and more delicate approach to cooking was being adopted. Quality not quantity reigned with a minimal aspect to the dishes; their meticulous presentation, mirroring the Japanese style, was a joy to behold.

Having moved from the sad, three-day-week of 70s London, Paris could not have been anything but exciting.

Breakfast, for the first few weeks, was at *Le Café de Flore*: the iconic Left Bank café on the Boulevard St Germain. In past times, these were the meeting places for artists, writers, philosophers and Left Bank intellectuals. Jean-Paul Sartre, Albert Camus and Simone de Beauvoir were among its regulars during the post war years. Having breakfast there was a treat. I loved the flurry of waiters in white aprons taking orders and welcoming their loyal clients by name. I sometimes caught a glimpse of Paloma Picasso and her Spanish designer friend Paco Rabanne, having coffee and croissants or eggs, the Flore's speciality, *oeufs coques trois minutes* (eggs, soft-boiled for 3 minutes). The eggs were perfectly cooked each time – soft whites and runny yolks –accompanied by some chilled butter and lightly toasted *mouilletes*. These are the slim fingers of bread that we call soldiers in English. The French word seems more apt to me as the word comes from the verb *mouiller*, meaning to soak or to wet. It brought to mind, my maternal grandmother's advice on how to cook a soft-boiled egg:

> *In order to prevent the egg whites becoming hard or rubbery, place the eggs in a pan of cold water. Gently bring to the boil on a medium-low heat. This might take 5 minutes. Once boiling, simmer for 2 minutes. Then remove the pan from the heat, leaving the eggs in the water for one more minute before serving. The whites will be cooked and the yolks runny. If you leave the eggs in the water for another minute, the yolks will be honey-like.*

The mini *madeleine* cake is inextricably linked with the French writer, Marcel Proust. Biting into the tea-soaked cake triggered, for him, a long-forgotten childhood memory which he describes so precisely in his novel *À la Recherche du Temps Perdu* (*In Search of Lost Time*):

> *"No sooner had the warm liquid mixed with the cake touched my palate than a shudder ran through me and I stopped, intent upon the extraordinary thing that was happening to me. An exquisite pleasure had invaded my senses ...."* *

Out of the blue, as if out of nowhere, a flavour or a scent can provoke an emotion, rooting out forgotten memories from the well of the unconscious. This experience is sometimes referred to as a Proust moment.

I must have been about three years old, and my first time in Paris, when I had my first bite of a *madeleine*. Since then, the taste and dainty shape of that miniature cake has stayed with me, reminding me of everything French.

* Marcel Proust, *In Search of Lost Time*.

Madeleines
Mini French Cakes

Most of the *madeleine* recipes stipulate to melt the butter. However, Felicity Cloake, in her 2015 Guardian article, *How to Make the Perfect Madeleines*, asks for the butter to be melted until it browns – becoming almost a *ghee*. I have tried both ways and liked both outcomes. I found that browning the butter gives a more nutty flavour and a lighter, fluffier cake.

The batter is poured into ribbed moulds and baked, during which time the *madeleines* invariably puff up with a typical bump on the top. This bump is the result of a thermal shock produced by a very hot oven on very cold batter and chilled baking tins.

MAKES 24

you can use any number of moulds. I use two tins of 12 moulds each making 24 cakes in all

120g/4¼oz/generous ½ cup unsalted butter

120g/4¼oz/scant 1 cup plain white flour

a small pinch of salt

1½ teaspoons baking powder

3 eggs, at room temperature

90g/3¼oz/scant ½ cup caster sugar

100g/3½oz/½ cup soft light brown sugar

3 tablespoons runny honey

3 tablespoons milk

2 teaspoons vanilla extract

grated zest of 1 lemon

- Melt the butter in a small pan on medium-low heat and cook until it turns a golden brown, about 12 minutes. Pour immediately into a heatproof bowl (strain if the milk solids have turned brown) and set aside to cool.
- Sift the flour, salt and baking powder into a separate bowl.
- Using a stand mixer or an electric whisk, beat the eggs, then slowly add both sugars, the honey, milk, vanilla extract and lemon zest. Whisk vigorously until the mixture is pale and fluffy and has doubled in size. Then mix in the cooled melted butter.
- Fold the flour mixture into the egg mixture in stages to avoid lumpiness. Once the batter is smooth, cover and refrigerate for at least 3 hours or overnight.
- Meanwhile, butter the madeleine moulds and refrigerate the tray(s) for an hour or place in the freezer for 30 minutes.
- Preheat the oven to 160°C Fan (180°C /350°F/Gas Mark 4).
- Fill each mould with a tablespoon of the chilled batter. Do not overfill as the batter will expand when baked.
- Bake for about 9–12 minutes until puffed up and golden.
- Once out of the oven, cool for a minute or so in the moulds, then turn out onto a wire rack and leave to cool completely.

Note: madeleines are best eaten fresh on the day they are baked, when they are soft and moist. If you have some leftover, you can freeze them, or keep them in an airtight container at room temperature for up to 3–4 days.

Steak frites came to represent a certain Paris for me.

The French sometimes call a steak *un bifteck*. The word is a compressed version of beef and steak. The expression *gagner son bifteck* literally means earning one's steak or, earning a living. The French nickname for the English is *les rosbifs* because of their famous Sunday roast and their great love of beef.

Steak frites (probably what hamburgers are to Americans) came to represent a certain Paris for me. Although most bistros offer the combination of steak with fries, it was the signature dish and claim to fame of L'Entrecôte, a chain of restaurants peppered all over Paris. One could not book a table as they had a first-come-first-serve policy, which was slightly annoying because it meant one had to queue. And a queue there was – always. I used to frequent the one in Porte Maillot where the queue of eager diners would snake all around the block – the only time I saw the French queuing patiently!

The restaurant served a set menu of a simple lettuce salad with a mustard vinaigrette topped with walnuts, followed by their famous *faux-filet* steak cut into thick slices, accompanied by a heap of crispy fries. The quality was always consistent. Thinking of it today, I realise how much meat had been a staple in those days, with vegetables almost an afterthought. I too indulged in large quantities of beef, always accompanied by a glass or two of red wine.

The only time I saw the French queuing patiently!

You can use various cuts such as rump, flank, or ribeye. I recommend ribeye (aged if possible) for its flavour and texture. An important point: the steaks should be at room temperature before cooking them and, once cooked, should be allowed to rest for a few minutes before serving. And it all depends on how you like your meat – well-done, medium, medium-rare or rare – as well as the cooking method you choose. I prefer medium-rare, where you see a nice pink line once the steak is cut. And I sear the steak in a hot dry pan (without oil or butter) rather than frying or grilling it. Use a good heavy-based pan. Frozen French fries, fried or baked, are an easy option. For condiments on the side, I usually use mustard and/or mayonnaise and sometimes ketchup! *Zut alors!* Such sacrilege! Only for the fries though!

Chiner and Le Petit Navire.

The very expressive French word *chiner* has no equivalent in English. It roughly means to go hunting for something or to pick up or buy something, usually in an antique or flea market. And *chiner* was one of my favourite pastimes, and still is. On some weekends, I accompanied my friend Michael, an antique dealer from London, to the flea markets of Clignancourt, situated just outside Paris.

Buzzing with French and foreign dealers and collectors, the place was a rich cornucopia of paintings, sculptures, bronzes, ceramics, glass, furniture and other exquisite items, mostly French. I went there stirred with a sense of expectation and excitement, determined to find a little treasure. Invariably, I ended up buying something. One of my treasured finds was a group of vases, plaster prototypes made in Luxembourg in the 1950s for Villeroy & Boch. I don't know whether these designs were ever approved and manufactured commercially, but the white plaster vases are still with me and have a prominent place in our living room.

After walking many kilometres up and down the various stalls, the highlight was always lunch at Le Petit Navire – a typical French bistro crammed with tables to accommodate all the fans of their speciality dish, *moules marinières.* The mussels were cooked in a buttery, parsley sauce which was a flavoursome slurping joy, delicious for mopping up with some crusty *pain de campagne*. This is what we ate every time we went to the market. I can still conjure up the flavour in my mouth today, although I no longer eat shellfish.

The dish is easy to make. The basic sauce (which you can use for fish too) consists of shallots, garlic, butter, dry white wine, lemon juice, sometimes cream, some fresh parsley, salt and pepper. You sweat some chopped shallots and garlic in butter, to which you add dry white wine, lemon juice and seasoning and boil together. Next, you throw in the fresh mussels (in shell), which cook in 3–4 minutes, then stir in some double cream (if using) and chopped fresh parsley. *Et voila!*

ONE STARTER I CAME TO LOVE WAS *Céleri-Rave Rémoulade*. The first time I tasted it was at a brasserie called Thoumieux, situated a few blocks from where I used to work, in the 7th *arrondissement*. At first sight, the dish looked nondescript, unremarkable. But on trying it, my taste buds sang and my nose twinkled. Its appearance belied the fire in its belly. The celeriac was the protagonist; yes, it filled the plate with its nutty white flesh, but the pungent sauce was the engine. And I loved it.

The celeriac is julienned or grated through a box grater or a food processor, then mixed in a mustardy mayonnaise sauce. It is best to prepare the *rémoulade* sauce first as the celeriac discolours quickly when left unadorned.

I usually make the mayonnaise from scratch. But a good brand of shop-bought mayonnaise will do just as well. The important thing to remember is that the sauce should taste of mustard and must be pungent to contrast with the bland celeriac. The *rémoulade* mayonnaise sauce is very versatile and any left over goes well with cold cuts of meat or chicken, spread on bread instead of butter to make a sandwich, or just used as a dip.

Céleri-Rave Rémoulade
Celeriac Rémoulade

A fresh celeriac is easier to grate or slice than an old one which will be spongier, more hollow and lighter in weight. The fresher the root, the crunchier the salad.

Celeriac root is usually large, weighing anything from 450–600g/1lb–1lb 5oz. Bear in mind that 250g/9oz serves about 3 people for a side salad. So if you buy one that weighs around 500g/1lb 2oz, then it will serve about 4–6. You can always cut the celeriac in half and use one half for a soup and the other half for this salad.

SERVES ABOUT 4–6

about 500–600g/1lb 2oz–1lb 5oz celeriac (see intro above), peeled and grated or julienned

THE REMOULADE SAUCE

¾ cup mayonnaise (page 197)

1 tablespoon water

3 generous tablespoons Dijon mustard

a pinch of salt

FOR THE GARNISH

1–2 tablespoons small capers or sliced gherkins, drained

2 tablespoons finely chopped fresh parsley

- Mix the *rémoulade* sauce ingredients well.
- Peel the celeriac to a smooth globe with a sharp knife. Then grate it using a box grater or a food processor.
- Transfer to a serving dish or salad bowl.
- Mix the celeriac with the *rémoulade* sauce and garnish with the capers and parsley.
- You can make this salad in advance, keep it in the fridge, then serve it as a starter or as a side dish to grilled chicken or fish.

Note: for a lighter sauce, you can replace the mayonnaise with a 250g/9oz mixture of crème fraîche and Greek yogurt, then add the same amount of mustard, salt and pepper.

La Coupole

*"As I ate the oysters with their strong taste of the sea and their faint metallic taste that the cold white wine washed away, leaving only the sea taste and the succulent texture... I began to be happy and to make plans."**

My first experience of oysters was most surprising and magical. I was dining with friends at La Coupole, the famous 1930s brasserie in the 14th *arrondissement* of Montparnasse. They ordered a plateau of oysters. I had never eaten an oyster before. Knowing this and my reluctance to eat them, they dared me to try one. I had images of it wriggling in my mouth. The oysters were turquoise and grey, a limp mass lying inert in their mother of pearl shells – until they were sprinkled with lemon juice. That made them wince. I hesitated, then took the plunge. This was, after all, a delicacy to be tasted at least once in one's life. *Un, deux, trois*, and I slid the shell's briny contents into my mouth. A surprising taste of the ocean filled it. There was no need to chew much, if at all, as the whole thing swirled and glided down my throat. Its shape and colour belied its delicious flavour. Fresh and saline, it tasted of the vast ocean. Truly, not of fish. Not fishy at all. It evoked the sea like nothing else. It was one of my happiest discoveries.
For our main course, we ordered a fish dish (the sea again; that evening was all about the sea) called *St Pierre a l'oseille* – John Dory with a sorrel sauce. I had not tasted sorrel before and found it surprisingly tart and lemony; its leaves resembling spinach but only in looks. The pairing of the sorrel sauce with fish was the invention of chef Pierre Troisgros in the 1960s, at the very beginning of the nouvelle cuisine era. His dish consisted of thin fillets of wild salmon served with a sorrel sauce which became an emblematic dish of French gastronomy. Our John Dory was served on a bed of rice topped with the delicious lemony sauce.

When I cook the dish today, I sometimes choose trout or salmon, sea bass or bream, the important ingredient being the sauce. I usually buy sorrel at a farmers' market, because supermarkets don't seem to stock it. So, spinach would be a good alternative. Remember to add a good dose of lemon juice and zest to imitate the tartness of the sorrel.

* Ernest Hemingway, *A Moveable Feast*.

Truite à l'Oseille
Trout Fillets with a Sorrel Sauce

SERVES 4

about 700g/1lb 9oz trout or salmon fillet, cut into 4 pieces

1 lemon, zested

THE SORREL SAUCE

30g/1oz butter

2 tablespoons olive oil

2 shallots, finely chopped

250ml/8fl oz/1 cup dry white wine

300g /10½ oz sorrel leaves, stems removed and finely chopped

150ml/5fl oz/½ cup water or fish stock

1 tablespoon bouillon powder

200ml/7fl oz/scant 1 cup thick cream

salt and pepper to taste

- Heat the butter and olive oil in a pan on medium heat and sweat the shallots for about 3–4 minutes. Add the wine and boil until it is reduced by half (about 10 minutes).
- Add the sorrel, the water and bouillon powder and bring to the boil again. Lower the heat a little and continue cooking for 10 minutes until the sorrel has wilted completely. The leaves will turn a dark dull green.
- Mix in the cream, the salt and pepper and cook until the sauce begins to thicken, stirring occasionally.
- Taste and adjust the seasoning.
- Lightly season the fish with salt and pepper and steam for 6–7 minutes or until cooked through. Arrange them on individual plates and ladle the sauce over them.
- Finish with a squeeze of lemon and a sprinkling of lemon zest.

→ Serve with plain basmati rice.

EVERY SATURDAY, the Boulevard des Batignoles in the 17th *arrondissement* would come alive with its animated fruit and vegetable market where I did my weekly shop. Herbaceous, earthy scents infused the air. Farmers from the neighbouring regions exhibited their produce on long tables. It was a visual feast of colour and plenty.

The tables of the smaller growers were of particular interest to me because, although they displayed only a small amount of produce – all in different shapes and sizes – the quality did not disappoint. Their lemons, thin-skinned and small, perfumed my kitchen for days with their citrusy fragrance. And their tomatoes had the true taste of summer – ripe and sweet, making the simplest and tastiest salads. And I must not forget to mention their figs, meltingly and achingly sweet. The produce on sale at the market was organic, '*bio*' as the French call it. And you could tell it was so by their irregular and surprising shapes and, ultimately, by their flavour.

Forty years on, I find it strange that today, most so-called organic fruits and vegetables that we find in our shops, are visually no different from the non-organic ones. That is to say, all are uniform: same size, same shape, same colour – grown to look enticing but sadly lacking in flavour, like those beautiful roses which attract by their beauty and charm, but are bereft of perfume.

DURING MY TIME IN FRANCE, I travelled extensively, discovering the culinary traditions of the various regions. I found the North and South quite disparate, both in climate and food. And the same goes for the East and West. I came to love many regional wines and cheeses. In the south-western part of France, below Bordeaux, there is a region or *département* called Les Landes with a long Atlantic Ocean coastline. There, I sampled local wines coupled with local cheeses and bread. Absolutely superb. Small wines you would not usually find in a supermarket that come direct from the wine grower or *vigneron*.

I remember well the taste of a wine which had an evocative name: *Le Vin des Sables*, literally translated, the wine of sand. It tasted of the soil. And it tasted of the Atlantic, of the sand, of that ocean, of the sweetness of that region, of Les Landes. I loved it so much that, on my return to Paris, I went searching for it. Of course, it wasn't easy to find, because it was what the French call a *petit vin*, a small wine, but I found a bottle of the same year in an expensive wine shop at a far higher price than in Les Landes. I bought the bottle anyway. Once back home, I prepared some lovely goat's cheese and fresh bread and poured the wine in anticipation. I sipped it, and sipped again, and was disappointed. Naturally! Neither the taste nor the experience was comparable. How could my flat in Paris match the open spaces of Les Landes and of the Atlantic Ocean...? Doubtless, the common wisdom that small wines do not usually travel well, rings true.

The Loire Valley, so rich in tradition, introduced me to its various local wines (I fell in love with the elegant taste of *Sancerre*) and its many delicious cheeses, not to mention the iconic regional dessert, *tarte tatin,* invented by the Tatin sisters who ran a restaurant and a hotel in the region. The story goes that the said *tarte* was initially a mistake.

One of the sisters was making an apple tart for a customer and, becoming distracted, baked it upside down. Distraught, she nevertheless flipped it on a plate and served it.

And the rest is history.

Tarte Tatin with Nectarines and Apricots

Although traditionally baked with apples, I took the opportunity of summer fruits to make this *tarte*. Halfway through assembling it, I realised that I needed one more nectarine which I did not have. So, I used two ripe apricots to fill the middle space and other gaps. You can, of course, use solely apricots or nectarines.

Tarte Tatin

Baked Nectarine and Apricot Tatin

SERVES 4–6

you will need a 20cm/8in shallow ovenproof pan or tart tin.

1–2 ripe apricots, sliced

4–5 ripe nectarines, halved

85g/3oz sugar

55g/2oz chilled butter, diced

300g/10½oz all-butter puff pastry

2 tablespoons flaked almonds

½ teaspoon ground cardamom

FOR THE GARNISH

1 tablespoon flaked almonds or crushed pistachios

1 tablespoon lemon juice

METHOD

- Preheat the oven to 160°C Fan (180°C/350°F/Gas Mark 4).
- Slice the apricots and nectarines in half and prise out the stones.
- If they are hard, the stones will be difficult to take out, so use a spoon to dig around the stone and then lift it out.
- Place the ovenproof pan on the hob on medium heat with the sugar. Shake the pan every so often but do not stir. Cook for about 5 to 8 minutes, then turn off the heat and add the butter.
- Once the butter has melted, arrange the nectarines snuggly in a circle around the edge of the pan first, then fill the empty spaces in the middle and other gaps with slices of apricots. There shouldn't be too many empty gaps in between.
- Cook covered for 5 minutes on medium heat.
- Roll out the puff pastry and cut a circle a little larger than the size of the pan, about 2–3 cm all round. (You can do this by putting a plate on top of the dough and cut around it.) Prick with a fork all over for the steam to escape.
- Lay the dough on top of the nectarines and gently tuck the extra dough down the sides of the pan. Prick with a knife in a few places to let the steam out.
- Bake for 30 minutes or so, until the pastry puffs up and turns crisp and golden.
- Take out of the oven and allow to cool down a little before inverting the *tarte* onto a serving dish. Do this with oven gloves in a swift and precise movement. Some juices will inevitably run out, but leave it to rest for about a minute or two before cleaning up around the plate if needs be.
- Sprinkle with the lemon juice, cardamom and slivered almonds or crushed pistachios.

→ Serve warm with some ricotta cheese, vanilla ice cream or double cream.

Note: if the tarte is not sweet enough for your taste, dust it with some icing sugar.

My work took me to various parts of France. I particularly liked the South of France. There I discovered *Provençale* and *Basque* dishes and sauces which exuded sunshine and summer for me. One herb mixture that is used abundantly is called *persillade*. Its name derives from the French *persil*, meaning parsley, and *ail*, meaning garlic. This simple mixture of chopped flat-leaf parsley and garlic is very versatile. You can toss it in a pasta dish with some olive oil and a few anchovy fillets; add it to a stir-fry of mushrooms; use it to spice up a potato salad; bake it over cod or haddock (page 155) or serve it as a delicious snack simply mixed with olive oil spread on a thick piece of warm bread with a slice of tomato atop. Ah, so many variations to be had! I absolutely love it.

Persillade
Parsley and Garlic Seasoning

7–8 plump garlic cloves, finely chopped

1 teaspoon salt

about 70g /2½ oz fresh parsley, finely chopped

2 tablespoons Aleppo pepper

2 tablespoons olive oil

toasted breadcrumbs (only add this if using the *persillade* immediately)

- Using a mortar and pestle, grind the garlic, measured salt, chopped parsley and Aleppo pepper together to make a paste and then mix in the olive oil. Use as necessary. Add the breadcrumbs on the day.
- Chop the parsley using a very sharp knife. A blunt(ish) knife would bruise its leaves and tear them rather than slice them neatly.
- If you do not have the patience to chop, use a food processor, but bear in mind that the parsley will be somewhat crushed as opposed to neatly sliced.

Note: while it is best used on the day it is made, should you make too much or have leftovers, keep it in the fridge (for no more than a couple of days) in a glass jar with a lid, totally immersed in olive oil. This stops it from oxidising and going mouldy.

Eglefin à la Persillade
Haddock Loins with a Persillade Mixture

I have made this dish a few times using various types of white fish like haddock, cod or sea bass. I usually use panko breadcrumbs, but you can use any dried breadcrumbs of your choice. Also, I favour butter to finish this dish as it moistens and enhances the flesh of white fish, which can be a little dry.

SERVES 4

6–7 plump garlic cloves, finely chopped

½ teaspoon salt

about 70g/2½ oz fresh parsley, roughly chopped

2 tablespoons Aleppo pepper

2 tablespoons olive oil

2 generous tablespoons panko breadcrumbs

800g/1¾ lb haddock loin or fillet (or use sea bass, cod or another white fish)

a good sprinkling of hot curry powder (about a tablespoon)

about 6 small round shallots, cut in half

4 knobs of butter

lemon juice, to drizzle

salt and freshly ground black pepper, to taste

- Preheat the oven to 180°C Fan (200°C/400°F/Gas Mark 6).

THE PERSILLADE

- Using a mortar and pestle, grind the garlic, measured salt, chopped parsley and Aleppo pepper together to make a paste and then mix in the olive oil and breadcrumbs.

THE FISH

- Cut the fish into four equal portions and place them in a single layer in an ovenproof dish. Season with salt and pepper.
- Sprinkle the curry powder evenly over the fish.
- Spoon the *persillade* mixture evenly over the fish to cover all the pieces.
- Arrange the shallot halves around the fish, then place a knob of butter on each piece of fish and finish with a drizzle of lemon juice.
- Bake for about 15–16 minutes until the fish is cooked through.

→ Serve accompanied by *tomates à la Provençale* (page 156).

Tomates à la Provençale
Baked Persillade Tomatoes

This simple dish makes a nice vegetarian starter and is best enjoyed in the summer when tomatoes are ripe, flavourful and juicy.

SERVES 4

PERSILLADE MIXTURE
(page 153)

2 tablespoons panko breadcrumbs (or any dried breadcrumbs of your choice)

2 tablespoons Aleppo pepper

4 large ripe tomatoes, each cut in half horizontally

20 black or green olives, stoned and roughly chopped

2–3 tablespoons olive oil

salt and freshly ground black pepper, to taste

- Preheat the oven to 180°C Fan (200°C/400°F/Gas Mark 6).
- Mix the panko breadcrumbs and the Aleppo pepper with the *persillade*.
- Place the tomato halves, cut-side up, in a single layer in an ovenproof dish. Season with salt and pepper and add a scant teaspoon of the chopped olives to each one. Top the tomatoes with the *persillade* mixture.
- Drizzle with the olive oil, cover the dish with foil and bake for about 10 minutes. Uncover and continue baking for another 10–12 minutes (by this stage, the tomatoes should be nicely cooked but not collapsing).

→ Serve hot or cold as a starter on a bed of rocket leaves or as an accompaniment to grilled fish or chicken.

Tian
A Southern French Baked Vegetable Dish

Tian is the name of both the earthenware vessel used for cooking and the *Provençale* speciality of thinly sliced seasonal vegetables such as courgettes, tomatoes and aubergines. A baked version of ratatouille in its ingredients, a *tian* is a delicious starter and also makes a good accompaniment to grilled chicken or meat.

SERVES 4

olive oil for cooking

2 onions, thinly sliced

2 garlic cloves, thinly sliced

1 teaspoon dried mixed herbs

a sprinkling of fresh thyme

1 aubergine, very thinly sliced

2 courgettes, thinly sliced

4 tomatoes, thickly sliced into rounds

salt and freshly ground black pepper, to taste

METHOD

- Heat 2–3 tablespoons of olive oil in a pan on medium heat and add the onions. Season with a pinch of salt and cook until soft, about 10–12 minutes. You can drizzle a little water over them to help them cook faster.
- Mix in the garlic and the herbs. Cook for a minute or two.
- Lightly oil an ovenproof dish. Arrange the onion mixture inside in a flat layer and set aside.
- Preheat the oven to 160°C Fan (180°C/350°F/Gas Mark 4).
- Prepare an ovenproof bowl of water to place on the bottom shelf to humidify the dish.
- Stir-fry the aubergine slices in 3 tablespoons of olive oil on medium heat for a few minutes, until softened. Do this in batches, removing each sautéed batch to a plate. Add more oil as needed.
- Arrange the sliced vegetables in the ovenproof dish, in overlapping and alternating rows on top of the onion layer: aubergines, then tomatoes and then courgettes.
- Season with salt and pepper. Sprinkle with an extra pinch of dried herbs and drizzle 3 tablespoons of olive oil all over.
- Cover the dish with foil and bake for about one hour or so. Half way through, uncover the dish and continue cooking until the vegetables are cooked through.

→ Serve warm or at room temperature. To deepen the flavour, this dish can be prepared a few hours in advance.

Piperade *can be prepared well in advance and stored in the fridge for up to a week.*

A south-western speciality, *Piperade* is a French and Spanish Basque relish comprising slow-cooked onions, red or green peppers and ripe tomatoes with a hint of heat from *Espellete* peppers. These are a type of mild chilli pepper cultivated in the Basque regions of Spain and France. You can use Aleppo pepper instead.

Piperade can be prepared well in advance and stored in the fridge for a week or so. You can spread it over toast to make a deliciously satisfying open sandwich; serve it over pan-fried or steamed fish, or use it as a base for simmering pieces of chicken or fish. It makes a rich pasta sauce too and accompanies most things savoury. I like to make an omelette or scrambled eggs with the relish.

Piperade
Basque Pepper and Tomato Relish

SERVES ABOUT 4
or more (depending on how you use it)

2 onions, grated

3 tablespoons olive oil

3 red peppers and 2 green peppers, deseeded, thinly sliced lengthways, then cut in half

1 fresh red chilli, finely chopped (optional)

1 jalapeño pepper, finely chopped

1 teaspoon Aleppo pepper

2 garlic cloves, finely chopped

400g/14oz tin plum tomatoes and their juice

1 teaspoon fresh thyme

1 tablespoon granulated sugar

1 tablespoon lemon juice

1 teaspoon salt

1 tablespoon roughly chopped fresh parsley, to garnish

- In a pot, sweat the onions in the olive oil on medium heat until transparent and soft, about 10 minutes. Do not brown.
- Add the red and green pepper slices, the chilli, jalapeño and Aleppo pepper to the pot. Cover and continue cooking on medium heat for another 20 minutes or so, stirring occasionally.
- Next, stir in the garlic, tomatoes (and their juice), the thyme and the sugar. Cover and simmer for another 20 minutes, stirring occasionally.
- Now add the lemon juice and season with the salt. Cook, uncovered, on medium heat until most of the liquid has evaporated. The vegetables should be soft and moist. Taste and adjust the seasoning.

→ Transfer to a serving dish and garnish with the parsley. You can serve piperade immediately or, for a deeper flavour, it will taste even better the following day, either cold or reheated.

Tips: you can poach fish or chicken pieces in the piperade. Simply lay them snugly in the mixture. Cover the pan and cook on medium heat for about 10 minutes or so until cooked through. If the piperade becomes too thick, mix in a cup of water as you go.

For poached eggs, shakshuka-style, make four wells in the hot piperade, break an egg into each well, then cover the pan and poach on low heat until the eggs are cooked to your liking.

Le Couscous Tunisien de Mon Ami Ali

IN MY NEIGHBOURHOOD, there were lots of bistros and brasseries, as well as mall restaurants offering various ethnic cuisines: Vietnamese, Senegalese, Berber and North African. A favourite of mine was an Algerian restaurant which I regularly frequented. They served a spicy couscous with pieces of lamb and loads of vegetables atop. The hot sauce poured over the dish was exquisite.

Of course, couscous is not a French dish. What makes it French for me is the fact that there are a multitude of North African restaurants in Paris serving this dish and, like curry for the English, it is almost a national dish for the French. And that is why I have included it here.

The recipe below was given to me in Paris by my friend, Ali, who learned it from his mother, a Tunisian Berber. Her recipe asks for rubbing and steaming the couscous grains three times. A quicker way is to pour boiling water on the grains and follow the instructions on the packet.

The most common spice blend is the Moroccan *ras el hanout*, which can consist of up to 20 different spices. It is an essential ingredient when making couscous. I use a shop-bought *ras el hanout* blend. You will need a *couscousier* or a large pot with a steamer section on top.

The hot sauce poured over the dish was exquisite.

Le Couscous Tunisien de Mon Ami Ali
Ali's Tunisian Couscous

SERVES 6 OR MORE

800g/1¾ slb boneless lamb shank or shoulder, cubed

500g/1lb 2oz medium couscous

4 tablespoons olive oil, plus extra for drizzling

2 onions, grated or finely chopped

3cm/1¼in piece of fresh root ginger, peeled and finely chopped

4 garlic cloves, finely chopped or crushed

2 tomatoes, grated or finely chopped

4 tablespoons tomato purée

2 litres/3½ pints/8½ cups water, plus more if needed

3 carrots, peeled and cut lengthways in half and then in half again

2 celery sticks, roughly chopped

3 turnips, peeled and quartered

400g/14oz tin chickpeas, drained and rinsed

3 courgettes, each cut in half lengthways

FOR THE SPICES

3 tablespoons ras el hanout

3 tablespoons harissa paste

1 teaspoon ground cumin

salt, to taste

- Heat 2 tablespoons of the olive oil in the *couscousier* or large pot and sauté the onions on medium heat until soft and golden, about 15 minutes.
- Add the ginger and stir-fry for 2 minutes.
- Mix in the garlic and cook on a low heat for another minute.
- Mix all the spices together with salt to taste, tip them in and stir-fry for a minute or so. Do not let them burn.
- Turn the heat up to medium-high, then add the lamb and the remaining 2 tablespoons of olive oil. Mix well and then brown the meat on all sides, stirring frequently.
- Once the meat is browned, cover and let it sweat for about 10 minutes on a low heat. Uncover the pan, raise the heat to high and stir the meat until it's sizzling again.
- Mix in the tomatoes and tomato purée and scrape the bottom of the pan to loosen the lovely brown bits. Add enough water to almost cover the meat.
- Bring to the boil, then reduce to a medium heat, cover and simmer for one hour until the meat is very soft.
- Once the meat is tender, add the carrots, celery and turnips. Cover with the rest of the water, then cook on medium heat for 15 minutes.

· Add the chickpeas and courgettes and cook, covered, for another 15 minutes. If you want more sauce, add a little more water and bring to a simmer.

· Meanwhile, prepare the couscous grains by following the instructions on the packet, or by immersing them for 10 minutes in the same volume of boiling water as the grains and cover. Fluff up the couscous with a fork. Drizzle some olive oil on top and fluff up again, separating all the stuck bits.

· Tip the couscous into the steamer on top of the *couscousier* or pot to steam while the vegetables are cooking underneath.

→ When you are ready to serve, arrange the couscous in a mound on a large serving dish. Add a sprinkling of olive oil to the grains and fluff up again with a fork. Then arrange the vegetables and meat around it. Pour a ladleful of the stewing sauce on top. Keep the rest of the sauce on the side for everyone to serve themselves.

Note: you can also serve the couscous in a serving dish on its own and serve the stew in a separate dish. You might put some extra harissa paste on the side for those who would like a spicier fare.

Ratatouille
Provençale Vegetable Stew

Ratatouille, from the Occitan word *ratatouiller*, meaning to stir, is a *Provençale* vegetable dish, the epitome of Mediterranean cooking and flavours. Much like another *Provençale* dish called *Tian* (page 157) which is baked, a ratatouille has a tomato sauce and is cooked on the hob like a stew. Similar vegetable dishes exist around the Mediterranean basin, for example, *tombet* in Majorca, *samfaina* in Catalonia or *caponata* in Italy.

There are many ways of cooking ratatouille. Some people put all the cubed ingredients in one pot, cover and cook for about 1½ hours. Others brown or sauté each individual ingredient separately, then cook them altogether for about 45–60 minutes. A friend of mine puts the aubergines and courgettes in the oven and bakes them for about 30 minutes before combining them on the hob with the other vegetables. The most important point for me is the aubergines. They have to be really well cooked and melting, not spongy. In this recipe, I sauté the diced courgettes and the aubergines first before adding the rest of the ingredients to the pan. You want a *confit* of vegetables (cooked slowly in their own fat or juices) not a stew with lots of sauce, so slow cooking is what I recommend.

Ratatouille goes very well with grilled chicken, fish or grilled lamb chops. You can serve it on its own with a nice piece of crusty bread. It is also delicious cold, spooned on a lettuce leaf or a thick piece of bread.

Ratatouille
Provençale Vegetable Stew

SERVES 4–6

olive oil, for drizzling and frying

1 large onion, finely chopped

2 medium aubergines, diced

2 courgettes, diced

2 red peppers, deseeded and cut into cubes

2–3 garlic cloves, finely chopped

5 large ripe fresh tomatoes or 4 tinned plum tomatoes, roughly chopped

a small handful of mixed fresh thyme and parsley, roughly chopped, plus extra parsley to garnish

salt and Aleppo pepper, to taste

½ teaspoon rose harissa (optional)

about 60ml/2fl oz/¼ cup water

about 8 Kalamata olives, stoned and roughly chopped

1 teaspoon capers in brine

2 tablespoons lemon juice, to finish

Note: if the stew has too much liquid, uncover and cook on a high heat for a few minutes.

- Heat 4 tablespoons of olive oil in a large pan or pot and sauté the onion on a medium heat until very soft and translucent, about 20 minutes.
- Add the diced aubergines and stir-fry until soft and lightly coloured (add more oil as needed). Then mix in the red peppers, the diced courgettes and garlic and stir to mix. Cook for about 15–20 minutes stirring occasionally, until softened.
- Add the tomatoes and the mixed thyme and parsley, the rose harissa (if using) season with some salt and Aleppo pepper, then cover and simmer on a medium-low heat for 5 minutes.
- Add the water and continue cooking on medium heat for another 40 minutes or so, stirring every so often. You want to achieve a honey-like consistency at the end.
- Once cooked, stir in the olives and the capers.
- This dish is best served after it has rested for a few hours or the following day. Enjoy it cold, hot or at room temperature.

→ Spoon the ratatouille into a large serving dish, or serve as a starter on individual plates. Drizzle the lemon juice on top and garnish with some extra chopped parsley.

Fish and Ratatouille

SERVES 4

olive oil, for greasing and drizzling

4 thick cod loins, about 600g/1lb 5oz in all

Aleppo pepper, for sprinkling (optional)

4 knobs of butter

salt and freshly ground black pepper, to taste

TO SERVE

a generous quantity of ratatouille

a squeeze or two of lemon juice

Of course, you can cook ratatouille specifically for this recipe (pages 164–66). But as I always cook a big batch of it, invariably I have some left over for the next day. That's when we enjoy it straight from the fridge on pieces of toast or spoon it inside lettuce leaves as a cold starter in the summer.

For a more substantial meal, I add a few fish pieces.

METHOD ONE

- Simply lay your raw fish in or over the ratatouille. Cover the pan and cook on medium heat for about 10–15 minutes or so until the fish is cooked through. You are actually steaming the fish on top of the vegetables. You can use any fillets of fish of your choice, I prefer to use a white fish because it contrasts well with the ratatouille.
- To avoid the ratatouille becoming too thick or dry, mix in 125ml/½ cup water before reheating it.

METHOD TWO

- Lightly oil an ovenproof dish with a little olive oil. Put the fish in the prepared ovenproof dish in a single layer. Season with some salt, pepper and Aleppo pepper (if using). Massage the pieces of fish with olive oil on all sides.
- Bake for about 20 minutes in the oven at 180°C Fan (200°C/400°F/Gas Mark 6) until cooked through.

→ Serve on a bed of warm ratatouille with a squeeze of lemon juice on the fish.

Le Gratin de Famille
Courgette Gratin

A summer dish that is very popular and homely all over France. Every household makes this dish during the hot summer months when there is an abundance of courgettes. The courgettes are sometimes sliced, grated or cubed, then steamed, stir-fried or blanched in water or milk, before being coated with a mixture of eggs, cream or crème fraîche and grated cheese. I make this dish with a breadcrumb gratin top very often. I serve it warm or cold with a simple salad on the side.

SERVES 4

you will need a 20cm/8in round or square ovenproof dish for a thicker gratin or a rectangular dish 20 × 35cm (8 × 14in) for a slim one

2 tablespoons olive oil

2 banana shallots, thinly sliced

½ teaspoon salt

½ teaspoon freshly ground black pepper

500g/1lb 2oz courgettes (about 3), thinly sliced using a mandolin or a sharp knife

2 large eggs

85ml/3fl oz/⅓ cup milk

3 tablespoons double cream or crème fraîche

a light grating of nutmeg (optional)

50g/1¾oz/⅓ cup finely grated Emmental or Gruyère cheese

50g/1¾oz/scant ¼ cup ricotta or cottage cheese

2 teaspoons cornflour, mixed with 4 tablespoons milk or water

FOR THE TOPPING

60g/2¼oz/½ cup finely grated Emmental or Gruyère cheese

1 tablespoon panko breadcrumbs

1 tablespoon butter, cut into 3 pieces, plus extra for greasing

- Butter an ovenproof dish and set aside.
- Heat the olive oil in a large pan. When hot, add the shallots, salt and black pepper. Stir-fry for a minute or so and then cover the pan and cook on a medium-low heat for 10 minutes, stirring from time to time, until the shallots soften a little.
- Mix in the courgette slices and cover the pan. Cook on medium heat for another 5 minutes. Then take off the heat and spread the vegetables in the buttered ovenproof dish in one even layer. Set aside to cool down.
- Preheat the oven to 160°C Fan (180°C/350°F/Gas Mark 4).
- Beat the eggs in a bowl, then mix in the milk, the cream or crème fraîche, the nutmeg (if using), grated cheese, ricotta or cottage cheese and the blended cornflour slurry. Pour the mixture over the cooled courgettes and spread evenly.
- For the topping, mix the breadcrumbs with the grated cheese and scatter evenly over the top of the creamy egg mixture. Pop the butter pieces on top.
- Bake for 30–40 minutes or until the top is golden brown.

→ Serve at room temperature with a leafy salad.

Clafouti
Baked Fruit Flan

Catherine, my friend from Poitiers, introduced me to *le clafouti*; her favourite dessert from the nearby Limousin region which she made very often during the summer. Consisting of a baked custard batter, it would be filled with a seasonal fruit, traditionally cherries which grow abundantly in that region, but it can also be made with other fruits such as apples, plums or pears. The name *clafouti*, meaning to fill, is not French. It comes from the Occitan language (*langue d'oc*) a branch of the Romance language of the Troubadours, that was spoken in southern France and north-eastern Spain in the 12th century.

In the summer, use cherries, apricots or strawberries. In the autumn, pears make delicious *clafouti*. In winter, you can choose frozen dark cherries or other frozen berries.

SERVES 6

you will need a 20cm/8in baking tin or ovenproof dish

a knob of butter for greasing

4 tablespoons granulated sugar

500g/1lb 2oz fresh cherries with stones in

cherry brandy or kirsch

icing sugar, to dust

FOR THE BATTER

50g/2oz/generous ¼ cup plain flour

70g/2½oz/⅓ cup caster sugar

a pinch of salt

3 eggs

200ml/7fl oz/scant 1 cup milk

75ml/2½fl oz/5 tablespoons double cream

½ teaspoon vanilla extract

50g/1¾oz/3½ tablespoons butter, melted

- Preheat the oven to 160°C Fan (180°C/350°F/Gas Mark 4).
- Oil the tin with the knob of butter, then sprinkle 2 tablespoons of the granulated sugar all over.
- Scatter the cherries in the tin. Sprinkle the remaining 2 tablespoons of granulated sugar over the fruit.
- For the batter, sift the flour, caster sugar and salt into a large bowl.
- Form a well in the middle, add the eggs, then whisk from the centre into the flour. Incorporate to make a smooth mixture with no lumps.
- Whisk in the milk slowly and then whisk in the cream, vanilla and melted butter, mixing to a smooth batter. Pour the batter evenly over the fruit.
- Bake for 30–40 minutes or until the top becomes golden brown.

→ Serve with 2–3 tablespoons of cherry brandy or kirsch drizzled over the *clafouti* and dust with icing sugar. This is best served warm soon after baking.

Note: leftovers can be kept in an airtight container in the fridge for 4–5 days, then enjoyed at room temperature or reheated until slightly warm.

AFTER MANY YEARS OF LIVING IN PARIS, away from my family, 'Frenchness' rubbed off on me. Like the French, I bought my daily baguette and *croissant-beurre* from the baker at the top of my road; like the French, I buttered my radishes and dipped them in salt; and like the French drank wine with every meal and every cheese. I spoke French, dressed French, and my friends were French. So, I persuaded myself that I could become '*Française*'; that I could conceive of putting down roots in this beautiful country and call it home.

That thought kept progressing and evolving in my mind for a long time, until... until the day my friend Catherine offered me some macaroons which her Lebanese friend had baked. The first bite flooded me with an immediate recognition! It was my Proust moment! This was mine, something I had perhaps forgotten. The rosewater in the macaroon filled my mouth like a familiar language; spoke to me, sang sweetly. Rosewater, which I had not tasted for many years, spelled family; the taste, the fragrance; my childhood. All the desserts I used to eat were perfumed with rosewater. And so were all grandmothers.

A voice within me asked, "*Mais tu es Française, non?*" "But you are French, now, aren't you?" The rosewater whispered, "Do you remember swimming in the Tigris river at dawn?"

Le vin et l'eau de rose. Wine and rosewater. Two stories. I have two stories within me.

*'We shall not cease from exploration,
and the end of all our exploring
will be to arrive where we started and
know the place for the first time.'*

T. S. Elliot, *Little Gidding, Four Quartets*

It's ironic how things turn out. Some walk the straight road all their life; others seem to take the less obvious path. I was searching for my 'place', a place where I felt I could belong, not realising that it was there all the while in the form of community – the Iraqi community that I had found too oppressive in my youth. But taking this path, exhilarating though it had been, was also very lonely. I made friends, of course, but I was always an 'exotic' outsider. And so I learned that identity is a complex construct. And attachment and detachment are a delicate balance to navigate. For those of us displaced or uprooted, for whom remnants of our past culture have undergone a gradual erosion, what endures is food and, if one is lucky, language and community.

I took another bite of the macaroon.

It was time to go home.

The Return Home

Chapter Six

The Return Home

London 1994

Sometimes one travels far. Very far. In search of something very near. Saliently under one's nose.

HOME IS WHERE MY STORY BEGAN. The return journey is where it ends. To London where my family lives. Where my home is now. Where I have a place. And a community. Where I met my husband. And where I reconnected with childhood friends. Warmly. Effortlessly. As if no time had passed. A thread of continuity making sense of me.

The London of 1994 had changed a lot. I found it more dynamic. More sure of itself than when I had left it. And more 'American'. The thing that surprised me, though, was the food. It was so much better than I remembered it. New restaurants were appearing serving delicious fusion food, creative dishes with new flavours. Modern British cooking was now exciting and forward-looking, easily overtaking the French by its sheer inventiveness.

One of the ambitions I cherished ever since I was a teenager was to open a small takeaway restaurant serving homemade Iraqi and Mediterranean food. But the project remained an idyllic dream for many practical reasons: time, or the lack of it, being one of them; I was still involved in my design practice; the high rents and the long-term financial investments required were another. Moreover, the stringent health and safety regulations were rather daunting, dampening my enthusiasm. Happily, sharing food and recipes, and hosting relaxed suppers and brunches, on a regular basis, mitigated my disappointment.

I am a home cook. Pottering in the kitchen is very natural to me. My cooking tends to be simple and spontaneous. The simpler the recipe, the better. And by simple, I don't mean bland. More and more I seem to shy away from elaborate dishes. In fact, on most days, I cook instinctively without the guidance of a recipe. What I have lurking in the fridge or larder dictates the meal I shall cook. And I am never afraid of leftovers. On the contrary, I treat them with respect. They are a precious ingredient to create yet another meal the following day. I like to cook in this flexible way. I like experimenting and as a result, many dishes continually evolve over time.

It always surprises me how a few humble ingredients, combined together with care and love, can give us such wonderful meals.

Bee Wilson in her book, *The Secret of Cooking*, writes "The problem with recipes is that nothing about cooking is obvious until you have done it at least once." And that is so true with everything. She quotes the journalist and novelist John Lanchester saying "A recipe is only ever scaffolding, not the building", which is a lovely metaphor, the point being that recipes are neither set in stone nor sacred. They are meant to be used as guides and to be followed, at least once, to help you understand a dish. And you can make them your own by adjusting and adapting them to suit your palate. This way, cooking becomes exciting and personal.

Our Family

An ingredient has a story, entwined in the history and stories of people: of geography and travel; of politics and trade.

Ingredients can enliven history lessons for children and young adults, becoming an educational and also a fun tool to pique their interest.

This way children will learn in a more tangible way about other countries and cultures and enrich their view of the world and our planet.

My Store Cupboard

SALT – of course. I use Maldon sea salt flakes and another herb-infused salt, appropriately called Herbamare. In her book, *An Everlasting Meal*, Tamar Adler's recommendation is to season water with salt before boiling or simmering anything in it. How much salt you ask? Well, it depends on the volume of water. But as a general rule, she advises that the water tastes pleasantly of the sea.

LEMONS, lemons, lemons, I cannot be a day without them – without the tang of sour to lift some dishes. After salt, lemons are the most important ingredient in my kitchen. We go through more than a dozen a week, some of which are unwaxed, which I use for their zest or to pickle, others go into sweet and sour stews, soups and various sauces or dressings.

Whenever I feel there is something missing in a dish, I ask my husband to taste. Often, his reply is "It's fine... but it needs more lemon." Of course, depending on the dish, this does not necessarily mean more lemon juice.

It could mean a pinch more of *amchur* (dried mango powder) or *sumac* (a tart substitute) lemon zest, tamarind, pomegranate molasses, vinegar, wine or dried lime. These souring agents are general inhabitants of my store cupboard. Of course, as with any seasoning, less is more. Also, remember to drizzle lemon juice on your cooked greens just before serving, as the acid will dumb down their bright green colour if put earlier.

OLIVE OIL The queen of trees for me is the great olive tree. From its small bitter drupes, it gives us rivers of gold. I would be bereft without it in my kitchen. I use extra virgin olive oil for everything: for frying, for baking, in cakes, in biscuits, in salads, on vegetables, in sauces and preserves. I also keep a bottle of walnut oil, light olive oil and sesame oil in the fridge for occasional use. And of course, olives, bitter green ones or black Kalamata, are always to hand.

ALEPPO PEPPER FLAKES are also known as *Halaby* (Aleppo in Arabic) because they used to be produced in the Aleppo region of Syria, and now in Turkey. It is my favourite chilli and I can be generous in using it because it is warm and fruity and milder than other chillies. I buy it by the kilo as I sprinkle it on many dishes and even on fruit.

ZAATAR. This is a wonderful mixture of sesame seeds, dried thyme, salt, and marjoram. I use it a lot sprinkled over boiled eggs and sliced mozzarella cheese, or mixed with olive oil it makes a delicious dip to dunk bread in.

MY OTHER FLAVOURING AGENTS are honey; marmalade; rosewater; orange blossom water; cardamom; sugar; saffron; turmeric; cayenne pepper; cinnamon; paprika; baharat; curry powder; tomato purée; cumin, fennel, and coriander seeds to be ground as required; fresh root ginger; garlic and onions.

Always to hand are various types of rice; lentils and dried or tinned beans; frozen peas; various nuts and seeds, as well as good-quality Lebanese tahina; harissa paste; soy sauce; tinned tomatoes, sardines, anchovies; and Dijon mustard.

FRESH HERBS such as parsley, coriander, mint and tarragon are bought on the day or weekly and kept in the fridge. To keep parsley fresh for a couple of weeks, I find that washing it and wrapping it in a cloth while damp, then inserting it into a plastic bag, does the trick. Don't be tempted to do that with fresh coriander or mint, as they rot when damp. Instead, trim off the ends of the stalks, place in a glass with just enough water to touch the ends, encase the leaves in a brown paper bag, secure the base of the bag to the glass with an elastic band, and store in the door of the fridge. Only wash the leaves as you need them.

NUTS. I keep almonds and walnuts in the fridge, and when I need them, I soak them in water overnight, restoring them to their former freshness.

PICKLES ARE A MUST IN MY STORE CUPBOARD. I consider them as staples and rely on them as another source of seasoning, in the same way as herbs and spices. Once I make them, I forget about them, until they are ready to be used. And I use them with restraint; a little goes a long way, as they can last for months. And the same goes for dips, although they should be used within a week or so of making them and kept refrigerated.

Preserved or pickled lemons are unique. Their complex flavour is intense and differs from the sharpness of natural lemons. Salt transforms them into something magical, into almost a new ingredient. They are indispensable in my kitchen. I always have a jar to hand and just a scant addition to a dish or sauce adds layers of flavour. They are especially delicious in salads with fish and chicken. Many cooks recommend discarding the flesh and using only the peel. I don't agree. I use the whole lemon because I find it imparts a more ample flavour.

The Moroccan way is to quarter the lemons, leaving them attached at the base, then stuffing each lemon with a tablespoon of salt then preserving them in lemon juice. I find dividing a lemon into eight pieces, or slicing it into very thin rounds, rather than quartering it, helps to pickle them more quickly.

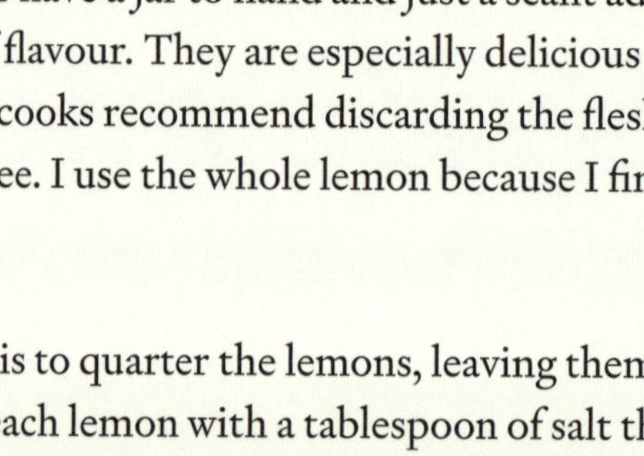

Pickles, Sauces, Dips and Nibbles

Preserved Lemons in Salt and Olive Oil

These are the star flavour in the famous Moroccan lemon chicken *tagine* dish (page 296). I also include them in my baked sea bass dish (page 280). I use garlic and chillies for flavouring, you can use any other herbs that you like instead.

you will need a 1.5 litre/ 2½ pint jar

8 unwaxed lemons

9 tablespoons salt

4 garlic cloves, peeled, crushed and cut in half

3–4 dried whole red chillies

olive oil, to cover

- Scrub the lemons thoroughly. Cut each into quarters, discarding the pips, and then halve them so that you end up with eight pieces. Place them in a bowl with the salt, garlic and chillies. Mix well, then cover and leave to marinate at room temperature for a few hours or overnight. The lemons will release some of their juice during this time.
- Give them a good stir every now and then.
- Pack the entire mixture into a sterilised jar. Pour in enough olive oil to cover and seal them completely. Gently tap the jar on the worktop to make sure there are no air bubbles lurking in between the lemons.
- I use a clean ramekin that just fits in the jar to keep the lemons under the oil.
- Close the jar and leave it in a cool, dry place for 3–4 months or until the rinds become very soft. The longer you leave them, the better they become.

→ I make a large jar which can last me a year.

Variation: if you want the lemons to mature faster, slice them into thin rounds, sprinkling some salt between each layer as you pack them in the jar. Then proceed as above.

Note: never use a wet utensil when picking out a piece of lemon, as this will start the moulding process; always use a clean, dry utensil.

DIAMETRO

Aubergine and Courgette Pickle

After preserved lemons, this pickle is one of the gems of my kitchen. Serve on toasted bread, or add it to grilled or steamed fish and chicken, or in a lentil and freekeh salad (page 217) to enhance the dish. This recipe is a twist on the Italian aubergine pickle, *melanzana sott'olio.* I have added two courgettes, a few walnuts as well as a few slices of a roasted red pepper, from a jar, for colour. If you don't like aubergines, the pickle works very well with just courgettes.

you will need a 750ml (25fl oz) jar

6–7 walnut halves, roughly quartered

1 medium aubergine

2 slim courgettes

4 tablespoons salt

500ml/18fl oz/2 generous cups apple cider vinegar

500ml/18fl oz/2 generous cups water

2–3 long slices of red pepper from a jar, roughly chopped (optional)

200ml/7fl oz/1 cup olive oil or more as needed

3 tablespoons apple cider vinegar

2 garlic cloves, roughly sliced

2–3 dried red chillies, crushed

1 tablespoon finely chopped fresh parsley

½ teaspoon dried mixed herbs (optional)

- Soak the walnuts in cold water overnight, then drain.
- Trim the ends of the aubergine. Peel and slice lengthways into 5mm/¼in slices. Thereafter, slice them into strips like short French fries.
- Trim the ends of the courgettes and slice them in half lengthways. Then proceed to cut them crosswise into half moon rounds.
- Put the aubergine and courgette slices in a colander and place it over a bowl. Sprinkle with the 4 tablespoons of salt. Mix well and cover the slices completely with a plate. Weigh down the plate with a heavy object (such as tins of beans or similar) to help extract most of the juice. Set aside at room temperature for at least 3 hours or overnight.
- The vegetables will have rendered a lot of their juices. Squeeze them to press out more of their juice – do this in batches and then set aside in a bowl.
- Pour the vinegar and water into a pan and bring to the boil.
- Tip in the aubergine and courgette and simmer for 10 minutes. Drain them well and set aside in a bowl.
- Mix in the red pepper slices (if using) and the walnuts.
- Add the olive oil, the 3 tablespoons of vinegar, garlic, chillies, parsley and dried herbs and stir to coat all the slices. Add a pinch of salt and adjust the seasoning.
- Pack into the sterilised jar, pushing down the slices to eliminate air bubbles. You need to completely cover the vegetables with the oil to prevent the formation of mould (so add more oil, if needed).
- Close the jar and leave at room temperature for at least 5 days before consuming. The longer the better. It will keep for several weeks.

Sauerkraut
Fermented Raw Cabbage

Sauerkraut is known to be beneficial for our gut and general digestive health. It is easy to make and can be enjoyed in many ways: straight from the jar, added to salads or vegetables, or on toast atop avocado slices. I sometimes mix it with a spoonful or two of kefir (page 192) or natural yogurt and spread it over a piece of toast.

You can use any type of cabbage. I like the pointed spring cabbage because it is softer in texture and releases its juices more easily. My favourite, though, is the red cabbage for its deep purple colour, which when mixed with kefir turns bright pink.

All you need is salt (2% of the weight of the cabbage) and a few spices. Just remember that successful fermentation occurs in an anaerobic situation, that is with no oxygen in the jar, otherwise unwanted bacteria can proliferate and the vegetable will go mouldy.

you will need a sterilised 750ml (25fl oz) jar

1 red cabbage or a pointed spring or white cabbage

salt as per % calculated

1 garlic clove, roughly chopped

½ tablespoon fennel seeds

½ tablespoon black peppercorns

- If using a very firm white or red cabbage, cut it in half and remove the hard core. (Don't throw this away, it can be used in soups or for making stock.)
- Slice the cabbage very thinly with a sharp knife, or grate it with a box grater or in a food processor.
- Weigh the shredded cabbage and calculate 2% of its weight in salt (for example, if your shredded cabbage weighs 500g/1lb 2oz you will need 10g/¼oz of salt).
- Mix the shredded cabbage, chopped garlic, the fennel seeds and the peppercorns with the salt in a large bowl. Using your hands, massage and scrunch the mixture for a few minutes. Leave to rest for 5 minutes, then massage it again. The cabbage will release some juice and that is what you want.
- Transfer the mixture into the jar. Keep pushing down to release the trapped air bubbles and to extract more juice. The cabbage has to be covered with its own juice. If not enough juice is released, wait 15 minutes and repeat.
- Should there still be insufficient juice to cover the cabbage, make a brine solution by dissolving 2g/½ teaspoon of salt in 100ml/scant ½ cup of cold water and pour this over the cabbage.

- Use something heavy to keep the cabbage under the brine. I use a sterilised ramekin that just fits into the jar. Screw the lid tightly on the jar and place it on a plate, in a dark place, at room temperature for about a week or two.
- Check the cabbage twice a week, uncovering the jar to release any gases, and pushing the contents down to release any air bubbles. Screw the lid tightly on the jar again.
- After a week or two the sauerkraut should be ready, but the longer it ferments, the more flavoursome it gets. It will keep for many months as long as the brine covers the cabbage.
- Enjoy it on its own; mixed with kefir (page 192); in salads or as an accompaniment to grilled meat or chicken. Remember to use a clean, dry utensil each time you take some from the jar.

Red cabbage sauerkraut mixed with kefir

Milk Kefir

Milk Kefir is a fermented milk drink, similar to a runny yogurt, made with kefir grains. If you are avoiding dairy, you can also make kefir with water (see the note below).

Homemade kefir is very easy to make. In fact, you have to do very little. Your task will be to feed the kefir grains (which resemble small cauliflower grains) with milk every 2–3 days. The beauty of homemade kefir is that it is thicker and more fermented than the commercial ones. It can have a slight fizz or bubbling due to the live fermentation, which is a good sign. A chemical process ensues when the grains are fed with milk (I use organic full-fat milk). While 'eating' the milk sugars, the grains discharge lactic acid and many strains of beneficial bacteria for our gut.

I bought my first batch of organic kefir grains online from Kombuchaorganic.uk and they include a leaflet with very precise instructions on how to proceed. Initially, I was surprised to see how little I was sent, no more than a tablespoon. But since then, the grains have grown so much that I am continually giving my surplus to friends who wish to have a go at making their own kefir.

Kefir is very versatile, we have it as a drink or pour it over porridge, cooked rice or vegetables. All you need is a sterilised glass jar, a piece of muslin, a plastic sieve, a glass or ceramic bowl and a plastic spoon or spatula.

Note: you can buy water kefir grains online (I use Happykombucha.co.uk as above) and follow the instructions which come with them. Also, check out an Instagram account called Hermann where Julius Fiedler explains how to make a delicious, fruit and pomegranate water kefir.

I leave the milk to ferment for three days as I like my kefir thick and sour. Some people leave it for as little as 24 hours which results in something similar to a thin yogurt. When the milk mixture separates into clumps and the clear liquid (the whey) appears, the kefir is ready.

At that point, pour it into a plastic sieve set on top of a bowl. Stir out all the liquid – this is the kefir, ready for use.

Creamy Tarragon and Tahina Sauce

Fresh tarragon is a favourite herb of mine. Mixed in this creamy sauce, its aromatic aniseed and liquorice notes complement a variety of dishes. You can whip up this easy sauce in no time at all, and I frequently pour it over baked salmon, trout (page 279) or chicken.

makes about 300ml (10fl oz/1¼ cups)

125ml/4fl oz/½ cup tahina

3 tablespoons lemon juice

6 tablespoons water

1 teaspoon salt

1 garlic clove, crushed to a paste

1 teaspoon small capers in brine, drained

a pinch of Aleppo pepper

a handful of fresh tarragon leaves, roughly chopped

5 tablespoons olive oil

- Put all the ingredients, except for the olive oil, in a clean jar with a lid.
- Shake the jar to blend the ingredients. Add the olive oil and shake again.
- Taste and adjust the seasoning and the lemon flavour.
- This sauce keeps in the fridge for a good week.

Salty Sunflower or Pumpkin Seed Nibbles

These little seed nibbles work their magic on any dish. I serve them on soups, dips and salads. They bring saltiness and a crunchy texture, enhancing any dish, savoury or sweet. Serve them with drinks or scattered over salads, soups, dips or ice cream.

55g/2oz/½ cup sunflower or pumpkin seeds

1 tablespoon light soy sauce

- Toast the seeds in a wide pan on a medium-low heat, shaking the pan and stirring frequently, until they start to colour. This will take about 10 minutes. Be careful not to burn them.
- Drizzle the soy sauce over the seeds and stir quickly so that all the seeds are coated.
- Take off the heat, leave them in the pan for a minute or so, and then spread them out in a single layer on a plate to cool down and dry out completely.

Chilli oil

This oil is great for salads, sauces and marinades. Elevate an avocado salad, plain rice, hard-boiled eggs or chicken with a spoonful of the garlic-chilli mixture; or as an appetiser just on its own over some bread. You won't be able to stop using it.

You can either heat up the oil before adding the garlic and chillies (left) or simply put the oil in a jar with the garlic and chillies (right). The latter infuses the oil and is less pungent. But either way, you have to like the heat of the chillies.

you will need a sterilised 500ml (18 fl oz) jar

400ml/14fl oz/1⅔ cups olive oil

12 garlic cloves, finely chopped

2–3 fresh red and green chillies, finely chopped or dried Kashmiri chillies, roughly chopped

- Heat the olive oil (very slightly) on medium heat. When the oil just begins to shimmer, take off the heat and add the garlic and chillies. Allow to cool down completely before closing the jar.
- The oil keeps for weeks.

Carrot Tops Spread

It is such a waste to throw away carrot tops. They make a lovely herbaceous dip which can be enjoyed as a snack with savoury biscuits or bread; mozzarella cheese or some crisp lettuce leaves or cauliflower.

makes about 300ml/10fl oz/ 1¼ cups

a bunch of fresh carrot tops, roughly chopped (use the stalks as well as the leaves)

a generous handful of fresh parsley, roughly chopped

2 small fresh green bird's eye chillies or 3 fresh jalapeño chillies

2 garlic cloves, peeled

30g/1oz flaked or blanched whole almonds

10g/¼oz raw cashew nuts

1 teaspoon capers in brine, drained

160ml/5¼fl oz/¾ cup olive oil

6 tablespoons lemon juice

1½ teaspoons salt, or to taste

- Put all the ingredients in a food processor and blend to a coarse texture.
- Transfer the mixture into a tall container and use a stick blender to achieve a smoother and creamier consistency. Taste and adjust the flavour to your preference.
- Of course, if you have a powerful machine like a Vitamix or a Thermomix, you can whizz all the ingredients together in one go.

→ Serve at room temperature. This spread keeps in an airtight container in the fridge for up to a week or so.

Note: see fennel fronds sauce too (page 221).

Mayonnaise

Homemade mayonnaise is a tasty condiment and very quick to rustle up; use it as a dip or add it to a vinaigrette to give an edge to your salad dressing; spread it in a sandwich or slather it over hard-boiled eggs. You can whisk the ingredients by hand, adding the oil gradually. But for a quick result, I use a handheld stick blender. Below is my mother's recipe.

I added a garlic clove because I love garlic, but that is optional.

1 tablespoon fresh lemon juice

1 generous tablespoon Dijon mustard

1 whole medium egg

1 garlic clove, chopped (optional)

175ml/6fl oz/¾ cup, olive oil or neutral tasting oil

½ teaspoon salt

½ teaspoon freshly ground black pepper

1–2 tablespoons water to loosen the texture

- Using a stick blender, combine all the mayonnaise ingredients, except the olive oil, in a narrow beaker. Blend together well.
- Add all the olive oil. Keep the blender firmly at the bottom of the beaker and blend for at least a further minute or two.
- Once you see a white creamy mixture forming at the bottom, then very carefully and slowly raise the blender up and down until all the oil is incorporated and the mixture is thick.
- Taste and adjust the seasoning (adding more lemon juice or salt, etc.) and loosen it if it's too thick by adding a tablespoon or two of cold water, then whizz again.
- Store in the fridge for 3–4 days.

Coriander Relish

Once you make this relish, you will start spooning it onto everything, it is that good. Ever since I was given the recipe by a lovely cook at a yoga retreat in Kerala, I have spread it on baked fish or chicken; over baked vegetables; in sandwiches in lieu of butter, or served it as a dip with crudités or bread. Some recipes include a mixture of mint and parsley with the coriander. I prefer the zingy taste of coriander on its own.

I tried making this relish with a stick blender only, but it took a long time and I had to chop the coriander leaves and blend them in stages. So, now, I always use my food processor first and then the stick blender. It does make for more washing up, but it's worth it, and you can use the tall container, which usually comes with the stick blender, as storage.

makes about 300ml/10fl oz/ 1¼ cups

a large bunch of fresh coriander (about 120g/4¼oz), roughly chopped (use the stalks as well as the leaves)

a small handful of fresh mint leaves, roughly chopped (optional)

2 small fresh green bird's eye chillies or 3 fresh jalapeño chillies

3 garlic cloves, peeled

2cm/¾in piece of fresh coconut or 1 tablespoon desiccated coconut (optional)

20g/¾oz unsalted cashew nuts

160ml/5½fl oz/⅔ cup olive oil

6 tablespoons lemon juice

1½ teaspoons salt, or to taste

· Put all the ingredients into a food processor and blend to a coarse mixture.

· Transfer the mixture into a tall container and use a stick blender to achieve a smoother and creamier consistency. Taste and adjust the flavour. If you find the texture too thick, blend in a tablespoon of water.

· Of course, if you have a powerful machine like a Vitamix or a Thermomix, you can whizz all the ingredients together in one go.

→ Serve at room temperature.

This relish keeps in an airtight container in the fridge for a week or so.

"May your crust be crisp and your bread always rise."

Peter Reinhart

TO LEAVEN MEANS TO LIGHTEN, TO ACTIVATE, to cause expansion; from the French *levain*, and from the Latin, *levare* (meaning to raise). Made from the oldest of grains, and as essential as rice for some nations, bread is food *par excellence*, a symbol of life, of Mother Nature's bounty. Incredibly, it begins life as a grass, which then produces seeds, from which we eventually make the different types of flours for baking.

Wheat and barley are Middle Eastern in origin, hence bread from these grains became an important and sacred ingredient in Bible stories.

When Jesus broke bread during his last Passover supper, usually called The Last Supper, it is believed that he broke the traditional unleavened barley cracker called matza. (I say barley and not wheat, because the barley harvest happens at the beginning of spring, which coincides with Passover and Easter, whereas the wheat harvest occurs two months later.) Unleavened means unraised by fermentation. Yeast and baking powder, as well as chickpea water (aquafaba) and yogurt, are all substances that cause rising by fermentation. This gives the bread and cakes a fluffier and softer texture. Unleavened bread is usually a flat bread made only with flour and water, where the dough does not ferment or rise. However, not all flatbreads today are made without yeast.

Bread and Baked Things

"How can a nation be great if its bread tastes like Kleenex?"

Julia Child

No-Knead Bread

I am not an instinctive baker. In fact, I have always been intimidated by baking and, as a result, I don't bake very often. But I chanced upon an article in the New York Times about an unbelievably easy method for baking bread without the requirement to knead it. And this delighted me. Basically, you mix everything in a pot with a wooden spoon, let it rest for a few hours and then you bake it. It sounded too good to be true. Intrigued, I searched the Internet for more information. I found a multitude of recipes and videos for different types of bread, all following the same 'no-knead' method.

It turns out that an English nutritionist, by the name of Doris Grant, discovered this ingenious method in the 1930s quite accidentally. One day, while baking bread, she realised she had forgotten to knead her dough before putting it in the oven. To her surprise, the outcome was a perfectly edible and tasty loaf. Elizabeth David mentions the Grant bread in her book, *English Bread and Yeast Cookery*.

My discovery stimulated and motivated me to start baking my own bread. I experimented with strong bread flour, wholemeal and white flour, and spelt flour. Canadian strong bread flour works best. Sometimes, I would add a herb or a seed, other times honey or a drop of olive oil. Once you follow the basic recipe, you can flavour it as you wish.

The proportion of flour to water is 2:1. This might vary slightly depending on the flour you choose. You will need an ovenproof pot with a cover or an ovenproof casserole. I use a *Le Creuset* pot with a cover, which traps the humidity inside the pot, helping to develop a nice crust.

375ml/13fl oz/1¾ cups warm water

1 teaspoon runny honey

350g/12oz/2½ cups strong white or wholemeal bread flour, plus extra for dusting

¼ teaspoon fast-action dried yeast

1 teaspoon salt

1 tablespoon olive oil

fine polenta, sesame seeds or finely ground oatmeal, to garnish

- Mix the warm water with the honey and set aside.
- Meanwhile, in a large bowl, sift the flour, add the yeast and salt and mix.
- Make a well in the middle of the flour and pour in the honey water and mix with a wooden spoon until the flour has absorbed all the water. Then mix in the olive oil. You want to arrive at a shaggy, sticky dough. This should take no more than a minute or two. You can use your hands but do not knead the dough much.
- Cover the bowl in cling film or a tea towel and set aside to rest at room temperature for 12–18 hours. (I leave it to rest overnight to achieve the sourdough effect.) The dough will be ready when it has more than doubled in size.
- Prepare another bowl and line it with baking parchment. You will be placing the dough in it.
- Using a rubber spatula, ease the dough onto your worktop in one go. You will notice the dough is stringy and sticky. Don't be tempted to add more flour.
- Using your hands or a dough scraper, stretch and fold the dough once towards you and then away from you. Do this about 8 times. Then nudge it into a ball.
- Place it in the parchment-lined bowl. Cover and let it rise in a warm place for at least 30 minutes.
- Meanwhile, preheat the oven to 210°C Fan (230°C/450°F/Gas Mark 8) and put the pot (with its cover) in which you are baking the bread on the lowest shelf and heat for 30 minutes.
- Then remove the pot from the oven, lift the dough with the parchment and plop it into the hot pot. This is a rather tricky manoeuvre so be very careful not to burn yourself.
- With a serrated knife, make a few shallow cuts on the surface of the dough and sprinkle with fine polenta, sesame seeds or finely ground oatmeal. Then cover the pot.
- Bake on the lowest shelf of the oven for 30 minutes, then uncover and continue baking for about 15 minutes or until the bread turns a deep golden colour.

→ Lift the bread out of the hot pot with the parchment and let it cool down completely on a wire rack before slicing it. It is best eaten freshly baked.

Sonia's Egyptian Rosquettes
Mini Wheat Bracelets with Cumin

This is my friend Sonia Shalam's Egyptian recipe for savoury *rosquettes*. The word *rosquettes,* comes from the Spanish *rosquitas* or *rosquillas,* which refers to round cookies with a hole in the middle. Claudia Roden, also from Egypt, calls them by their Arabic name, *ka'ak. Rosquettes* are generally sweet, but Sonia's are salty with a pronounced cumin flavour and it's impossible to eat just one.

MAKES ABOUT 80 ROSQUETTES

500g/1lb 2oz/3½ cups plain flour

1 generous tablespoon ground cumin

1 generous tablespoon ground coriander

1 tablespoon cumin seeds

1 teaspoon nigella seeds

1½ teaspoons salt

1 teaspoon/4g/1⁄8oz fast-action dried yeast

250–275ml/8–9fl oz/ generous 1 cup warm water (you might need less or more)

60ml/2fl oz/¼ cup light olive oil

1 egg, beaten with 1 tablespoon water

a mixed handful each of sesame and nigella seeds, to garnish

- In a bowl, mix all the dry ingredients together. Mix in most of the warm water until you get a shaggy dough. Add the olive oil and a little more water and knead it for a few minutes. If the dough is still too dry, add a little more water.
- Continue kneading the dough for another 5 minutes, adding more of the water if needed. You should end up with a soft and smooth dough, not sticky or too dry.
- Cover the bowl with cling film or a tea towel and place it in a warm place for a few hours until the dough doubles in size.
- Gently punch it down to deflate it. Cover again and leave it to rest in a warm place for another 15 minutes.
- Meanwhile, preheat the oven to 170°C Fan (190°C/375°F/Gas Mark 5).
- Line two oven trays with baking parchment.
- Take a walnut-sized piece of dough and roll it into a long, thin sausage about 14–15cm/5½–6in in length. Form it into a small ring, then press the ends together. Place it on the lined tray. Repeat until you have used up all the dough.
- Brush the top of each *rosquette* with the egg wash and then sprinkle them with the mixed seeds to garnish.
- Bake for about 30 minutes or until golden brown.

→ Remove from the oven, then transfer to a wire rack to cool. They should be crisp and crunchy once cool and ready to serve.

Note: the rosquettes can be stored in an airtight container in the fridge for a week or two or in the freezer for up to a month. Defrost before serving at room temperature.

Pão de Queijo
Brazilian Cheese Bread

Vanessa Rea is my Brazilian nephew's wife. A few years ago, she introduced me to *pão de queijo*, the famous Brazilian cheese bread which is served in coffee bars all over Brazil. These small cheesy bread rolls, made with sweet manioc flour (from the cassava root) are a very popular snack, consumed mostly at breakfast time. Easy to make and the chewiest bread ever. The gluten-free *pão de queijo* is very similar to the French cheesy breads called *gougères*. The main difference is the flour. The French breads are made with wheat flour which contains gluten.

MAKES ABOUT 60–70 BALLS/ROLLS

500g/1lb 2oz/5 cups sweet manioc flour*

250ml/8fl oz/1 cup milk

250ml/8fl oz/1 cup water

½ teaspoon salt

75g (2¾oz/⅓ cup unsalted butter

3 eggs

100g/3½oz mozzarella cheese), grated

150g/5½oz Parmesan cheese, finely grated

olive oil (or extra softened butter), for greasing hands

*You can buy sweet manioc flour online or from Portuguese and Brazilian shops.

- Put the flour into a bowl.
- Heat the milk, water and salt together in a pan on a medium heat for a minute or two. Add the butter and stir until it melts, then bring to the boil.
- Once the mixture starts boiling, remove from the heat, pour it over the flour and mix with a wooden spoon until you get a rough and gooey dough, about 4 minutes. Set aside to cool down before adding the eggs.
- When the dough has cooled, add the eggs, one at a time, and mix well.
- Mix in the mozzarella and Parmesan with a wooden spoon and then knead with your hands until everything is well combined. Cover the bowl and refrigerate the dough for about an hour.
- Preheat the oven to 180°C Fan (200°C/400°F/Gas Mark 6).
- Line an oven tray (you might need two) with a non-stick baking mat or baking parchment.
- Grease your hands with olive oil or softened butter. Roll the dough into balls, each about the size of a golf ball. Arrange them on the lined oven tray(s), leaving a little space between each one, until all the dough has been used.
- Bake for about 20–25 minutes until the balls puff up and turn golden. The longer you bake them, the crispier the outer crust will be.

→ Place immediately on a serving dish and enjoy hot or warm.

Note: leftovers will keep in an airtight container in the fridge for up to 5 days. You can also freeze them for a month or two, reheating them in a moderate oven, straight from the freezer or fridge before serving.

Gluten-free Buckwheat Seed Crackers

Buckwheat does not contain gluten. For this recipe, I use a mixture of buckwheat and rice flour and four types of seeds to make the dough. I roll this out very thinly then bake it to a crisp sheet which I then break up into pieces. The recipe below was given to me by my cousin Carina, twenty-five years ago. I have been baking these healthy and very tasty crackers ever since, and continue to teach others to do so as well.

I use a measure of ¼ cup (about 4 tablespoons) to make this recipe

makes enough dough to be thinly spread across one 60cm/23½in oven tray

1 measure of buckwheat flour

1 measure of rice flour

1 measure of sunflower seeds

1 measure of pumpkin seeds

1 measure of sesame seeds

1 measure of linseeds

½ measure of olive oil

2½ measures of boiling water, plus another ½ measure if needed

- Preheat the oven to 130°C Fan (150°C /300°F/Gas Mark 2).
- Mix all the dry ingredients together in a bowl. Add enough boiling water to make the dough smooth and elastic.
- Prepare two sheets of baking parchment the same size as your oven tray. Line the tray with one sheet. Tip the dough onto it, cover it with the second sheet and flatten it evenly with your hand. Then carefully roll it out with a rolling pin, the thinner the better. You should have an even thickness throughout. Carefully take off the top parchment.
- Pop it into the oven and bake for about 40–45 minutes. You want it very crisp and nicely toasted.

→ Remove from the oven and leave to cool on the oven tray. Break it up into pieces to serve.

Note: leaving out the linseeds makes for a less dense and lighter cracker. In that case, increase the other seeds by a third.

Slightly Sweet Seed Clusters

My friend, Caroline Haim, made these some years ago and I remember how much I loved them. In this recipe, I use flaked almonds and three different seeds. You can also add some roughly crushed pistachio; the recipe is quite flexible.

Delicate and elegant gems to crunch on, at tea time or any other time; they take no longer than 30 minutes to make from start to finish.

MAKES 25–30

3½ tablespoons sugar
2 medium egg whites
½ cup sunflower seeds
½ cup sesame seeds
1 cup pumpkin seeds
⅓ cup flaked almonds

- Preheat the oven to 170°C Fan (190°C/375°F/Gas Mark 5).
- Lightly beat the egg whites with the sugar. Add the seeds and mix well.
- Line an oven tray with baking parchment.
- Place a tablespoon of the seed mixture on the parchment. Flatten it gently with the spoon. Do the same with the rest of the seed mixture.
- Bake for about 18–20 minutes or until the seeds are slightly toasted.

→ Remove from the oven, then transfer to a wire rack to cool completely before handling them.

Note: they can be stored in an airtight container in the fridge for a week or two or in the freezer for a month or so. Defrost before serving at room temperature.

"Salad is an evolving dish of possibilities."

THE WORD SALAD ORIGINATES FROM THE LATIN *SAL*, meaning salt. So, originally, a salad was any mixture of vegetables that was salted or dressed in a salty dressing. I have a predilection for salads, all kinds of salads: whether it be a *tabbouleh*, a leafy or vegetable mix, a warm or a cold one, a spicy or a fruity one. I love to compose them and delight in the colours and textures of the various ingredients.

Apart from the combination of ingredients and its pleasing visual aspect, what makes a good salad for me is, above all, its dressing. My mother, who was very particular about her salad dressings, taught me this at an early age – I must have been 10 years old when I mixed my first vinaigrette under her appraising eye.

A salad dressing has two main components: an oil and an acidic ingredient such as lime juice, lemon juice or vinegar. To vary the flavour of your salad dressing, you can change the ingredients you habitually use. For example, instead of olive oil, try a walnut oil to give it a lighter, more subtle note. Instead of lemon juice, use a variety of vinegars such as apple cider, sherry or balsamic vinegar. You can also season with a dash of mustard and Aleppo pepper. Adding honey, garlic or a dollop of natural yogurt or tahina will define its character further. Different fresh herbs such as parsley, mint, coriander or basil will also make a subtle difference to the taste. Small changes can bring new flavours.

The following proportions should be borne in mind:

- For 2 tablespoons of lemon juice, mix in 4 tablespoons of oil. In other words, double the amount of oil to lemon juice.
- If using vinegar, you multiply the amount of oil by three.
- And if you add mustard to your vinaigrette, up the oil a little.

Salads

- Always combine the seasoning in the vinegar or lemon juice before adding the oil, as it mixes better that way. The other method that I also use is to put all the dressing ingredients into a clean jar with a screw-top lid and shake thoroughly just before use.

I must admit, though, I don't always follow the above measures religiously. I often just generous drizzle of olive oil on whatever salad leaves or vegetables are in the bowl, mix and then add a squeeze of lemon juice, season with salt and pepper and fluff the whole thing lightly; but trust your own palate, taste and make some adjustments, if needs be.

For leafy salads, I usually use a lot of lemon and orange juice rather than vinegar, unless it is balsamic. When using vinegar, I add some honey to mellow its sharpness. A trick that I find works well, is to taste the dressing before mixing it with the salad. Do this by dipping a leaf, or another ingredient you are using in the salad, into the dressing and taste. You will know if it needs adjusting. It's easier to do so at this stage rather than later. I find having to fiddle and adjust after the salad is dressed can reduce the whole thing to a somewhat soggy mess.

Extra virgin olive oil is my choice of oil, which I sometimes combine with walnut oil for more subtle and complex flavours. Toasted sesame oil is wonderful too but must be used sparingly as it can overpower everything else.

Tahina, which is sesame butter, brings yet another texture to the dressing. Try adding a teaspoon of it to your basic dressing and you will get a creamy sauce that is wonderful on cooked vegetables.

For robust salads of say, chickpeas or carrots, I like adding some finely chopped preserved lemon (page 186) or some harissa paste to the dressing (I usually use rose harissa paste by Belazu). This addition to a basic dressing gives a very interesting flavour to your dish and a certain '*je ne sais quoi*'.

Steamed Aubergine Salad in a Sweet Vinegar Dressing

This is a most refreshing salad that goes well with the poached mackerel in honey and vinegar (page 274) You can either steam the aubergines or poach them in water.

SERVES 2 OR MORE

1 shallot, thinly sliced

2 aubergines, washed, green top cut off

1 teaspoon fresh root ginger, finely chopped

2 small tomatoes, finely chopped

FOR THE DRESSING

2 tablespoons apple cider vinegar

2 tablespoon olive oil

1 tablespoon lemon juice

3 tablespoons runny honey

½ teaspoon salt or soy sauce

sprinkling of chopped fresh coriander to finish

- Tip the sliced shallot in a small bowl and cover with water to soften their pungency. Soak for 10 minutes or so, drain and set aside.
- Steam the aubergines for about 15–20 minutes or until very soft and set aside. (Cut the aubergines in half to fit them in the pan).
- When cool enough to handle, peel off their skin, chop them roughly and squeeze the flesh to drain off all the excess water. Place them in a salad bowl and mix in the rest of the ingredients.
- Mix all the dressing ingredients together and pour over the salad. Garnish with some chopped coriander.

→ Serve at room temperature or chilled.

Cauliflower Tabbouleh

This is a gluten-free salad using cauliflower instead of bulgur wheat. Cauliflowers are usually large and quite heavy, so you can always cut yours in half and save the other half for a soup or side dish.

SERVES 4–6
as a side dish

200–250g/7–9oz cauliflower, quartered, outer greens removed

40g/1½oz fresh flat-leaf parsley, finely chopped

150g/5½oz fresh mint leaves, finely chopped

2 spring onions, finely chopped

3 tomatoes, finely diced

FOR THE DRESSING

4 tablespoons lemon juice

7–8 tablespoons olive oil

1–2 tablespoons chilli oil (page 195)

1 garlic clove, finely chopped

1 teaspoon salt, or to taste

1 teaspoon Aleppo pepper

a sprinkling of freshly ground black pepper

- Grate the cauliflower using a box grater. You want to achieve a sandy consistency, similar to fine couscous. You can also use a food processor and pulse until you achieve the same consistency.
- Tip the grated cauliflower into a large, heatproof bowl and blanch by pouring boiling water over it, leaving it for a minute in the water (this will eliminate some of the bitter taste, but will keep the cauliflower crunchy). Drain, then scatter the cauliflower over a tea towel to dry and cool completely.
- Tip the blanched cauliflower into a salad bowl and fluff up with a fork.
- Mix in the chopped parsley, mint and spring onions, then add the diced tomatoes.
- Shake all the dressing ingredients together in a jar with a lid, then pour over the salad and fluff again.
- Taste and adjust the seasoning.

→ Serve with grilled meat or other *mezze* dishes.

Freekeh and Lentils with Pickles

Freekeh is a grain of wheat or barley grown in the Middle East. The young grains were traditionally harvested green, before maturity, dried in bunches and set alight to char their outer husk. The husk was then discarded by the action of rubbing, imbuing a smokiness to the green grain. Hence the name *freekeh* which comes from the Aramaic and Arabic meaning 'to rub'. It has a nutty texture and can be used instead of brown rice. I cook it for about 25–30 minutes or follow the instructions on the packet.

You can cook the Puy lentils from scratch. For less work, I very often buy cooked Puy lentils which are very tasty. This recipe works well with brown rice too. If you have not made the pickled vegetables (page 188), add a sour pickle of your choice.

SERVES 4

550ml/18½fl oz/2½ cups water

½ teaspoon salt

180g/6¼oz/1 cup freekeh

1 courgette, cubed

300g/10½oz/4 cups cooked Puy lentils (see introduction)

1 tomato, peeled and finely chopped

3 tablespoons vegetable pickle (page 188)

2 tablespoons olive oil

2 tablespoons chilli oil (page 195)

a handful of parsley, finely chopped

FOR THE DRESSING

2 tablespoons lemon juice

4 tablespoons olive oil

½ teaspoon Dijon mustard

½ teaspoon salt

a pinch of cayenne pepper

- Boil the water with the salt. Add the *freekeh* and bring to the boil again. Cook on medium heat for 30–35 minutes. Drain well and tip into a salad bowl.
- Blanch the cubed courgette in boiling water for a minute. Drain and add to the *freekeh*.
- Stir in the lentils, tomato, pickles, olive oil, chilli oil and parsley, and fluff up with a fork.
- Put the dressing ingredients in a jar with a lid. Shake to emulsify and pour over the salad. Add the parsley to garnish.

→ Serve warm or at room temperature with grilled fish or chicken.

Samphire Salad with Tomatoes and Broccoli

I put together this simple summer salad very often. It is delicious on its own, or as an accompaniment to baked or grilled fish or chicken. I love samphire in salads or with fish. If you don't have samphire, add a few chopped olives instead. I sometimes add avocado and red pepper to this salad.

SERVES 4 AS A SIDE DISH

2 tablespoons pine nuts, toasted
2–3 fresh ripe tomatoes
2 handfuls of fresh samphire, rinsed
250g/9oz broccoli florets
1 shallot, finely sliced
1 small red pepper, finely sliced (optional)
1 ripe avocado, cut in half and sliced crossways (optional)

FOR THE DRESSING

4 tablespoons lemon juice
3 tablespoons olive oil
1 teaspoon Dijon mustard
1 small garlic clove, crushed
½ teaspoon salt

- In a pan over medium heat, toast the pine nuts until lightly golden, stirring from time to time. Set aside.
- With a sharp knife, lightly score the tomatoes.
- Put the samphire in a pot of boiling water with the tomatoes. After a minute or so, remove the tomatoes with a slotted spoon and set aside to cool. Add the broccoli to the pot and continue simmering for 3 minutes.
- Meanwhile, peel the skin off the tomatoes, place them in a salad bowl and cut them into quarters. The tomatoes will be soft and will bleed a bit, which is what you want. Salt them lightly.
- Drain the samphire and broccoli. Add them to the salad bowl with the shallot and red pepper slices, if using. Set aside to cool. Then, top with the avocado, if using.
- Put all the dressing ingredients into a screw-top jar and shake to emulsify. Pour over the salad and mix.

→ Garnish with the toasted pine nuts.

Cucumber Spaghetti Salad

I use a julienne peeler to get thin strands of cucumber for this salad. I also like to have paper-thin ribbons instead, and use an ordinary peeler to make these. The salad is very versatile. If you don't like cucumber, you can use a mixture of carrots and courgettes. The toasted sesame seeds bring an added layer of flavour to the salad.

SERVES 4
as a side dish or starter

3–4 tablespoons sesame seeds

500g/1lb 2oz Middle Eastern cucumbers or standard cucumbers

¼ red pepper, deseeded and sliced into thin strips

¼ yellow pepper, deseeded and sliced into thin strips

FOR THE DRESSING

3 tablespoons apple cider vinegar

1 teaspoon granulated sugar

½ teaspoon salt, or to taste

½ teaspoon Aleppo pepper

- Lightly toast the sesame seeds in a small frying pan on a medium heat until golden brown, about 5–6 minutes. Stir frequently to prevent the seeds from burning. Once toasted, set aside.
- Wash the cucumbers and, using a julienne peeler, slice the cucumbers into spaghetti-like strands.
- Arrange them in a salad bowl with the red and yellow peppers.
- Mix all the dressing ingredients together in a small bowl until the sugar has dissolved, then pour over the cucumber salad and mix.

→ Garnish with the toasted sesame seeds and serve.

Fennel Salad with Potatoes and Fennel Fronds Sauce

You can sometimes find a whole fennel with its fronds at a farmers' market or a good grocery shop. I urge you to buy one to make this delicious salad. You can use the whole vegetable: the fronds to make a lovely sauce which keeps well in the fridge for a week or so; and the bulb is chopped and simmered with slices of lemon to soften. You can use the leftover sauce as a dip for crudités or as a spread over toast and other vegetables. The potato gives it a creaminess and marries well with the lemon and fennel. It makes a perfect accompaniment to fish.

SERVES 2 OR MORE

1 fennel bulb, thickly sliced

1 unwaxed, lemon, sliced into rounds

1 small starchy potato, diced

1 teaspoon salt

60ml/2 fl oz/¼ cup olive oil

1 tablespoon lemon juice, to finish

FOR THE SAUCE

a generous handful of fronds and stalks, roughly chopped

1 lemon, zested and juiced

1 large orange, juiced

3 garlic cloves, roughly chopped

1 ripe avocado, roughly sliced

½ teaspoon salt

½ teaspoon cayenne or Aleppo pepper

- Blend all the sauce ingredients until smooth. If it is very thick, add a little more orange or lemon juice.
- Boil the fennel and lemon slices for about 20 minutes until softened. Drain and place in a salad bowl.
- In a pot of water, add the salt and the potatoes and bring to the boil. Cook for about 30 minutes. Drain and add to the fennel.
- Season the warm vegetables with salt and coat them with the olive oil and lemon juice.
- Spoon some of the sauce over the vegetables, keeping the leftover sauce in a small bowl on the side.

→ Serve warm or at room temperature.

Warm Trout Salad with Piedmont Black rice

I just love this Venus black rice from the Piedmont region. It is wholegrain with a nutty texture, similar to brown rice, and has a dramatic depth of purple black colour that stands out. It is available in most supermarkets and health shops. Cook this rice as you would pasta in a lot of boiling water. I often serve it on its own; with grilled chicken, or in a salad mixed with vegetables such as butternut squash and broccoli. For this recipe, I am using trout. Its orange colour makes a beautiful contrast to the black rice.

SERVES 4

200g/7oz/1 cup black Venus rice

2 tablespoons olive oil

½ teaspoon salt

about 300g/10½ oz trout fillets

½ teaspoon salt

1 tablespoon lemon juice

1 tablespoon olive oil or chilli oil (page 195)

1 tablespoon honey

½ teaspoon Aleppo pepper

200g/7oz frozen edamame beans

1 small shallot, finely sliced

FOR THE DRESSING

1 tablespoon cider vinegar

2 tablespoons lemon juice

1 tablespoon honey

4 tablespoons olive oil

- Rinse the rice in running water. Bring a large pan of water to the boil. Stir in the rice and return to the boil. Cover and simmer gently for 25–30 minutes until cooked through but with a bite. Once cooked, remove from the heat and drain. Place in a serving dish and drizzle with a tablespoon of olive oil and a pinch of salt. Cover to keep warm and set aside.
- Meanwhile, preheat the oven to 180°C Fan (200°C /400°F/ Gas Mark 6).
- Place the fish fillets in an ovenproof dish and season with salt and Aleppo pepper, drizzle with the lemon juice, olive oil or chilli oil and honey. Bake for about 18–20 minutes or until cooked through.
- In the meantime, tip the edamame beans in boiling water and cook for 5–6 minutes. Drain and mix with the rice. Keep the dish covered.
- Once the fish fillets are cooked, break them up and scatter them with the shallot slices over the rice.

→ Drizzle with the dressing and serve warm or at room temperature.

Variation: substitute the fish with butternut squash thereby keeping the contrast of colours and making it a vegan dish. Choose a small squash about 500g/1lb 2oz, peeled, deseeded and diced. Tip into a bowl and drizzle with olive oil, honey and salt. Spread over a lined oven tray. Bake for 35 minutes until cooked and lightly golden. Once cooked, scatter them over the rice. Drizzle with the dressing.

Mushroom, Chickpea and Rocket Salad in a Harissa Dressing

This is a warm salad which you can serve as a light meal or as a side dish. I find I use less oil by first cooking the mushrooms in a dry pan until they render their own juices, before stir-frying them with olive oil and garlic. When I can, I buy organic mushrooms (usually shiitake and oyster) from a farmers' market near me. You can buy them from a supermarket too. If you can't find shiitake mushrooms, chestnut mushrooms work well too. The rocket leaves give a pleasant bitter flavour to the salad. And I like the way they wilt when the hot mushrooms are spooned over them. Nowadays, you can buy harissa paste from most supermarkets and, of course, from Middle Eastern shops too.

SERVES 2 AS A MAIN DISH, OR 4 AS A SIDE DISH

450–550g/1lb–1lb 4oz mixed oyster and shiitake mushrooms, tough stalks removed, roughly chopped

2 tablespoons olive oil, plus extra to serve

1 garlic clove, finely chopped

a generous handful of fresh parsley, finely chopped

180g/6¼oz/¾ cup (drained weight) chickpeas from a tin or jar, rinsed and drained

1 tablespoon harissa paste

2 tablespoons olive oil

about 50g/1¾oz rocket leaves, roughly chopped

salt and freshly ground black pepper, to taste

FOR THE DRESSING

1 tablespoon lemon juice

2–3 tablespoons olive oil

2–3 tablespoons harissa paste

¼ teaspoon salt

- Season the mushrooms with salt and place in a wide pan with no oil. Cover the pan and sweat them on a medium heat for about 15 minutes. They will give off some of their juice. Give them a good stir once or twice.
- Once the juice has evaporated, mix in the olive oil, garlic and the parsley and stir-fry for another minute or two.
- Meanwhile, tip the chickpeas into a salad bowl. Mix in the harissa paste and olive oil. Season with salt and pepper.
- Throw in the rocket leaves on top.
- Spoon the hot mushrooms over the salad.
- Mix all the dressing ingredients in a jar with a screw-top lid and shake to emulsify. Pour the dressing over the salad.

→ Serve immediately or at room temperature accompanied by a glass of red wine.

Bright Pink Cabbage Salad with Orange Segments

When purple cabbage comes into contact with the juices of a citrus fruit, it blushes and turns bright pink! This is due to a chemical reaction which changes the colour of its pigments, making this salad vibrantly colourful.

SERVES 6 AS A SIDE DISH

1 red cabbage (about 650g/1lb 7oz), core removed and finely grated or sliced using a mandolin

1 orange (blood orange if available)

a few walnut halves, roughly chopped

grated zest of 1 lemon

3 tablespoons fresh parsley and a few mint leaves, finely chopped to garnish

FOR THE DRESSING

juice of 1 lemon

4 tablespoons olive oil

1 teaspoon Dijon mustard

1 teaspoon runny honey

1 tablespoon capers in brine, drained

salt and freshly ground black pepper, to taste

- Steam the shredded cabbage over a pan of boiling water for about 7–8 minutes or until it has wilted slightly. Drain, tip it into a salad bowl and set aside to cool.
- Meanwhile, zest the orange, then segment it (discarding the pith and membranes). Set aside.
- Mix all the dressing ingredients in a jar with a screw-top lid and shake to emulsify. Pour the dressing over the cabbage and mix well.
- Arrange the orange segments on top of the cabbage.
- Scatter the walnuts, lemon and orange zests and the parsley and mint over the salad to finish.

→ Serve at room temperature or chilled.

Spring Greens Tagliatelle

For this salad, you make a tight roll of the spring greens leaves, which you then slice very thinly into strands, steam for a few minutes or stir-fry before coating them with a mustard dressing. Eat this warm salad almost like tagliatelle on account of its thinly cut strands. And those who do not usually like their greens somehow devour this dish.

SERVES 4
as a side dish

500g/1lb 2oz spring greens

FOR THE DRESSING

grated zest and juice of 1 lemon

½ teaspoon salt

½ teaspoon freshly ground black pepper

½ fresh red chilli, deseeded and finely chopped (optional)

¼ teaspoon Dijon mustard

4 tablespoons olive oil

FOR THE GARNISH

a handful of Kalamata olives, stoned

1 tablespoon pine nuts or chopped walnuts

a few pomegranate seeds

- Wash the spring greens leaves thoroughly and drain.
- Taking a few leaves at a time, roll them tightly lengthways to make a slender cigar shape. Slice the cigar lengthways down the middle. Then, still holding it tightly together, slice it widthways very thinly. Try to get wafer-thin slices. Do this with all the leaves.
- Bring a pan of water to the boil. Add the greens and cook for 6–7 minutes to soften them. Alternatively, you can steam them for about 10 minutes. The greens should still have a slight bite to them. It's better not to cook them for much longer as they will lose their emerald green colour.
- Drain well and place in a salad bowl.
- Mix all the dressing ingredients in a jar with a screw-top lid and shake to emulsify.
- Pour the dressing over the salad and mix well to coat all the greens.

→ Garnish with the olives, pine nuts or walnuts and pomegranate seeds. Serve warm or at room temperature.

Baked Beetroot and Butternut Squash Salad

A very satisfying autumnal salad with a delicate sweetness. You can also use pumpkin or sweet potato instead of butternut squash. I don't peel the squash as it has a nice texture, so wash it thoroughly. I put a hint of Lebanese tahina in the sauce for extra creaminess, but this is optional.

SERVES 4
as a side dish

400g/14oz beetroots, washed and trimmed

400g/14oz butternut squash, washed, deseeded and diced

2 tablespoons fresh parsley, roughly chopped

2 tablespoons of pomegranate seeds

FOR THE DRESSING

2–3 tablespoons lemon juice

½ teaspoon Dijon mustard

½ teaspoon runny honey

1 teaspoon tahina (optional)

2 tablespoons olive oil

a pinch of salt and cayenne pepper

- Preheat the oven to 200°C Fan (220°C /425°F/Gas Mark 7).
- Wrap the whole beetroots in foil. Do the same with the butternut squash pieces. Bake for about an hour.
- After about 40 minutes, check if the butternut squash is cooked. If so, take it out of the oven, unwrap and set aside to cool.
- When the beetroots are cooked, unwrap and set aside to cool. When cool enough to handle, slide the skins off and cube them. Place them in a serving dish and add the butternut squash cubes.
- Scatter the parsley leaves and pomegranate seeds on top.
- Mix all the dressing ingredients in a screw-top jar, then pour over the salad.

→ Serve at room temperature or chilled.

Variation: you can crumble some feta cheese on top. Its saltiness will complement the sweetness of the root vegetables.

Fennel Salad with Pear and Kalamata Olives

The sweetness of the pear and fennel complements the saltiness of the olives. And the addition of walnuts gives a nice crunch to the salad. You can also make a lovely sauce with the fronds (page 221).

SERVES 4
as a side dish

1 medium fennel bulb, cut in half lengthways, then thinly shaved using a mandolin

½ red onion, very thinly sliced

1 conference pear, thinly sliced (discard any pips)

about 10 Kalamata olives, stoned and halved

about 10 seedless black grapes, halved

2 tablespoons fresh tarragon leaves, roughly chopped

FOR THE DRESSING

2 tablespoons lemon juice or apple cider vinegar

3 tablespoons olive oil

¼ teaspoon salt

a pinch of Aleppo pepper

FOR THE GARNISH

a few fresh tarragon leaves

a few walnut halves, roughly chopped

- Mix all the salad ingredients together in a salad bowl.
- Mix the dressing ingredients together in a jar with a lid and shake to blend.
- Pour the dressing over the salad and toss to mix.
- Garnish with the tarragon leaves and chopped walnuts.

→ Serve chilled or at room temperature.

I REMEMBER READING A BOOK, a few years ago in Kerala, where Gandhi was paraphrased as saying "*Chew your soup and drink your food*". And that has always stayed with me, reminding me to chew my food well and savour it slowly.

Soups are usually soft, creamy or sometimes even bland. To make them a little more interesting, I like to add a bit of texture to them, bringing that happy surprise while eating. And texture can come in the shape of croutons, various nuts or seeds or some raw vegetables. I frequently use salted pumpkin and sunflower seed nibbles (page 194) or roughly chopped walnuts in my soups.

Vegetables are part of almost every meal in our home. One of our favourite vegetables is aubergine. I have cooked it in many different ways – I have fried, steamed, poached and baked it. Once in a while I make a big batch of ratatouille (page 166) but when I'm short of time, I cook a very lazy but still tasty version. I cube 2 aubergines and 2 courgettes, season them with salt and pepper, lightly drizzle them with olive oil and bake them in a medium oven for about 25–30 minutes. Meanwhile, I make a rich tomato sauce by simmering a mixture of tinned plum tomatoes, garlic, chillies, thyme and salt for about 30 minutes, until the sauce is reduced and thickened. I, then, tip the aubergine and the courgettes into the sauce. Give it a good mix, simmer for another minute, and serve the stew garnished with parsley. I accompany this simple stew with couscous or short grain brown rice.

Try it with or without the courgettes and you'll be making it frequently.

Soups and Vegetables

My Effortless Pea Soup

This is one easy and simple soup for busy people to prepare, yet it's so tasty. The flavour is subtle and the texture is so creamy you'd think there must be cream added to it. Well, the recipe does not call for cream nor frying either. Boiling the onions rather than frying them makes the soup light and brings a layer of sweetness to it. I make it very often for a light supper accompanied by steamed vegetables and some lovely sourdough bread. It will keep for a few days in the fridge, but it is best consumed on the day or the day after.

SERVES 2

1 onion, roughly chopped

2 garlic cloves, roughly chopped

400ml/14fl oz/1⅔ cups vegetable stock or water

150g/5½oz/1¼ cups frozen petits pois or garden peas

½ teaspoon vegetable bouillon powder (optional)

½ teaspoon salt

½ teaspoon freshly ground black pepper

2 tablespoons olive oil

FOR THE GARNISH

a few salty sunflower or pumpkin seed nibbles (page 194)

4 tablespoons crumbled feta cheese (optional)

Aleppo pepper, for sprinkling

- Add the onion, garlic and stock or water to a saucepan, bring to the boil, then simmer until the onion is soft, about 15–20 minutes.
- Add the peas, bouillon powder (if using), salt and black pepper. Simmer for about 10 minutes until the peas are very soft. Don't overcook them though, as they will turn a dull green colour.
- Whizz everything together in the pan using a stick blender. Add the olive oil and blend again. The soup should be very creamy. If it is too thick, mix in a little more water. Taste and adjust the flavour.

→ Serve hot in individual soup bowls, garnished with the salty seed nibbles, the feta (if using) and a sprinkling of Aleppo pepper.

ACCIDENTS IN THE KITCHEN ARE NOT ALWAYS A DISASTER. They can lead to new discoveries, to something unexpected. And this is how this soup came about. I was going to make a hearty warming soup of butternut squash and swede but I baked them in the oven for a little too long. The squash survived as it was cut in half but the cubed swede got burnt so it couldn't go in the soup. I thought I'll just use the butternut squash for the soup. But as I had four people to feed, the squash was not enough. So I had to think of what else to put in to stretch it. I didn't have any potatoes or carrots which could have worked. I then remembered that I had a baked beetroot, leftover from another dish lurking in the fridge. I blended it with the squash. The mix of the two earthy vegetables produced the most beautiful colour and flavour. And so it was, because of the burnt swede, I had a new soup recipe which I have since made several times!

Butternut Squash and Beetroot Soup

This soup has a mixture of sweet and savoury flavours. It is on the sweet side but the garnish of feta cheese balances the sweetness with its saltiness. The dill adds an interesting herby taste and the croutons give the soup some texture. I like to enhance this soup with a sprinkling of cayenne pepper and some yogurt. Enjoy this wonderful soup!

SERVES 5–6

400g/14oz butternut squash, deseeded and diced

1 beetroot, peeled and diced

6 banana shallots, peeled and cut in half

2 tablespoons runny honey

1½ teaspoons Aleppo pepper

½ teaspoon vegetable bouillon powder (optional)

½ teaspoon salt

2 tablespoons olive oil

500ml/18fl oz/generous 2 cups water or vegetable stock

1 tablespoon lemon juice

FOR THE GARNISH

swirls of yogurt

1 tablespoon finely chopped fresh dill

- Preheat the oven to 180°C Fan (200°C/400°F/Gas Mark 6).
- Put the butternut squash, the beetroot and the shallot halves in an ovenproof dish.
- Mix the honey, Aleppo pepper, bouillon powder (if using), salt and olive oil. Then massage the vegetables with the mixture. Cover the dish with foil and bake for about 40 minutes until the vegetables are soft when pierced with a fork.
- Tip the roasted vegetables into a saucepan and pour in the water or stock. Bring to the boil, cover the pan and simmer on medium heat for about 5 minutes.
- Carefully blend together in the pan using a stick blender until smooth.
- Add the lemon juice and more hot water if the soup is too thick.
- Taste and adjust the flavour to your liking.

→ Serve hot in individual soup plates with the garnishes on top of each portion.

Watercress and Spinach Soup

A delicate tasting soup for the beginning of spring. It is very easy and quick to rustle up. You can add more watercress if you like.

SERVES 2

300g/10½ oz floury potatoes, peeled and diced

1 large onion or leek, finely sliced

750ml/25fl oz/3 cups water or vegetable stock

½ teaspoon salt

200g/7oz watercress, roughly chopped

a generous handful baby spinach

½ teaspoon Aleppo pepper

a knob of butter (optional)

FOR THE GARNISH

a handful of croutons

a drizzle of olive oil

a few watercress leaves

- In a saucepan, add the measured water or stock, the salt, the potatoes and onion or leek to the boil. Cover and cook for 20 minutes on medium heat.
- Mix in the watercress and spinach, cover the pan and continue cooking for another 15 minutes.
- Using a stick blender, whizz everything together in the pan. Add the Aleppo pepper, butter (if using) and blend again. The soup should be smooth. Add a little water if too thick. Taste and adjust the seasoning.

→ Serve hot in individual soup plates. Garnish with a few croutons, a few watercress leaves and a drizzle of olive oil.

Celeriac Parsnip and Pear Soup

The celeriac root is a little bland and the parsnip quietly sweet, but together they come alive with the addition of a pear and that of cumin, ginger and garlic. The toasted pitta bread pieces and salty sunflower nibbles give texture and a crunchiness to this velvety soup. If you don't have white wine to hand, add another tablespoon of apple cider vinegar.

SERVES 4–6

3 tablespoons olive oil

1 onion, finely chopped

1 small celeriac, peeled and coarsely chopped

3 parsnips, peeled and coarsely chopped

1 pear, peeled and coarsely chopped

2–3 plump garlic cloves, finely chopped

¼ teaspoon cumin seeds

½ teaspoon ground ginger

½ teaspoon ground cumin

1 tablespoon apple cider vinegar

60ml/2fl oz/¼ cup dry white wine

1 teaspoon salt

1 teaspoon Aleppo pepper

600ml/20fl oz/2½ cups vegetable stock or water

FOR THE GARNISH

4 tablespoons full-fat natural yogurt (optional) or kefir

a handful of toasted pitta bread crushed into pieces

a few salty sunflower or pumpkin seed nibbles (page 194)

- In a heavy-based pan, heat the olive oil and fry the onion on a medium heat until golden, about 15 minutes. Add the celeriac and parsnips and stir-fry for 2–3 minutes or so.
- Mix in the pear, garlic, cumin seeds, ground cumin and ginger, vinegar, wine, salt and Aleppo pepper. Stir, then cover and leave to sweat on a low heat for about 5 minutes.
- Pour in the vegetable stock or water then bring to the boil. Cover and simmer on a medium-low heat for about 30–35 minutes until the vegetables are soft, stirring occasionally.
- Taste and adjust the seasoning.
- Using a stick blender in the pan, blend everything together into a smooth and velvety soup. If the soup is too thick then mix in a little more water.

→ Serve hot in individual soup plates with a swirl of yogurt (if using), pumpkin seed nibbles and toasted bread pieces.

Tofu with Mushrooms and Harissa Sauce

This is a satisfying 'meaty' vegetarian dish. I buy organic extra firm tofu (it has the least amount of water) and a variety of mushrooms which you find in most supermarkets. Choose portobello, shiitake, oyster or chestnut mushrooms or a mixture. As for the harissa paste, I use rose harissa but plain harissa is fine. I happened to have leftover steamed broccoli, so I added a few small florets as a garnish. You can also add chopped spring onions.

3–4 tablespoons sesame seeds

450–550/1lb–1lb 4oz mixed chestnut and shiitake mushrooms, tough stalks removed, roughly chopped

1 teaspoon salt

3–4 tablespoons olive oil

1 garlic clove, finely chopped

1 teaspoon cayenne pepper

a generous handful of fresh parsley, finely chopped

about 280g/10oz extra firm tofu

1 teaspoon salt

1 teaspoon Aleppo pepper

2 tablespoons arrowroot or cornflour

3 tablespoons apple cider vinegar

2 tablespoons light soy sauce

2 tablespoons rose harissa

garnish with the toasted sesame seeds, a sprinkling of chopped parsley or small cooked broccoli florets

- Lightly toast the sesame seeds in a small frying pan on medium heat until golden brown, about 5–6 minutes. Stir frequently to prevent the seeds from burning. Once toasted, set aside.
- Season the mushrooms with the salt and place in a wide frying pan. Cover the pan and sweat them on a medium heat for about 15 minutes. They will give off most of their juices. Give them a good stir once or twice.
- Once the juice has evaporated, mix in 2 tablespoons of the olive oil, garlic, cayenne pepper and the parsley and stir-fry for another minute or two. Then tip the mushrooms into a serving dish, cover and set aside.
- Meanwhile, wrap the tofu in a kitchen towel and gently press it with your hands to drain its excess moisture.
- Pat dry and cut the tofu into bite-sized pieces, cubes or slices, and tip them with the the arrowroot, salt and Aleppo pepper in a resealable bag. Seal the bag and gently shake to cover and season the tofu.
- Using the same pan, heat the rest of the olive oil on a medium heat. Add the tofu pieces one by one, in one layer. Do not disturb them. Cook for about 5–6 minutes until golden. Turn them over and cook for another 4 minutes. Shake the pan every so often but do not stir.
- Mix together the vinegar, soy sauce and harissa and pour over the tofu. Shake the pan and cook on a medium heat for a scant minute.

→ Remove from the heat and gently tip the tofu with the sauce over the mushrooms. Garnish with the toasted sesame seeds and chopped parsley or broccoli florets. Serve warm.

Variation: for a substantial meal, serve the tofu and mushrooms on a bed of cooked quinoa with finely chopped green chillies.

Baked Sweet and Sour Aubergine Stew

Always make this dish a few hours or even a day in advance to allow the flavours to intensify. It is also delicious served cold or at room temperature.

SERVES 6

8 stoned dried prunes, roughly chopped

4 medium aubergines, sliced into 1cm/½in-thick rounds

6–8 tablespoons olive oil

2 large onions, very thinly sliced in rings

1 teaspoon granulated sugar

5 large tomatoes, sliced into thick round rounds

salt, to taste

FOR THE SAUCE

2 tablespoons tomato purée

2 tablespoons tomato ketchup

3 tablespoons sugar

juice of 2 lemons

1 tablespoon olive oil

1 tablespoon pomegranate molasses

a pinch of cayenne pepper

salt and freshly ground black pepper, to taste

- Soak the prunes in water for 10 minutes. Drain and set aside.
- Place the sliced aubergines in a colander. Salt liberally, making sure all the slices are covered, and then leave for 30 minutes.
- Rinse the aubergines, drain and pat dry and set aside.
- Heat 2 tablespoons of the olive oil in a large frying pan and fry the onion rings with the sugar on a medium heat for about 15 minutes until soft, stirring every so often. Remove to a plate and set aside.
- In the same pan, heat 2 tablespoons of olive oil and fry the aubergine slices in batches on a medium heat until soft, turning once. Remove to a plate and set aside. Add 1–2 tablespoons of olive oil for each subsequent batch.
- Preheat the oven to 180°C Fan (200°C /400°F/Gas Mark 6).
- Lightly oil a large, ovenproof dish and set aside.
- Arrange half the aubergine slices in a single layer at the bottom of the ovenproof dish, followed by a layer of half the tomato slices, then a layer of all the onions and prunes. Top off with a layer of the remaining aubergines followed by the tomato slices.
- Mix all the sauce ingredients together in a screw top jar and shake until the sugar has dissolved, adding salt and pepper to taste. It should taste sweet and sour with a slightly spicy note from the cayenne pepper.
- Pour the sauce evenly over the vegetables and then cover the dish with foil or baking parchment. Bake for 50–60 minutes, uncovering the dish halfway through.

→ Serve hot, cold or at room temperature with plain white rice and/or grilled meat or fish.

Courgette, Aubergine and Bean Curry

This is such a comforting and delicately flavoured curry dish. It has become a family favourite. The aubergine and courgettes are a happy combination, and the white beans and coconut milk give a creaminess and texture to the generous sauce. Enjoy it ladled over some fluffy basmati rice.

SERVES 6

1 aubergine, cubed

4 tablespoons olive oil

1 onion, grated or very finely chopped

1 small fresh green chilli, finely chopped

4cm/1½in piece of fresh root ginger, peeled and finely chopped (see note below)

2 garlic cloves, finely chopped

1 large ripe tomato, cut into chunks

500ml/18fl oz/generous 2 cups water

2 courgettes, cubed

400g/14oz tin white beans, drained and rinsed

400ml/14fl oz tin coconut milk

FOR THE SPICES

1 teaspoon mild curry powder,

1 teaspoon ground coriander

1 teaspoon Aleppo pepper

1 teaspoon salt

½ teaspoon ground cumin

½ teaspoon freshly ground black pepper

2 tablespoons water

FOR THE GARNISH

grated zest of ½ lime

1 tablespoon chopped fresh coriander or parsley

- Stir-fry the aubergine cubes in 2 tablespoons of the olive oil on a medium heat for about 10 minutes until softened. Set aside on a plate and cover.
- In the same pan, heat the rest of the oil and stir in the onion. Cover the pan and simmer on a low heat for about 20 minutes until softened, stirring occasionally.
- Add the chilli and stir-fry on a medium heat for about 2 minutes.
- Add the ginger and stir-fry for 2 minutes, then the garlic and cook for another minute.
- Mix in all the spices and add them to the pan with the 2 tablespoons of water. Cook for about 1 minute, stirring occasionally, until the water has evaporated.
- Add the tomato chunks and water to the pan and bring to the boil. Cook for about 10 minutes.
- Tip in the fried aubergine cubes, cover and cook for another 1 minute.
- Add the courgettes and beans. Cover the pan, reduce the heat and simmer for about 5 minutes or until the courgettes have softened. Stir occasionally.
- Pour in the coconut milk and simmer, uncovered, for another 4 minutes.
- Taste and adjust the seasoning.
- Garnish with the lime zest and coriander or parsley.

→ Serve with fluffy white basmati rice.

Note: if you have a mortar and pestle, rather than chopping them, pound the ginger and garlic into a paste with a pinch of salt, then stir-fry as above, just for a minute or two.

OKRA, CALLED LADY'S FINGERS because of its slender and long tapering shape, is not a favourite with everyone. Many people tend to avoid it because of its gelatinous texture. And okra can certainly be slimy, but it all depends on how you prepare it. The more you slice it, the slimier it becomes. But if you cook it whole, it does not release its gooey substance. Until recently, I only cooked okra one way: in a sweet and sour tomato sauce with lemon juice, tamarind paste or pomegranate molasses. But, on one of our trips to India, I had the pleasure of eating a raw, very fresh, pod just picked off the plant. It was crisp and deliciously refreshing. So I can say that okra pods can be eaten raw when very fresh. They can also be steamed, stir-fried or cooked in a sauce.

I remember Nana, my paternal grandmother, used to string fresh okra into necklaces and leave them to dry in the sun during the summer. This way we had okra in the winter when it was out of season.

Okra and Cavolo Nero Duo

I like to use a soft-leaved kale like cavolo nero for this dish, but other varieties are good too. When you massage kale with salt and a little olive oil, the leaves begin to wilt and their texture softens. This way you can eat them raw, if you like. Make sure the okra is fresh, that is to say, not limp at the tip, and try to buy small dainty ones if you can. The flavour of cumin and ginger work particularly well here, adding a warming and earthy note to the vegetables.

SERVES 2 AS A MAIN DISH, OR 4 AS A SIDE DISH

250g/9oz cavolo nero (or a kale of your choice), roughly chopped

1½ tablespoons cumin seeds

4 tablespoons olive oil

1 small shallot, finely sliced

2 garlic cloves, finely sliced

2cm/¾in piece of fresh root ginger, finely chopped

1 fresh green or red chilli, finely sliced

¼ teaspoon salt

250g/9oz fresh okra, trimmed and cut in half

a squeeze of lemon juice

salt and freshly ground black pepper, to taste

a drizzle of chilli oil (page 195), (optional)

- Cook the cavolo nero in a pan of boiling water for 5 minutes, then drain well and set aside.
- Meanwhile, heat a wok or a pan on medium heat until hot. Then dry-fry the cumin seeds for about 30 seconds or so until they release their fragrance.
- Add 3 tablespoons of the olive oil and the shallot slices to the pan. Stir-fry for about a minute, then mix in the garlic, ginger, chilli and salt. Stir-fry for about 2 minutes, stirring frequently.
- Stir in the okra, cover the pan and let the vegetables sweat on a medium-low heat for about 3 minutes, stirring from time to time.
- Mix in the drained cavolo nero. Add the remaining olive oil and season with salt and pepper. Stir-fry on a medium heat for another 2 minutes (or longer if you like your okra soft).

→ Serve with a squeeze of lemon juice and a drizzle of chilli oil (if using) to finish.

Spiced Cauliflower Nuggets with Kefir

My family is fond of cauliflower, whether it be raw or cooked. Although mild-tasting, it comes alive with a creamy sauce or a spicy dip. This recipe makes a tasty vegetable side dish to grilled chicken, or a vegetarian meal on its own served with a simple lettuce salad.

SERVES 2 AS A MAIN DISH, OR 4 AS A SIDE DISH

1 medium cauliflower (about 500g/1lb 2oz), outer greens removed

FOR THE SPICE MIXTURE

1 teaspoon ground turmeric

1 teaspoon *zaatar* (optional)

2 teaspoons smoked paprika

2 teaspoons hot curry powder

2 teaspoons ground cumin

1½ teaspoons salt

120ml/4fl oz/½ cup olive oil

FOR THE GARNISH

1 tablespoon fresh parsley leaves, finely chopped

125ml/4fl oz/½ cup kefir (page 192) or natural yogurt

- Mix all the ingredients for the spice mixture together in a large bowl. Set aside.
- Put the whole cauliflower, floret side up, in a deep pan and pour in boiling water almost to the top of it. Cover the pan and bring to the boil, then simmer for about 5–6 minutes until slightly softened.
- Take out the cauliflower and leave aside to cool down.
- Preheat the oven to 180°C Fan (200°C /400°F/Gas Mark 6).
- Once cool enough to handle, break the cauliflower into small florets and finely dice the stem. Place them in the bowl containing the spice mixture and gently mix with your hands until coated all over.
- Transfer to an ovenproof dish, loosely cover with foil or baking parchment and bake for 30 minutes or until golden brown.

→ To serve, drizzle the kefir or yogurt over the spiced cauliflower and garnish with the chopped parsley.

Creamy Sweet Potato and Beetroot Stew

If I have time, I prefer to use fresh beetroots for this dish, which I either roast or steam. Shop-bought cooked beetroots work well too. The bright orange colour of the sweet potatoes makes a vivid contrast to the wine-red beetroots, and their creamy sweet flavour is tempered with a hint of sourness from the pomegranate molasses.

SERVES 4 OR MORE

350g/12oz raw or cooked beetroots

4 tablespoons olive oil

1 onion, grated or very finely chopped

1 small fresh green chilli, finely chopped

3 garlic cloves, finely chopped

200ml/7fl oz/1 cup water

400g/14oz tin plum tomatoes

400g/14oz sweet potatoes, peeled and thickly diced

2 tablespoons pomegranate molasses

400ml/14fl oz tin coconut milk

1 tablespoon lemon juice

FOR THE SPICES

1 tablespoon hot curry powder

1 teaspoon ground coriander

½ teaspoon ground cumin

½ teaspoon freshly ground black pepper

1 teaspoon salt

1 teaspoon Aleppo pepper

1 tablespoon fresh coriander or parsley roughly chopped, to garnish

- If using raw beetroots, steam or roast them until soft, then peel off the skin.
- Slice the cooked beetroots and set aside.
- Heat 2 tablespoons of the olive oil in a large pan. Stir in the onion, then cover and cook on a medium-low heat for about 20 minutes until softened, stirring occasionally.
- Add the chilli and stir-fry on a medium heat for about 2 minutes.
- Add the garlic and stir-fry for another minute.
- Mix in all the spices and the remaining olive oil. Cook for about a minute or so, stirring occasionally.
- Add 2 tablespoons of the water and keep cooking and stirring occasionally, until the water evaporates.
- Stir in the tinned tomatoes with their juice. Add the remaining water and bring to the boil. Turn down to a gentle simmer and cook for about 15 minutes, stirring occasionally.
- Add half the diced sweet potato, the beetroot slices and pomegranate molasses. Cover and cook for another 10 minutes. The sweet potato will melt and thicken the sauce.
- Add the rest of the sweet potato and the coconut milk. Half-cover the pan and simmer for about another 5 minutes or until they are tender.
- Stir in the lemon juice. Taste and adjust the seasoning.

→ Garnish with the chopped coriander or parsley. Serve with fluffy white basmati rice.

I LIKE THE LIAISING QUALITY OF AN EGG; the way it embraces ingredients, gathering them to its bosom. So, you can include pretty much anything into an egg mixture, and your leftovers are ideal. Baked in the oven or cooked on the hob, they will make a substantial dish.

For my soft-boiled eggs, I enjoy them scooped into a small bowl, sprinkled with some *zaatar*, freshly ground pepper and a drizzle of olive oil.

For a fried egg for one person, I always use my blinis pan and fry the eggs for 3–4 minutes. Then season it as above and enjoy it with some fresh pitta bread.

As for hard boiled eggs, I love them with a dollop of homemade mayonnaise (page 197) and a touch of harissa paste. I use rose harissa by Belazu.

If I have some leftover rice, I like to add a fried egg on top. It make a tasty meal.

Eggs and Cheesy Things

"Probably one of the most private things in the world is an egg until it is broken."

M.F.K. Fisher, *Love in a Dish and Other Pieces*

Mushroom and Parsley Tortilla

I used a mixture of oyster and Chestnut mushrooms for this recipe. Portobello or shiitake mushrooms work well too. I find I use less oil by first cooking the mushrooms in a dry pan until they render their juices, before stir-frying them with olive oil and garlic.

SERVES 4–6

About 700g/1lb 9oz mushrooms, roughly sliced

½ teaspoon salt

3 tablespoons olive oil

1 garlic clove, finely chopped

a handful of fresh parsley, finely chopped

8 eggs

a pinch of cayenne pepper

- Season the mushrooms with the salt and place in a wide pan. Cover the pan and sweat them on a medium heat for about 15 minutes. They will give off some of their juices. Give them a good stir once in a while.
- Once their juices have evaporated, mix in the olive oil, the garlic and the parsley and stir-fry for another minute or two.
- Beat the eggs and pour over the mushrooms. Cover the pan and cook over medium-low heat for about 10 minutes.
- Turn on the grill.
- Uncover the pan and place it under the hot grill to cook the top until it becomes golden brown.
- Let the omelette cool down a little before sliding it out of the pan onto a serving plate.

→ Cut into sections and serve with a simple tomato and lettuce salad.

Ajja B'jebben
Cheesy Egg Buns

Literally translated in Arabic, *Ajja b'jebben,* is a storm of cheese (meaning a lot of cheese). *Ajja* means a storm and *jebben* means cheese. This makes a lovely starter or a very light meal. Use a 12-hole cupcake or muffin tin.

I usually serve them on a bed of rocket or lettuce leaves with a few diced cucumber and tomato, simply dressed with lemon juice and olive oil.

MAKES 12 BUNS

4 eggs

350g/12oz mixture of grated halloumi cheese and cheddar cheese in equal proportions (175g/6oz of each)

1 tablespoon milk or water

2 tablespoons self-raising flour

½ teaspoon Aleppo pepper

freshly ground black pepper, to taste

1 tablespoon olive oil

salad leaves of your choice, finely chopped

- Preheat the oven to 180°C Fan (200°C/400°F/Gas Mark 6).
- Beat the eggs in a bowl. Add the cheeses, the milk or water, flour and Aleppo pepper and mix well. Season to taste with black pepper.
- With a piece of kitchen paper, grease a non-stick, 12-hole cupcake or muffin tin with the olive oil.
- Pour the cheese mixture into the moulds, dividing it evenly.
- Bake for 25 minutes or until the tops become golden.
- Meanwhile, arrange the salad leaves on a serving plate, or on individual plates and drizzle a little olive oil and lemon juice over them.

→ Place the buns on top of the salad and serve warm.

Leftover buns can be stored in an airtight container in the fridge for a few days. Enjoy them as a snack, warm or at room temperature.

Note: if you don't have a muffin tin, you can make a tortilla instead (follow the instructions for the mushroom tortilla on page 257). Decorate it with thin round slices of cucumber. Then divide it in equal triangular portions and serve with a salad.

Torta Talong
Aubergine Omelette

This *torta talong* recipe was given to me by a Filipino cook. The aubergine's smoky flavour works well with the egg. And the omelette makes a substantial snack or light meal. I prefer to use slim aubergines for this recipe.

SERVES ONE

1 aubergine

2–3 eggs

1 small fresh green chilli, finely chopped (optional)

½ teaspoon light soy sauce

2 tablespoons olive oil

salt and freshly ground black pepper, to taste

- Prick the aubergine all over with a fork. This will stop it from bursting while being charred or grilled.
- Chargrill the skin of the whole aubergine directly over the flame of a gas hob, turning it over every so often, until it turns completely black and very soft. If you don't have a gas hob, you can do this under a preheated hot grill instead – it will take longer, about 40 minutes.
- Place the aubergine on a plate and set aside for a few minutes to cool down.
- In the meantime, beat the eggs in a bowl. Add the green chilli, soy sauce and a pinch of pepper and beat again.
- Once the aubergine has sufficiently cooled down, peel off the skin, keeping the calyx (the green top) intact. The flesh should be quite soft and cooked.
- Place it on a plate and gently flatten the flesh with a fork, keeping it attached at the calyx.
- Pat the flesh dry with kitchen paper (it will have watered a little) season with salt and pepper, then gently dip it in the egg mixture to coat.
- Heat the olive oil in a small frying pan until hot. Carefully place the aubergine in the hot oil and then pour the rest of the egg mixture on top, avoiding the calyx. Cover and cook on a gentle heat until the eggs are done, about 5–6 minutes.
- Put the pan under a preheated hot grill to get a lightly browned top.

→ You can garnish with chopped coriander leaves and an extra sprinkling of soy sauce. Serve warm or at room temperature with some pickles and crusty bread.

Leftovers Tortilla Cake

Whether you have chicken, potatoes, cheese, vegetables, pasta or rice as leftovers, you can envelop them in the all-encompassing egg mixture, pouring the melange into an ovenproof pan or dish, and then bake. You can also add a few extra ingredients to your leftovers if they are not substantial enough. The amount of eggs can vary, depending on the volume of your leftovers. As a rule, more is better as you don't want a scrambled dish but an upstanding tortilla, with the leftovers within it.

SERVES 4

180–200g/6¼–7oz/1½–2 cups cooked leftovers (such as chicken, potatoes, cheese, vegetables, pasta, rice), roughly chopped

1 teaspoon smoked paprika

1 teaspoon mild curry powder

a pinch of cayenne pepper

1 teaspoon salt

2 tablespoons olive oil

a handful of fresh parsley leaves, finely chopped

8 eggs

- Preheat the oven to 180°C Fan (200°C/400°F/Gas Mark 6).
- Line a 20cm/8in ovenproof pan or dish (that has a cover) with baking parchment.
- In a bowl, season the leftovers with the paprika, curry powder, cayenne pepper and salt. Mix in the olive oil and parsley.
- Beat the eggs in a separate large bowl.
- Tip the seasoned leftovers into the eggs. Mix well.
- Pour the whole mixture into the prepared pan/dish. Cut away the extra parchment that protrudes around the edges and cover the pan.
- Bake for 25 minutes.
- Uncover and bake for a further 5 minutes or until the top becomes brown.
- Remove from the oven and let the omelette cool down for a few minutes, before lifting it out of the pan with the baking parchment and slide it onto a serving plate.

→ Cut into sections and serve it warm or cold with some coriander relish/dip (page 198) and a simple tomato and lettuce salad.

How to Make Your Own Soft Cheese

This is easy and fun to make. The quality of the milk is important. Use raw milk if you can get it or pasteurised full-fat milk, preferably organic. Do not use ultra-pasteurised or homogenised milk because they do not set properly. I season the cheese with honey, olive oil and *zaatar*, and my husband mixes it with some quince jam or sweet pickles on his bread. Feel free to add the seasoning of your choice.

MAKES ABOUT 500G/1LB 2OZ SOFT CHEESE

you will need a large non-reactive saucepan (i.e. one that is neither aluminium nor copper), a large sieve, a large bowl and a large piece of cheesecloth or muslin

2 litres/3½ pints/8½ cups full-fat milk

½ teaspoon salt

5 tablespoons lemon juice or apple cider vinegar

runny honey, olive oil and *zaatar* (optional)

- Gently heat the milk and salt to just below boiling. Take the pot off the heat and stir in the lemon juice or vinegar. Cover and let it sit for 10–15 minutes.
- Place the sieve over the bowl and line it with the cheesecloth (if using muslin, which is thinner, fold it a few times first).
- Pour the mixture into the centre of the cheesecloth and close the sides.
- Tie it tightly with a rubber band or string so as to make a sack in the shape of a ball.
- When cool enough to handle, gently squeeze the cheese and extract as much of the liquid (whey) as possible while retaining the ball shape.
- Leave the sack in the sieve in the fridge for at least 4–5 hours, or better still, overnight.

→ To serve, unwrap and place the ball of cheese on a plate. Drizzle with the runny honey, olive oil and a sprinkling of *zaatar*.

Enjoy as a spread over toast or crusty bread. It will keep in an airtight container in the fridge for up to a week.

THERE ARE SO MANY DIFFERENT VARIETIES OF RICE and as many ways to cook it. Most of the time, I use long grain basmati rice or short grain brown rice; and, occasionally, black rice which I love because of its colour and nutty texture. I am frequently asked what is the correct amount of water to obtain a fluffy basmati rice. By the absorption method, the guidelines are simple: if you have rinsed and soaked your rice, the proportion of water to rice is 1¼ measures of water to 1 measure of rice. If you have rinsed but not soaked it, use 1½ measures of water. Another more *ad hoc* method which works well is to add water to two fingers above the level of the rice. Of course, each variety of basmati cooks slightly differently, varying by just a few minutes in some cases. In addition, your pots and ovens might differ from mine, so you must experiment within these guidelines to see what works for you in your own environment.

The other way which insures a very fluffy basmati rice is the Persian *chelo* method. This is done by half-cooking the rice in a lot of water as you would pasta. It is then drained, rinsed and layered into the pot in batches. A hole is made in the middle of the rice to let the steam circulate. Thereafter, the pan is tightly covered and the rice is steamed on a low heat in its residual moisture. Herbs and marinated chicken or fish are sometimes added, making the rice dish a complete nourishing meal.

The important first step to follow is to rinse the rice thoroughly until the water runs clear, thus removing as much of the starch as possible (this way you will have fluffier grains). Then soak it in cold water for a good 30 minutes or more before cooking (some soak their rice for 24 hours). Soaking makes it cook much faster. When I am in a hurry though, I just rinse the rice and proceed to cook it.

The second important point is your pot: if you want the *hakaka* (the crispy crust at the bottom of the pot), you need a good-quality, non-stick pot with a heavy thick base. A cheap one can result in burnt rice at the bottom. Once cooked, to insure the *hakaka* is successfully detached, place the pot in some cold water for a few minutes, before turning it upside down. I must admit, I do not usually do this either, but it is a good tip to remember for releasing anything that is stuck to a pan.

Rice

The sweet newly weds
On their heads like a blessing
A shower of rice

Saffron Rice with Hakaka

I buy extra long basmati rice in 5 kilo bags from Middle Eastern shops. There are many brands, I use the one called *Kamran*. Of course, you can use your usual brand. Just bear in mind that each type cooks differently.

In this recipe, you will boil the rice first as you would pasta and then cook it in its own steam.

SERVES 4 OR MORE

350g/12 oz/1¾ cups white basmati rice

1 teaspoon ground saffron or about 10–15 saffron strands

5 tablespoons boiling water

About 1.5 litres/2½ pints/6 cups water

1 teaspoon salt

2 tablespoons olive oil

- Rinse the rice several times until the water runs clear, then leave to soak in cold water for 30 minutes or so and then drain.
- Steep the saffron in 5 tablespoons of boiling water and set aside.
- In a large, heavy-based pot, bring the water and the salt to the boil. Tip in the drained rice and bring back to the boil. (The water has to generously cover the rice, as when cooking pasta.)
- Keep the water boiling for about 8–9 minutes or until the rice is almost cooked or al dente. Rinse and drain.
- Wipe the pot dry, heat the olive oil, then scatter a few handfuls of rice into the pot.
- Drizzle half the saffron water over the rice and then continue scattering in the rest of the rice. Don't dump all the rice into the pot in one go. You want it to be light and airy so that the steam can reach every grain.
- Drizzle in the rest of the saffron water. Use the handle of a wooden spoon to make 2–3 holes in the rice to allow the steam to circulate, then drizzle 3 tablespoons of water over the rice.
- Wrap the lid in a tea towel and place it securely on the pot.
- Cook the rice on the lowest heat for about 1 hour. Although the rice will now be cooked, to ensure you have some *hakaka*, keep it on the hob for another 35–45 minutes.
- Turn off the heat and let the rice rest, covered, for a good 5 minutes.

→ Serve it like a cake. Do this, wearing oven gloves. Uncover the pot, put a plate on top of the pot, hold it down firmly with one hand and then carefully turn the pot upside down with the other hand to release the rice 'cake' onto the plate.

Spicy Mushroom and Wild Garlic Brown Rice

I use oyster and shiitake mushrooms in this dish. Portobello and chestnut mushrooms or a mixture will also work. I cook this rice very often and particularly during the first few weeks of spring when we go foraging for wild garlic, which grows abundantly at that time. I particularly like to decorate the dish with the white garlic flowers. When I can't find wild garlic, I use parsley instead. The nutty texture of the brown rice works well with the softness of the mushrooms.

SERVES 4

280g/10oz/1¼ cups short-grain brown rice

700ml/24fl oz/scant 3 cups water

2 teaspoons salt

about 550g/1lb 4oz mixed oyster and shiitake mushrooms (tough stalks removed), roughly chopped

2 tablespoons olive oil

2 garlic cloves, finely chopped

1½ teaspoons Aleppo pepper

1 teaspoon ground cumin

1 teaspoon ground turmeric

1 teaspoon hot paprika

½ teaspoon cumin seeds

a few wild garlic leaves or parsley, finely chopped, to garnish

- Rinse the rice thoroughly, then drain. Bring the water to the boil in a saucepan. Tip the rice in, add the salt and bring back to the boil.
- Lower the heat to medium, then cover and cook for 35–40 minutes, or until tender.
- Meanwhile, season the mushrooms with a pinch of salt and place them in a wide pan. Cover the pan and sweat them on medium heat for about 10–15 minutes, giving them a good stir a couple of times, until most of their juices have evaporated.
- Mix in the olive oil, garlic and all the spices. Continue cooking and stirring for a further 5 minutes.
- Drain the rice, then tip it into the pan with the mushrooms and stir to mix.
- Drizzle some extra olive oil over the top. Taste and adjust the seasoning (you might need a little more salt).

→ Transfer to a serving dish and scatter the chopped wild garlic or parsley leaves over the dish.

Rice with Dates and Lentils

Dishes of rice and lentils came to us from India. In the Middle East, each country has its own rice and lentil dish; in Iraq, we have *kichri*, in Lebanon, *mujaddara* (page 83) and in Egypt, it is *koshari*. The recipe below is a variation, sweetened by the addition of dates and raisins, resulting in a salty, sweet and mildly spicy dish.

SERVES 4

350g/12oz/1¾ cups white basmati rice

150g/5½oz/¾ cup dried Puy lentils

5 tablespoons olive oil

2 tablespoons raisins or sultanas

5 Medjool dates, stoned and roughly chopped, plus a few extra stoned whole dates to garnish

1 onion, finely chopped

1 garlic clove, finely chopped

½ teaspoon ground cumin

½ teaspoon hot curry powder

½ teaspoon freshly ground black pepper

500ml/18fl oz/generous 2 cups water or stock

1 teaspoon salt

fresh parsley sprigs, to garnish

- Rinse the rice several times until the water runs clear, then leave to soak in cold water for 30 minutes or so.
- Meanwhile, rinse the lentils well and cook them for about 25 minutes. They should be soft but not mushy. Drain and transfer to a bowl. Mix in a tablespoon of olive oil to keep them moist and set aside.
- Stir-fry the raisins or sultanas and the dates in 2 tablespoons of the olive oil on a medium-low heat until they plump up, about 5 minutes, shaking the pan from time to time. Set aside.
- In the same pan, add another tablespoon of olive oil and sweat the onion on a medium heat for about 15 minutes.
- Mix in the garlic, cumin, curry powder and black pepper and continue cooking for about a minute, stirring frequently. Set aside.
- Heat the water or stock in a non-stick, heavy-based pot, then add the salt and 1 tablespoon of olive oil. Bring to the boil.
- Drain the rice and tip it into the boiling water. Bring back to the boil, then reduce the heat to low, cover and cook for about 20 minutes.
- Thereafter, uncover it, combine the raisins or sultanas, dates, spicy onion and the lentils with the rice. Mix gently with a fork so as not to crush the ingredients. Adjust the seasoning to taste.
- Cover again and simmer on the lowest heat for another 10 minutes or up to 40 minutes should you wish to obtain a *hakaka* crust at the bottom (page 266).

→ Serve garnished with parsley sprigs and a few extra stoned whole dates.

WHEN FISH IS VERY FRESH, IT IS DELICATE and does not smell. And that should be your guideline. I buy my very fresh fish online from a company called The Upper Scale, located in Billingsgate Market in London. So far, their quality has not disappointed.

I have never been a fan of frying fish at home, principally because of the pernicious smell which invades every corner of the house. I have an oven and a hob. I don't have a barbecue, but were I to have one, I am sure I would use it to cook many things, including fish. I usually bake, poach or steam fish. Of course, it all depends on the type of fish and whether it is filleted or whole, how large it is and what the recipe calls for.

There are many ways of steaming fish. You can put it directly in a steamer, or, together with herbs and spices, enclosed in a parcel made out of baking parchment (*en papillote*) or wrapped in some pliable natural leaf, such as Swiss chard or banana leaf. Another way is to lay the fish on a bed of simmering vegetables, cover and let it steam gently for a few minutes.

Fish

Poached Mackerel with Honey and Vinegar

Mackerel's texture changes and becomes very tasty when marinated and poached in vinegar and honey. The fish can be enjoyed hot or cold accompanied by steamed vegetables and a salad.

SERVES 2

300ml/10fl oz/1¼ cups apple cider vinegar

4 tablespoons runny honey

½ teaspoon salt

½ teaspoon cayenne pepper

2 mackerel fillets, about 170g/6oz each

1 onion, finely sliced

½ cup water

a few parsley leaves, roughly chopped

- Mix the vinegar with the honey, salt, and cayenne pepper.
- Score the skin of the mackerel in three places and arrange on a plate skin side down. Pour the vinegar mixture over the fish. Set aside for 10 minutes.
- Scatter the onion slices in a saucepan, add the water and simmer for 5 minutes to soften.
- Place the mackerel over the onions and pour the vinegar mixture over the fish. Cover the pan and bring to the boil, then simmer on medium-low heat for about 5–6 minutes, or until the fish is cooked.
- Take off the heat, keep the pan covered and let the fish rest for a few minutes.
- Transfer the fillets to a serving dish and pour the vinegar mixture with the onions over them. Garnish with the chopped parsley.

→ Serve at room temperature accompanied by steamed sweet potatoes and the steamed aubergine salad (page 213).

Easy Salmon with a Marmalade Dressing

This is a very quick and tasty dish to prepare. It bakes in no time at all and the marmalade's bitter-sweet flavour compliments the oiliness of the salmon. You can also use trout instead of salmon.

SERVES 4

- 4 salmon fillets, about 170g/6oz each
- a drizzle of lemon juice
- a pinch of salt
- a sprinkling of Aleppo pepper
- 2 spring onions, finely sliced

FOR THE SAUCE

- 1 tablespoon olive oil
- a pinch of salt
- 1–2 teaspoons Aleppo pepper
- 6–7 tablespoons of marmalade
- 2 tablespoons lemon juice
- 4 tablespoons balsamic vinegar

FOR THE GARNISH

- 3 tablespoons sesame and pumpkin seeds, toasted
- a sprinkling of chopped coriander

- Preheat the oven to 180°C Fan (200°C/400°F/Gas Mark 6).
- Arrange the fillets in an oven dish. Season with salt and Aleppo pepper and drizzle with lemon juice. Then scatter the spring onions over them.
- Bake for about 18–20 minutes or so, or until the salmon is cooked through.
- Meanwhile, toast the pumpkin and sesame seeds until lightly golden and set aside.
- Pour the sauce ingredients in a jar with a lid and shake to blend.
- Remove the fish from the oven and ladle the sauce on each fillet.
- Garnish with the toasted seeds and the chopped coriander.

→ Serve with some steamed vegetables

Hake Marinière with Mushrooms

I cook the mushrooms in a dry pan until they render their own juices *(à l'étouffée*, as the French say) before adding the oil and butter. The mushrooms absorb less oil that way. For this dish, I have used hake. You can use haddock or any other white fish fillets instead.

SERVES 4

450g/1lb chestnut mushrooms, finely sliced

2 tablespoons olive oil

55g/2oz/4 tablespoons butter

2 banana shallots, finely sliced

2 garlic cloves, finely chopped

½ teaspoon salt

200ml/7fl oz/scant 1 cup dry white wine

120ml/4fl oz/½ cup water or vegetable stock

a pinch each of salt and freshly ground black pepper

a pinch of Aleppo pepper

4 fillets of hake, about 180g/6¼ oz each

120ml/4fl oz/½ cup double cream

15 saffron strands, steeped in 2 tablespoons boiling water for a few minutes (optional)

2 tablespoons fresh parsley, finely chopped

1 tablespoon lemon juice

· Tip the mushrooms into a pan (wide enough to lay the fish in a single layer). Cover and cook on a medium heat, stirring from time to time, until the mushrooms have released their liquid, about 10–15 minutes. Uncover the pan and cook until most of the juices have evaporated, about 5 minutes.

· Stir in the olive oil, butter and shallots. Cook until the shallots are translucent, about 5–6 minutes.

· Stir in the garlic and salt and cook for 1 minute.

· Add the wine and water or stock and bring to the boil, then cook on medium heat until the liquid is reduced by about half.

· Meanwhile, season the fish portions on both sides with the salt, the black pepper and the Aleppo pepper.

· Place the fish in the pan with the mushrooms in a single layer. Cover and cook on medium heat for about 5 minutes, until cooked through.

· Uncover the pan, pour in the cream and the saffron liquid (if using) and sprinkle in the parsley. Shake the pan gently and baste the fish with the sauce. Cover and simmer for a further minute.

· Arrange the fish on a serving dish. Pour the mushrooms and sauce over the top.

· Drizzle with the lemon juice. You can garnish with some extra chopped parsley and chives.

→ Serve with fluffy white basmati rice or mashed potatoes.

Pollock in a Mustard Sauce

You can use hake steaks, haddock or cod loins instead of pollock for this recipe.

SERVES 4

2 garlic cloves, roughly chopped

½ teaspoon Aleppo pepper

a pinch of salt

4 tablespoons olive oil

4 pollock steaks, about 170g/6oz each

a handful of fresh tarragon, finely chopped, to garnish

FOR THE SAUCE

3 tablespoons mayonnaise or tahina

2 tablespoons Dijon mustard

2 tablespoons lime or lemon juice

½ teaspoon salt

5 tablespoons water

2 tablespoons fresh tarragon, roughly chopped. If you don't have fresh tarragon use fresh coriander or parsley

2 tablespoons olive oil

- Using a mortar and pestle, crush the garlic cloves with the Aleppo pepper and a pinch of salt into a paste.
- Mix in the olive oil, then massage the fish steaks all over with the mixture.
- Place the fish in a single layer in a frying pan, then cover and cook on a high heat for 30 seconds.
- Reduce the heat to low, then cook (still covered) for about 5 minutes, or until the fish is cooked. Remove from the heat and set aside to rest, still covered, for 2 minutes. It will continue cooking.
- Put all the sauce ingredients in a jar with a lid and shake to emulsify.

→ Arrange the fish on a serving plate. Pour the sauce on top. Serve garnished with some more chopped tarragon.

Salmon with a Tahina and Tarragon Sauce

This is a favourite dish in our household. It doesn't take long to prepare and is my go-to recipe that I cook for 2, 4 or 6 people. The tarragon is the star herb here (my French influence) and its hint of aniseed goes well with the delicate flavour of the salmon without overpowering it. You can, of course, use trout, if you prefer. If your fish is super fresh (sashimi-grade) undercook it slightly, leaving the middle a little pink.

SERVES 4

4 salmon fillets, about 170g/6oz each

½ a preserved lemon (page 186), drained and finely chopped

2 spring onions, finely sliced

4cm/1½in piece of fresh root ginger, finely chopped

juice of ½ lemon

2 tablespoons olive oil

a few fresh tarragon leaves, to garnish

FOR THE SAUCE

3 tablespoons tahina

3 tablespoons lemon juice

1 heaped teaspoon Dijon mustard

4–5 tablespoons water

1–2 garlic cloves, finely chopped

4–5 tablespoons olive oil

1 teaspoon salt

½ teaspoon cayenne pepper or Aleppo pepper

1 tablespoon small capers in brine, drained

3–4 tablespoons fresh tarragon leaves, roughly chopped

- Preheat the oven to 180°C Fan (200°C/400°F/Gas Mark 6).
- Place the salmon fillets in a single layer in an ovenproof dish.
- Scatter the preserved lemon, spring onions and ginger evenly over the fish, then drizzle the lemon juice and olive oil on top.
- Bake for about 20–25 minutes until the fish is cooked.
- Put all the sauce ingredients in a screw-top jar and shake to emulsify.

→ Serve the fish in the baking dish and pour the sauce over the top. Sprinkle over a few tarragon leaves to garnish. Plain white rice, steamed spinach and mashed potatoes are good accompaniments.

Sea Bass with Capers and Preserved Lemon

This is a very easy dish to rustle up. The preserved lemon (page 186) gives it its sharp, complex flavour. If you don't have preserved lemons, I suggest scattering the grated zest of an unwaxed lemon along with a few thin slices of lemon over the fish. This will work well although the flavour will be different. You might need to add a pinch more salt too.

SERVES 4

- 4 sea bass or sea bream fillets, about 170g/6oz each
- 2 spring onions, finely sliced diagonally
- 2 tablespoons capers in brine, drained
- ½ a preserved lemon (page 186), drained and finely chopped
- 3cm/1¼in piece of fresh root ginger, finely chopped
- 2 tablespoons lemon juice
- 2 tablespoons olive oil
- a sprinkle of salt
- a sprinkle of *zaatar* (optional)
- a few cherry tomatoes, cut in half
- a few broccoli florets, roughly chopped (optional)

· Preheat the oven to 180°C Fan (200°C/400°F/Gas Mark 6).

· Arrange the fish fillets in a single layer in an ovenproof dish (you might need two dishes).

· Scatter the spring onions, capers, preserved lemon and ginger over the fish, then drizzle the lemon juice and olive oil on top.

· Finally, sprinkle over a little salt and *zaatar* (if using) and finish with the cherry tomatoes and broccoli florets (if using).

· Bake for about 15–17 minutes, or until the fish is cooked.

→ Serve with mashed potatoes, some steamed vegetables of your choice or fluffy white basmati rice.

Sweet and Sour Trout with Caramelised Onions

The sweetness of the caramelised onions, tempered by the capers, briny olives and vinegar, complements the oily trout perfectly, resulting in a dish of complex and elegant flavours.

SERVES 4

3 tablespoons olive oil

4 trout or salmon fillets, about 170g/6oz each

6 red onions, thinly sliced

3 tablespoons water

2 tablespoons sugar or runny honey

½ teaspoon salt

a few grindings of black pepper

½ teaspoon cayenne pepper

FOR THE SAUCE

1 tablespoon capers in brine, drained

grated zest and juice of 1 orange

3 tablespoons lemon juice

1 tablespoon balsamic vinegar

2 tablespoons runny honey

3 tablespoons olive oil

1 small garlic clove, finely chopped

½ teaspoon salt

3 tablespoons Kalamata olives, stoned and coarsely chopped (or any other brined olives)

FOR THE GARNISH

2 tablespoons fresh parsley, finely chopped

a drizzle of pomegranate molasses or balsamic vinegar

- Wipe a large frying pan with olive oil.
- Add the fish fillets to the pan in one layer and fry on medium-high heat for about a minute on each side, then set aside on a plate and cover to keep warm.
- In the same pan, heat the olive oil and fry the red onions on medium heat until soft, about 15 minutes. Stir occasionally.
- Mix in the water, sugar or honey, salt, black pepper and cayenne pepper and cover the pan. Cook on medium-low heat for another 15–20 minutes, stirring from time to time. You want the onions to be very soft.
- Meanwhile, put all the sauce ingredients into a jar with a lid. Shake to emulsify, taste, and adjust the seasoning and flavour. The sauce should be sweet and sour.
- Arrange the fish fillets on top of the onions in the pan. Pour the sauce over them. Cover the pan and simmer on medium-low heat for 5 minutes.
- Garnish with the chopped parsley and a drizzle of pomegranate molasses or balsamic vinegar.

→ Serve with a purée of parsnips and sweet potatoes.

Trout Fillets in Spring Greens Parcels

I cook fish in a parcel quite often. For this recipe, I have used large leaves of Swiss chard or spring greens. If the single leaves are not large enough, I put two leaves together to make the parcel. Cut off the very wooden stalks to facilitate the folding of the parcels. Although this recipe calls for lemon slices, you can certainly use thin slices of preserved lemon instead (page 186).

SERVES 4

4 large spring green leaves

4 trout fillets, about 170g/6oz each

2 tablespoons fresh dill or parsley, finely chopped

2 tablespoons fresh root ginger, finely chopped

½ a lemon, cut thinly into 4 rounds

2 tablespoons lemon juice

olive oil, for drizzling

a sprinkling of salt and freshly ground black pepper

FOR THE SAUCE

4 tablespoons olive oil

1 tablespoon Dijon mustard

2 tablespoons lemon juice (use the other half of the lemon)

2 spring onions, finely chopped

1 tablespoon capers in brine, drained

1 tablespoon fresh parsley, finely chopped

1 teaspoon salt

½ teaspoon Aleppo pepper or cayenne pepper

- Cut off the wooden stalks of the spring green leaves.
- Place a trout fillet onto each leaf and sprinkle with the dill or parsley, the ginger and a sprinkling of salt and pepper. Place a slice of lemon atop each one.
- Then, drizzle the lemon juice and a little olive oil over each fillet.
- Wrap the leaves around the fillets to make a parcel, enclose them securely. Then gently place them in a steamer.
- Steam over a pan of boiling water for about 7–8 minutes.
- Put all the sauce ingredients in a jar and shake to emulsify.
- Carefully transfer the fish parcels to a serving dish and pour the sauce over them.

→ Serve with my coriander relish (page 198) or my carrot tops spread (page 196) and some boiled potatoes.

Rose Harissa Marinated Baked Haddock

One dish that is a firm favourite with everyone is baked haddock (sometimes cod) steeped in a mild rose harissa marinade (I use the Belazu brand, but feel free to use any other harissa paste). It's a very simple dish with a lot of flavour. It takes a few minutes to prepare and no more than 25 minutes in the oven.

SERVES 4

4 haddock fillets, 185g/6 ½oz each

4 garlic cloves, peeled

2 spring onions, finely sliced diagonally

2 large tomatoes, sliced into thick rounds

200g/7oz/1 cup medium couscous grains

a drizzle of olive oil

salt and Aleppo pepper, to taste

FOR THE MARINADE

4 garlic cloves, pressed

1 teaspoon salt

3 tablespoons rose harissa paste

1 teaspoon smoked paprika

½ teaspoon Aleppo pepper

6–7 tablespoons olive oil

2 tablespoons lemon juice

FOR THE GARNISH

a small handful or fresh parsley, roughly chopped

2 tablespoons pomegranate seeds (optional)

- Preheat the oven to 180°C Fan (200°C/400°F/Gas Mark 6).
- Put all the marinade ingredients in a jar with a lid and shake to emulsify.
- Place the fish fillets in a roasting tray or large ovenproof dish (do not overlap them). Pour the marinade all over them, then gently massage it into the fish. I usually leave the fish to marinate for about 10 minutes.
- Scatter the garlic, spring onions and tomatoes around the fish.
- Bake for about 20 minutes (depending on the thickness of your fish), or until the fish is cooked.
- Meanwhile, put the couscous in a heatproof bowl and follow the instructions on the packet. Another option is to stir in the same volume of boiling water as the couscous and cover immediately. Let the grains rest for 10 or so minutes to absorb all the water.
- Uncover and fluff up the couscous with a fork. Add a drizzle of olive oil and a sprinkling of salt and Aleppo pepper. Mix to get rid of any lumps and then keep covered until you are ready to serve the fish.
- Once the fish is ready, turn off the oven, leaving the fish to rest there for a minute or two.
- Remove from the oven and baste the fish with any remaining marinade in the ovenproof dish.

→ Serve each fillet on a bed of couscous on individual plates. Garnish with the parsley and pomegranate seeds (if using).

Escabèche

Escabèche is a dish that came to us from the exuberant cuisine of the Persian Empire, which dates back more than 2,000 years. Its Persian name was *el sikbaj*, which translates as a vinegar stew: a dish of lamb cooked in vinegar, bitter oranges or lime, and sweetened with fruit, sugar or pomegranate molasses and spices. It relied on an acidic ingredient to alleviate the fattiness of the lamb.

The concept of marrying sweet and sour flavours is typical of Persian cooking. And this culinary tradition made its way to the Iberian Peninsula and North Africa during the medieval Arab conquest. In fact, the dishes of Tunisia, Algeria and Morocco, of meat and fish cooked with fruits, cinnamon and honey, are a testament to the Persian influence. To this day, the Babylonian Jewish diaspora continue to cook sweet and sour dishes.

While under Arab rule, the Spanish and Portuguese adopted *el sikbaj* among other culinary delights, modifying and adjusting the flavours to suit their local diet. They called it *escabèche* by a corruption of the Persian name, and in turn, introduced the dish to their various colonies in South America and the Philippines. Today, *escabèche* is a general name usually given to a fish dish cooked in a vinegary marinade, sometimes sweetened, with each country having its own variation. It is believed that *ceviche*, the raw fish cooked by the acid in limes and lemons, could have been a by-product of *escabèche*.

Escabèche of Mackerel

You can choose another oily fish instead of mackerel, if you prefer, such as sardines, salmon or trout. The acidity of the marinade lends itself to oily fish. The idea is to pan-fry the fish very lightly, then allow the hot marinade to finish the cooking. Be sure to score the skin so that the fillets don't buckle when fried. This dish should be prepared a day in advance, to be enjoyed cold or at room temperature the following day.

SERVES 4

2 tablespoons olive oil

4 mackerel fillets, about 180g/6¼oz each

a sprinkling of salt and freshly ground black pepper, to taste

FOR THE MARINADE

1 tablespoon olive oil

1 shallot, very finely sliced

1 carrot, peeled and finely sliced

4cm/1½in piece of fresh root ginger, finely sliced or grated

3 garlic cloves, thinly sliced

½ teaspoon coriander seeds, lightly crushed

½ teaspoon smoked paprika

1 lemon, finely sliced into rounds

1 teaspoon capers in brine, drained

2 sprigs of fresh thyme

300ml/10fl oz/1¼ cups apple cider or white wine vinegar

300ml/10fl oz/1¼ cups water

8 red peppercorns

2–3 tablespoons runny honey

- Season the fish with salt and pepper and score the skin twice.
- Heat the 2 tablespoons of olive oil in a frying pan on medium heat, then reduce the heat to low and place the fish in a single layer in the frying pan and cook for about 2 minutes on each side. (Cooking here is very light because the vinegar will do the rest.)
- Transfer the fish in a single layer to a deep serving dish (large enough accommodate the marinade). Set aside.
- Now to make the marinade, heat 1 tablespoon of olive oil in the same frying pan, and sweat the shallot, carrot and ginger on medium-low heat for 3–4 minutes, stirring occasionally.
- Stir in the garlic, crushed coriander seeds and the smoked paprika. Cook for a minute or so.
- Add the lemon slices, capers and thyme.
- Shake the pan, pour in the vinegar and simmer for 5 minutes.
- Add the water, red peppercorns and honey. Bring to the boil. Once boiling, reduce the heat and simmer for a good 5 minutes.
- Pour the hot marinade over the fish and cover the dish.
- Once the fish has cooled to room temperature, refrigerate it for 6 hours or ideally overnight before serving.

→ Serve at room temperature with a simple salad.

Halibut in a Mediterranean Sauce

Gently poached tomato, garlic and parsley in olive oil is, for me, the epitome of the Mediterranean flavours that I have always loved. While the sauce is simmering, you add in the various vegetables and the fish. Sea bass and haddock fillets are a good alternative to halibut.

SERVES 2

2 halibut fillets, about 170g/6oz each

6 tablespoons olive oil

5 tomatoes, each sliced into 4 rounds

a pinch of salt and pepper

a handful of fresh parsley, finely chopped

2 garlic cloves, finely chopped

a pinch of Aleppo pepper

a few olives, stoned and roughly chopped

a handful of spinach

- In a wide pan, heat the olive oil. Add the sliced tomatoes in one layer. Season with salt and pepper and poach in the oil on low heat for about 10 minutes.
- Add the parsley, garlic, Aleppo pepper, and the olives. Cover the pan and keep simmering for a minute or two.
- Place the halibut fillets in the pan, cover and cook on medium heat for 5–6 minutes. Baste the fish with the sauce occasionally.
- Scatter the spinach on top and cover the pan. Cook on low heat for another 2 minutes.
- Take off the heat, keep the pan covered and let the fish rest for a few minutes.

→ Serve on a bed of mashed potatoes.

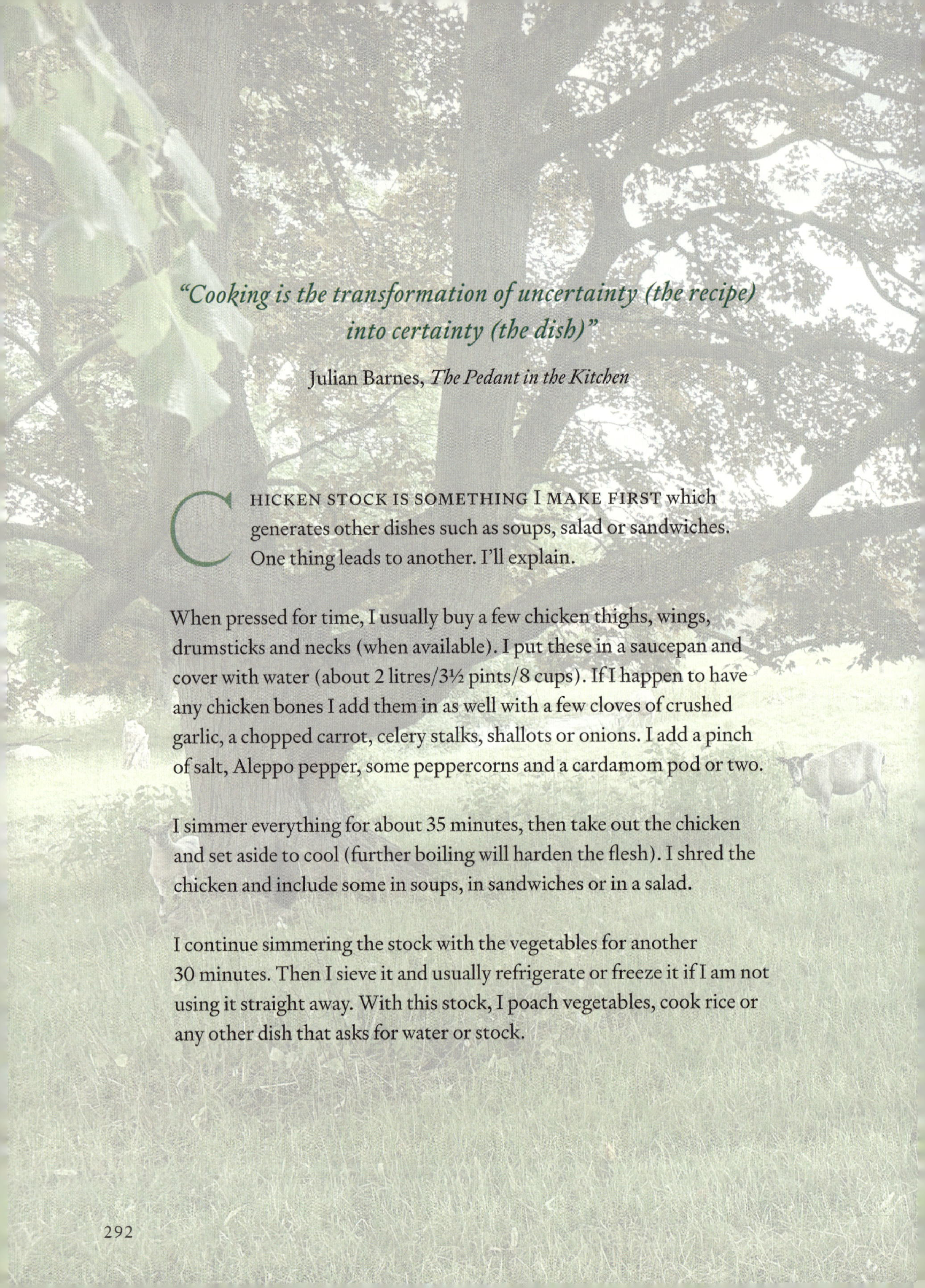

"Cooking is the transformation of uncertainty (the recipe) into certainty (the dish)"

Julian Barnes, *The Pedant in the Kitchen*

Chicken stock is something I make first which generates other dishes such as soups, salad or sandwiches. One thing leads to another. I'll explain.

When pressed for time, I usually buy a few chicken thighs, wings, drumsticks and necks (when available). I put these in a saucepan and cover with water (about 2 litres/3½ pints/8 cups). If I happen to have any chicken bones I add them in as well with a few cloves of crushed garlic, a chopped carrot, celery stalks, shallots or onions. I add a pinch of salt, Aleppo pepper, some peppercorns and a cardamom pod or two.

I simmer everything for about 35 minutes, then take out the chicken and set aside to cool (further boiling will harden the flesh). I shred the chicken and include some in soups, in sandwiches or in a salad.

I continue simmering the stock with the vegetables for another 30 minutes. Then I sieve it and usually refrigerate or freeze it if I am not using it straight away. With this stock, I poach vegetables, cook rice or any other dish that asks for water or stock.

Lamb and Chicken

Grilled Chicken on a Warm Quinoa and Vegetable Salad

I use mayonnaise, rather than yogurt, to tenderise the chicken and it really works. I suggest you prepare the marinade and marinate the chicken in the morning or a few hours before cooking the dish. You can use peas instead of Brussels sprouts or any other vegetable of your choice. I happened to have some leftover steamed sweet potato in the fridge which I added to the salad.

SERVES 4

550g/1lb 4oz chicken thighs, skinless and boneless

200g/7oz red or mixed quinoa

150g/5½oz broccoli florets, roughly sliced

5 Brussels sprouts cut in half

FOR THE MARINADE

5 tablespoons shop-bought mayonnaise or homemade (page 197)

4 tablespoons olive oil

3 garlic cloves, crushed

½ teaspoon each, ground cumin, ground turmeric

¼ teaspoon cayenne pepper

½ teaspoon salt

2 tablespoons water

FOR THE SALAD DRESSING

2 garlic cloves, pressed

½ teaspoon salt

2 tablespoons olive oil

2 tablespoons lemon juice

¼ teaspoon honey

½ teaspoon Aleppo pepper

a sprinkling of finely chopped parsley, to garnish

- Cut the chicken into equal bite-sized pieces. Mix all the marinade ingredients together in a bowl, tip in the chicken and mix until all the pieces are covered. Then, refrigerate for about an hour or two.
- An hour before serving, rinse the quinoa thoroughly and cook according to the instructions on the packet. Drain and set aside in a bowl.
- Steam the broccoli florets and Brussel sprouts for 5 minutes and add to the quinoa.
- Mix the salad dressing ingredients together and pour over the quinoa mixture.
- Thread the chicken pieces on to your skewers (keep the rest of the marinade for brushing). Put the grill on high heat and cook the chicken for about 3 minutes on each side or until cooked through and golden brown (avoid overcooking the chicken as it dries out).

→ Spoon the quinoa mixture on a serving plate and arrange the chicken skewers on top. Brush the chicken with any leftover marinade and garnish with the chopped parsley.

Baked Lemon Chicken with Olives

This is my adaptation of the famous Moroccan dish *Tagine b'Djaj*. Traditionally, a whole chicken is cooked in a *tagine* on the hob. Instead, my recipe calls for chicken pieces, mixed with spices and preserved lemon, then baked in a low oven for an hour. There isn't much faffing at the hob, the oven does it all – well, most of it. The fragrant combination of the chicken and the preserved lemon is truly delicious.

SERVES 2

2 tablespoons olive oil

1 medium onion, finely chopped

½ a stock cube

200ml/7fl oz/scant 1 cup boiling water

4 chicken thighs, bone-in, skin-off

1 whole preserved lemon, finely chopped

3 tablespoons olive oil

8 black olives in brine, drained

1 tablespoon capers in brine, drained

a generous handful of fresh coriander, finely chopped

a generous handful of fresh parsley, finely chopped

THE SPICES

1 teaspoon ground turmeric

½ teaspoon cinnamon

1 teaspoon ground ginger

2 garlic cloves, finely chopped

2cm fresh root ginger, finely chopped

1 teaspoon Aleppo pepper

a generous handful of fresh parsley, coarsely chopped, to garnish

- Heat 2 tablespoons olive oil in a pan. When hot, fry the onion until soft (about 8 minutes).
- Add the spices and stir-fry for one minute or until the aroma is released.
- While the onion is cooking, dissolve the stock cube in the hot water and set aside.
- Preheat the oven to 160°C Fan (180°C/350°F/Gas Mark 4).
- In a bowl, mix in the chicken pieces with the preserved lemon, 3 tablespoons olive oil, the olives, capers, parsley and coriander. Then, mix in the cooked onion, the spices and the stock. Set aside for about 10 minutes to allow the flavours to mingle.
- Transfer to an ovenproof dish, cover with foil or baking parchment and bake for 75–85 minutes until the chicken is thoroughly cooked.

→ Garnish with the chopped parsley and serve with white basmati rice, couscous or bulgur wheat.

Spicy Pulled Lamb with Chickpeas and Sweet Potato Mash

Slow cooked lamb is one of the easiest and most flavoursome dishes you can put on your table. And it does not involve you in its cooking either. An almost hands-free recipe. Here you will prepare the shanks *en papillote*, that is wrapped in a parcel, baked in a low oven for an hour or more, and served on a bed of slightly smashed chickpeas and sweet potato purée. Any leftover lamb can be wrapped in some flat bread with a slice of tomato, a lettuce leaf and a drizzle of tahina to make a delicious snack. If cooking chickpeas from scratch, don't forget to soak them overnight with a teaspoon of bicarbonate of soda. When I am feeling lazy, I use shop-bought cooked chickpeas instead.

SERVES 4

400g/14oz jar or tin of chickpeas

4 bone-in lamb shoulder shanks, about 400g/14oz each

1 chicken stock cube

1 teaspoon vegetable bouillon powder

1 teaspoon 5-spice powder

2 sweet potatoes, peeled and diced into cubes

juice of ½ lemon

a pinch of Aleppo pepper

a drizzle of olive oil

a pinch of salt

- Preheat the oven to 210°C Fan (230°C/450°F/Gas Mark 8).
- Empty the jar or tin of chickpeas into a pan, cover and cook for 10 minutes on medium heat. Drain, lightly crush some of them and set aside in a bowl and cover.
- Prepare 2 sheets of baking parchment large enough in which to wrap 2 shanks in each one. Place 2 shanks in the middle of each sheet.
- Crumble the stock cube, the vegetable bouillon powder and the 5-spice powder over them. Rub the seasoning well into the lamb.
- Wrap the shanks very tightly in the parchment. Then wrap the parcels in foil. The parcels need to be airtight so that no moisture is lost during the roasting.
- Transfer the parcels to an ovenproof dish and bake for 10 minutes at high temperature. Then lower the oven temperature to 160°C Fan (180°C/350°F/Gas Mark 4) and bake for 60–90 minutes.
- While the lamb is cooking, steam the diced sweet potatoes until soft. Then, using a fork, mash into a smooth purée. Cover and set aside.
- After an hour, check that the lamb is cooked to your liking. Spread the sweet potato mash on a serving dish and tip the chickpeas on top. Sprinkle with a little salt, a pinch of Aleppo pepper, a drizzle of olive oil and the lemon juice. Shred the lamb off the bone and place on top of the chickpeas. You can save the bones for stock.

Variation: serve the lamb shanks on a bed of saffron rice (page 266) or on a bed of seasoned couscous or fine bulgur wheat.

Chicken Liver, Chocolate and Pastis

Pastis is the aperitif of the South of France *par excellence*. Slightly bitter-sweet, it has a complex herby aniseed and liquorice flavour and goes white when added to water. Do not use Pernod for this recipe as it is much drier and has not the same sweet complexity of flavour.

The dark chocolate is my cheeky flavour surprise ingredient, but it is optional.

SERVES 4

2 tablespoons olive oil

1 shallot, finely sliced

1 garlic clove, finely chopped

450g/1lb chicken livers, thinly sliced

a pinch of cayenne pepper

a pinch of salt and black pepper

3 generous tablespoons runny honey

2 tablespoons apple cider or balsamic vinegar

3 tablespoons pastis

a sprinkling of cacao powder, to garnish (optional)

· In a large frying pan, heat the olive oil on a medium-low heat and cook the shallot slices for about 10 minutes until softened.

· Stir in the garlic and cook for about 30 seconds.

· Add the liver with the cayenne pepper, salt and black pepper. Shake the pan a little and cover. Cook on medium heat for about 3–4 minutes.

· Then turn the livers over. Tip in the honey and vinegar, shake the pan to mix. Cover the pan and cook for another 3–4 minutes (or longer if you like the livers well done).

· Take off the heat and add the *pastis* and shake the pan to mix.

→ Serve on a bed of butternut squash or sweet potato purée and sprinkle the cacao powder on top (if using).

Beetroot and Apricot Lamb Stew

This dish can be cooked a day or two in advance giving the flavours a chance to mingle and intensify. My preference here is for lamb but beef or chicken work well too.

SERVES 4–6

You will need 4 medium cooked beetroots

4 tablespoons olive oil

1 onion, grated or very finely chopped

1 small fresh green chilli, deseeded and finely chopped

3 garlic cloves, finely chopped

600g/1lb 5oz cubed lamb

70ml/2½ fl oz/⅓ cup water

70g/2½oz dried apricots, roughly chopped

3 medium cooked beetroots, peeled and cubed

200ml/7 fl oz/scant 1 cup passata or tinned tomatoes finely chopped

400ml/14 fl oz tin coconut milk

1 tablespoon lemon juice

THE SPICES

½ teaspoon ground cinnamon

1 tablespoon hot curry powder

1 teaspoon ground coriander

½ teaspoon ground cumin

1 teaspoon salt

1 teaspoon Aleppo pepper

- Heat 2 tablespoons of the olive oil in a large pan. Stir in the onion, then cover and cook on a low heat for about 15 minutes until softened, stirring occasionally. Do not allow it to burn or caramelise.
- Add the chilli and stir-fry on medium heat for about a minute.
- Stir in the garlic and cook for about 30 seconds. Do not allow the garlic to burn.
- Mix in all the spices and the remaining olive oil and cook for about another minute, stirring occasionally.
- Add the lamb and brown on all sides, stirring frequently. Once the meat is browned all over, cover, turn the heat down to medium-low and let it sweat for about 10 minutes.
- Add 70ml of water and scrape the bottom of the pan to loosen the lovely brown bits.
- Turn up the heat to high and bring to the boil. Then, lower the heat to medium-low, cover and simmer for 35 minutes.
- Meanwhile, finely blend all the sauce ingredients, except the lemon juice.
- Before adding it, uncover the pan, raise the heat to high and stir the meat until sizzling.
- Then pour in the sauce and bring to the boil. Cook uncovered for about a minute or so to allow the sauce to thicken slightly.
- Cover the pan, lower the heat to medium-low and simmer for another 30 minutes or until the lamb is very tender.
- Add the 3 cubed beetroots with the apricots, the coconut milk and the passata or tinned tomatoes, and bring to the boil.
- Turn the heat right down to a gentle simmer and cook for about another 15 minutes, stirring occasionally.
- Just before serving, stir in the lemon juice. Taste and adjust the flavour if too sour add more sugar if too sweet add more lemon juice.

→ Garnish with the chopped coriander or parsley. Serve with fluffy white basmati rice.

FOR THE BEETROOT SAUCE

1 cooked beetroot

1 tablespoon tomato paste or passata

1 tablespoon apple cider vinegar

1 tablespoon sugar

½ teaspoon salt and pepper each

150ml/5 fl oz/⅔ cup water

2 tablespoons lemon juice

2 tablespoons sugar

1 tablespoon chopped fresh coriander or parsley, for the garnish

FRUITS ARE ONE OF MY FAVOURITE SWEETS. There's nothing sweeter than a platter of ripe seasonal fruit. However, I do have a predilection for cooking fruit, especially when they are not quite ripe, because the cooking process intensifies and brings out their essence. Plums, pears, apples and especially quince, are my favourite when baked or poached. In Baghdad, we accompanied ripe figs and juicy watermelons with a salty white cheese. The combined sweet and salty flavours go so well together. Cheese and jam is another very similar flavour combination. My husband Frank takes great delight in eating a cheesy omelette, *Ajja* (page 258), with homemade jam. And I occasionally cook lamb with poached quince or apricots (pages 39 and 302).

Our Middle Eastern sweetmeats were never served as desserts after a meal. They were traditionally prepared for special occasions or offered at tea time to guests or impromptu visitors.

Sweet Things

Beetroot Halva

One of the desserts that I loved eating in Kerala was carrot *halva*: grated carrots with nuts and coconut milk, sweetened with *jaggery*. It is a common sweet in the South of India. The recipe below was given to me by a lovely cook called Angela from Bangalore. Her recipe, which I have modified slightly, using less butter, calls for beetroots instead of carrots. Traditionally, the beetroots are blended and then sieved, using only their extracted juice to make a jelly. I have used the whole vegetable not wanting to waste any of it.

SERVES 6

You will need a 20 × 15cm/ 8 × 6 in tin or oven dish

2 tablespoons raw unsalted cashew nuts, roughly chopped

2 tablespoons flaked almonds, roughly chopped

1½ tablespoons raisins, roughly chopped

2 small dates, roughly chopped

about 550g/1lb 4oz raw beetroots, peeled and roughly chopped

250ml/8fl oz/1 cup water

5 tablespoons cornflour

3 tablespoons water

2 tablespoons butter or ghee

150g/5½oz/¾ cup sugar

1 teaspoon ground cardamom

GARNISH FOR THE BOTTOM OF THE TIN

2 teaspoons sesame seeds

1 small date, roughly chopped

1–2 tablespoons flaked almonds

1 tablespoon pistachios, roughly chopped

- You can either stir-fry the nuts, raisins and dates in some ghee or butter, or as I do, put them in a bowl and pour boiling water over them and soak them for about 10 minutes. Then drain and set aside.
- Place the beetroot in a blender with the cup of water and blend to a creamy mixture.
- In a bowl, mix the cornflour with 3 tablespoons of water to make a smooth slurry and set aside. Make sure that you eliminate all the lumps.
- Line your tin or oven dish with baking parchment.
- Mix the garnish ingredients together and sprinkle them evenly in the tin.
- Heat a pan on medium heat, add a tablespoon of butter or ghee and mix in the blended beetroot, and the soaked nuts, raisins and dates. Stir frequently. After about 15 minutes mix in the sugar, cardamom and another tablespoon of ghee or butter. Stir continuously for another 10 minutes then add in the cornflour mixture.
- Keep stirring until most of the water evaporates and the paste thickens to a pudding-like consistency. The mixture is ready when it becomes quite dry and does not stick to the sides of the pan.
- Pour the mixture into your tin and let it cool to room temperature. Refrigerate for a few hours to allow the *halva* to stiffen.
- Then invert the tin on a serving dish and gently peel off the baking parchment. When inverted, the top of the *halva* will be incrusted with the nuts and sesame seeds.
- Cut the *halva* into slices like a cake or into small squares or diamond shapes as a *baklava*.

→ Garnish with more nuts and serve on its own or with cream.

Poached Pears in a Turmeric and Ginger Syrup

Poached pears delicately perfumed with orange zest, cinnamon and stem ginger in syrup, are a dream of a dessert. I poach them in turmeric for a hint of colour. They are delicious served chilled or at room temperature, with crème fraîche or vanilla ice cream. To allow the flavours to mingle, make this dessert a good few hours before serving or a day in advance and refrigerate. I buy a 400g jar of stem ginger balls in syrup from supermarkets. You will be using all the syrup of the jar and 4 balls for this recipe. Keep the rest of the ginger in the refrigerator to use again with homemade syrup.

SERVES 4 OR MORE

4 large Conference pears, not too ripe

1 tablespoon turmeric

½ teaspoon cinnamon (optional)

zest or thinly-peeled skin of 1 orange (use a peeler to form ribbons)

1 teaspoon vanilla extract

400g/14oz jar candied ginger balls in syrup

zest of 1 orange, to garnish

- Peel the pears and slice them in half lengthwise. Core and leave the stem on one half.
- Put them in one layer in a wide pan of water to just cover the pears, add the turmeric, the cinnamon (if using), the orange zest or thinly-peeled skin and the vanilla extract. Bring to a boil and then lower the heat, cover and simmer gently for 10 to 15 minutes (the pears must not become too mushy).
- In the meantime, finely chop 4 ginger balls and set aside.
- When the pears are done, gently lift them out with a slotted spoon and arrange them on a serving dish.
- Tip the ginger syrup over them and scatter the chopped ginger all over.

→ Garnish with the orange zest and serve with crème fraîche or vanilla ice cream.

Cream Cheese and Yogurt Cake

This cheesecake is so very light and does not have a traditional biscuit base. You can bake it a day in advance because it can keep in the fridge for four days or more. The topping of flaked almonds gives it a nice crunchy texture. You can also top it with roughly ground pistachios.

SERVES 6

You will need a 20cm/8in round cake tin.

220g/8oz/1 cup full fat cream cheese

80g/3oz/⅓ cup thick Greek yogurt

4 eggs, yolks and whites separated

180ml/6fl oz/¾ cup condensed milk

1 teaspoon vanilla extract

zest of 1 lemon

FOR THE GARNISH

a good sprinkling of flaked almonds

- Line the inside of the cake tin with baking parchment or use shop-bought 20cm/8in cake tin liners.
- Preheat the oven to 160°C Fan (180°C/350°F/Gas Mark 4).
- Blend the egg yolks with the cream cheese and yogurt using a hand or electric whisk.
- Whisk in the condensed milk until very smooth.
- Mix in the vanilla extract and the lemon zest.
- Beat the egg whites until stiff, then gently fold them into the egg yolk mixture until well incorporated. Do not stir as this will eliminate the air in the egg whites and consequently the lightness of the cake.
- Pour the mixture into the cake tin. Cover the top with a good sprinkling of flaked almonds. Gently tap the tin on the worktop a few times to release any air bubbles.
- Bake for 35–40 minutes until the almonds turn a golden brown.
- Thereafter, switch off the oven but do not open the oven door immediately. Leave the pudding to cool down inside it. (If you take out the cake too quickly, the height will reduce to half and the soufflé effect will disappear.)
- Once cold, carefully transfer to a serving dish and refrigerate for an hour or so.

→ Serve chilled or at room temperature.

Note: this cake will keep in the fridge for at least 4 days.

Exotic Black Rice Pudding

I like to use black rice for its nuttiness and colour. And I often wondered what it would be like to make it into a pudding as in a white rice pudding. What I didn't realise was that both black and white glutinous rice are traditionally used in South Asian and Filipino sweets. I bought my black Thai rice from my local supermarket but you can also order it online. I have added ground cardamom which is optional.

SERVES 2–4

75g/2¾oz/⅓ cup black Thai rice, rinsed and soaked for 30 minutes

350ml/12fl oz/1½ cup water

200ml/7fl oz/scant 1 cup coconut cream

2 tablespoons sugar

1 teaspoon vanilla extract

a good pinch of cardamom (optional)

20g/¾oz flaked almonds

flaked almonds or vanilla ice cream, to garnish

- Tip the rice into a saucepan with the water and bring to the boil, then cover and simmer gently on the lowest heat for 40–45 minutes until all the water has evaporated.
- Mix in the coconut cream, sugar, vanilla extract and cardamom (if using). Cover and continue simmering for another 15 minutes, stirring frequently.
- At this point, add the flaked almonds and bring to the boil. Take off the heat, give the rice a stir and cover to cool down, then refrigerate. If too dry mix in 1 or 2 tablespoons of water.

→ Serve in individual bowls at room temperature or chilled with a handful of flaked almonds or a blob of vanilla ice cream as a garnish. You can also top the pudding with some sliced fruits like mango, papaya or banana.

Baked Plum Dessert

An easy and delicious dessert that I often bake in the summer months. I bake the plums with their stones in (of course, alerting everyone to be careful when eating them). You can also fish them out after the plums have been baked. I use a glass Pyrex dish with a cover – that way I can see when the plums are starting to melt.

SERVES 4–6

1kg/2¼lb dark red plums

a drizzle or two of rosewater (optional)

a few dollops of thick natural yogurt, double cream or crème fraîche

a sprinkling of chopped pistachios or flaked almonds, to decorate

Note: when the plums are in season, they are juicy. However, once out of the oven, if you find that the plums did not release much juice, you can mix in a tablespoon or so of water.

- Preheat the oven to 190°C Fan (210°C/410°F/Gas Mark 6½).
- Wash the plums and place in a deep Pyrex or ovenproof dish. Cover and bake for 35–45 minutes or until the plums have melted and their juices have oozed out. Test to see if they are done by squashing one with a fork. If not, bake them for a little longer.
- Remove from the oven. At this point, I usually squash the plums a little to extract more of their juice and mix well.
- Let the fruit cool down, then place in a covered container in the fridge.
- Serve cold in individual bowls with a drizzle of rosewater (if using) and top each serving with a dollop of thick yogurt, double cream or crème fraîche. Decorate with some chopped pistachios or flaked almonds.

Sagu de Vinho Tinto
Tapioca Pearls in Red Wine

The first time I tasted this sagu dessert was when my Brazilian nephew's wife, Vanessa Rea, made it for me. These pearls, either called *sago* or *sagu*, are made from the starch of the cassava plant which grows widely all over Brazil. I was surprised by the colour of this dessert; it wasn't white but ruby red – because wine is used instead of milk – a speciality of the Italian immigrants who settled in the South of Brazil in the early 1900s. This is a 'grown-up' dessert, as one of my friends put it. For children though, grape juice is used in place of wine. An integral part of this dessert, though, is a runny custard or a crème Anglaise which is mixed with it giving it a hint of sweet creaminess.

SERVES 4 OR MORE

120g/4¼oz small sago pearls

600ml/20fl oz/2½ cups water

a pinch of ground cinnamon

a pinch of ground cloves

500ml/18fl oz/generous 2 cups red wine

250ml/8fl oz/1 cup red grape juice

3–4 tablespoons granulated sugar

vanilla ice cream or runny custard, to serve

- Put the sago pearls, water, cinnamon and cloves into a heavy-based pan and bring to the boil, then reduce the heat and simmer for about 20 minutes until the pearls begin to turn translucent.
- Mix in the red wine, grape juice and sugar and bring to the boil once more. Taste to adjust the sweetness by adding another tablespoon of sugar if needs be. Reduce the heat to medium and cook for about 20–25 minutes, stirring frequently, until the balls are totally translucent and the consistency a little gelatinous. The longer you cook it, the thicker and more gelatinous it will become. Bear in mind, also, that it will thicken even further as it cools down.
- Pour into a serving bowl. Once cool, cover and refrigerate for an hour or more until chilled.

→ Serve at room temperature or chilled with a spoonful of vanilla ice cream or some runny custard on top.

Quince

A SEDUCTIVE EXOTIC FRUIT, quince comes into its own when cooked, becoming soft and moist, turning the colour of deep amber. This autumnal fruit is available from November for a good two to three months. They are grown in the UK, but those from the Near East are the most fragrant. Choose ripe yellow ones and avoid the ones with a green tinge. You can find them in most Arab and Iranian shops. I buy them in November and December to make jam or various desserts. Their heady perfume pervades my kitchen while they linger in a large fruit bowl on my worktop, waiting patiently for me.

Slow cooking is its best friend, but patience will reap its rewards. One thing to remember, quince needs something sweet like honey or sugar to cook with so as to soften its tartness. You can poach it for 30 minutes, dust it with some sugar and cinnamon and bake it with a crumble topping or in a pie; you can make a delicious jam out of it or as an accompaniment to a meat dish, and if you have the patience, make some quince cheese, our traditional *louzina* (page 41). The Spanish have a similar, slightly softer paste called *dulce de membrillo,* traditionally paired with a salty hard cheese like *Manchego*. On our many sojourns in Spain, my husband's first purchases are *membrillo*, *Manchego* and fresh goat cheeses which he enjoys together with a good piece of bread.

My Quince Almond Crumble

Although the inclusion of the apple is optional, I find it complements the quince rather well. You can of course, bake the quinces on their own without adding the apple. My preference is to poach the quinces first before baking them. It shortens the cooking time.

SERVES 4–6

500g/1lb 2oz quince (about 2–3 quinces) halved and cored

5 tablespoons sugar

500ml/18fl oz/ generous 2 cups water

1 apple, peeled, halved and cored

½ teaspoon ground cardamom

1 tablespoon rosewater

FOR THE TOPPING

20g/¾oz almonds with skin

1 tablespoon rolled oats

2 tablespoons brown or Demerara sugar

Some cream, ice cream or yogurt, to serve

- Slice the quinces into eight 3cm/1in wedges.
- Put them in a pot with the sugar and the water.
- Bring to the boil then lower the heat to a simmer, cover and cook for 30 minutes or so or until the fruit is very soft. You can verify this by piercing a slice with the tip of a sharp knife.
- Preheat the oven to 190°C Fan (210°C /410°F/Gas Mark 6½).
- In the meantime, slice the apple (if using) into eight 3cm/1in wedges.
- Tip the quince wedges with their water into an ovenproof dish. Arrange the apple around or in between the quinces and sprinkle with the ground cardamom and rosewater.
- Cover the dish and bake for 40–45 minutes or until the apple has softened.
- Put all the topping ingredients in a coffee grinder or a mini-chopper and roughly grind them. Then sprinkle the hot fruit with some of the topping. This will sink into the fruit.

→ Serve warm, with a dollop of ice cream or yogurt, sprinkled with the rest of the topping mixture.

'No Bake' Chocolate, Tahina and Nut Truffles

These dark chocolate truffles are very easy and fun to make. I find that Lindt baking chocolate has a good balance of sweet and bitter flavours. The tahina gives a creamy smoothness to them and the pinch of paprika leaves a warm, spicy feeling in the mouth right at the end.

MAKES ABOUT 40 BALLS

100g/3½oz/⅔ cup Lindt baking chocolate, broken into pieces

3 tablespoons Menier unsweetened cacao powder (or one of your choice), plus extra for dusting

60g/2¼oz/½ cup walnuts, finely ground

60g/2¼oz/½ cup blanched whole almonds, finely ground

40g/1½oz/⅓ cup cashew nuts, finely ground

3 tablespoons tahina

a generous pinch of paprika

sesame seeds, for coating

Note: these truffles will taste better the following day. They also keep well in an airtight container, either at room temperature, or in the fridge, for at least a month – if they last that long!

- Place the chocolate pieces in a heatproof bowl set over a pan of gently simmering water, ensuring that the bottom of the bowl doesn't touch the water underneath. Heat until melted.
- Remove the bowl from the heat. Add the cacao powder, all the ground nuts, the tahina and paprika and mix to make a smooth dough.
- Cover and leave to rest in the fridge for an hour or so to stiffen up a little. After resting, if the dough is too wet, mix in a little more cacao powder.
- Take tablespoonful pieces of the dough and shape into balls (you will make about 40 in total). Roll them first in the sesame seeds (for more texture), then in some extra cacao powder, covering them completely.
- Arrange them in a single layer on a flat serving dish and leave them for a few hours to firm up at room temperature or in the fridge before serving.

Orange Zest, Walnut and Chocolate Spread

This is such an easy chocolate spread to make in the morning for kids (and, between you and me, for adults too!) A substitute for Nutella, it is my take on our Iraqi mixture of tahina and date syrup which we have for breakfast on crackers or bread. In this recipe, I use tahina and organic cacao powder to bind them into a delicious paste. A garnish of orange zest gives it a pleasant citrusy flavour.

100ml/3½ fl oz/½ cup tahina

2½ tablespoons cacao powder

2 tablespoons maple syrup or honey, or more to taste

some crushed walnuts or hazelnuts for texture (optional)

zest of 1 orange, to garnish

- Pour the tahina in a bowl. Add the cacao powder and, with a spoon, blend it slowly starting from the middle. Make sure there are no lumps and all the cacao has been incorporated.
- Now, add the maple syrup or honey and mix well. Taste and adjust the flavour.
- Add some crushed walnuts or hazelnuts into the mixture to give it more body.

→ Garnish with the orange zest.

Cardamom-Infused Almond Cookies

Deliciously chewy with a hint of cardamom and rosewater, these macaroons are traditionally baked for our Passover feast. Nowadays though, I make these cookies all year round – great as a sweet snack with tea or coffee.

MAKES ABOUT 35

270g/9 oz/2¾ cups almond flour

150g/5½ oz/⅔ cup caster sugar

2 large egg whites, lightly beaten until frothy

1½ teaspoons ground cardamom

rosewater

- Preheat the oven to 140°C Fan (160°C/325°F/Gas Mark 3).
- Mix the almonds, sugar and cardamom together in a bowl. Add in the egg whites and knead into a malleable dough. Cover and leave to rest in the fridge for a couple of hours or overnight.
- Line an oven tray with baking parchment.
- Pour a little rosewater in a bowl. Lightly wet your hands with the rosewater and take a little of the dough, the size of a walnut, and shape it into a ball. Arrange on a tray, flattening the top a little with your finger and place a pistachio in the centre. Space the balls a little to a void them sticking to each other when baked.
- Bake for about 15 to 20 minutes or until lightly golden.
- Leave to cool completely before handling.

→ Serve at room temperature. Store in an airtight container in the fridge or freezer where they will keep for a long time.

Chocolate and Coconut Bonbons

I have put my own twist on this traditional Indian recipe which uses condensed milk instead of eggs. I have added pure cacao powder to the milk turning the bonbons into a milk chocolate with a dusting of cardamom and bitter cacao on top to give them an edge. The cardamom is optional, but tasty.

MAKES ABOUT 35–40 BONBONS

297g/10½ oz tin condensed milk

2 tablespoons unsweetened cacao powder, plus extra for dusting

200g/7oz/2 cups unsweetened desiccated coconut, plus 1 tablespoon extra for dusting (optional)

- Pour the condensed milk into a heavy-based pan over a medium heat.
- Mix in the cacao powder, smoothing out any lumps, and stir continuously. When the mixture heats up and starts to gently bubble, add the coconut and mix vigorously.
- Continue mixing and folding for about 10 minutes until you get a more solid consistency that you will be able to roll. Be careful not to burn the mixture.
- Remove from the heat and tip it into a heatproof bowl, and wait for the dough to cool down a little.
- Sprinkle some of the desiccated coconut onto your work surface.
- Take about a teaspoonful of dough and roll it into a ball with your palms, then into the coconut to coat. Depending on the size of your bonbons, you should make about 35–40.

→ Transfer to a serving plate and place in the fridge to firm up. Serve slightly chilled.

Note: the bonbons will keep in an airtight container in the fridge for several weeks.

Orange-Zested Courgette and Chocolate Cake

I love this cake. The flavours of orange zest and bittersweet dark chocolate (60–70% cacao) work so well together. And the mixture of the grated courgette, almond and self-raising flour bakes into a moist and serious chocolate cake. I sometimes add a few chopped walnuts for texture, but that is optional.

you will need an 18cm/7in or 20cm/8in cake tin

1 courgette, about 200g/7oz

200g/7oz dark chocolate broken into pieces

2 tablespoons olive oil

zest of 1 orange, plus extra to garnish

½ teaspoon paprika

3 eggs, separated in 2 bowls

100g/3½ oz/½ cup caster sugar

1½ teaspoons vanilla extract

a pinch of salt

35g/1¼oz/generous ¼ cup almond flour

60g/2¼oz/½ cup self-raising flour

½ teaspoon baking powder

4 walnut halves, roughly chopped (optional)

icing sugar and more orange zest for the top

- Wash the courgette, top and tail it and grate it finely. Set aside.
- Place the chocolate pieces in a heatproof bowl set over a pan of gently simmering water, ensuring that the bottom of the bowl doesn't touch the water underneath. Heat until melted.
- Remove the bowl from the heat. Mix in the olive oil, the orange zest and paprika and set aside.
- Preheat the oven to 160°C Fan (180°C/350°F/Gas Mark 4).
- Line your cake tin with baking parchment.
- Beat the egg yolks with the sugar until creamy and light in colour. Mix in the grated courgettes, vanilla and salt and then slowly pour in the cooled chocolate stirring vigorously.
- Sift the almond flour, self-raising flour and baking powder over the chocolate mixture, stirring slowly all the while to incorporate well. Mix in the walnuts, if using.
- Using an electric whisk, beat the egg whites, at medium speed, until they start to thicken and turn into soft creamy peaks. Then, gently fold into the chocolate mixture until thoroughly incorporated.
- Pour the mixture into the lined cake tin and bake for 30–40 minutes, until a knife inserted in the middle of the cake comes out dry. Remove from the oven and leave to cool for about 10 minutes in the tin. Then turn out on a wire rack to cool completely.

→ Serve with a sprinkling of orange zest and icing sugar accompanied by a dollop of cream.

Acknowledgements

This book – a long toyed-with idea – took over five years of hard work and perseverance to take shape, changing from one concept to another, while always remaining rooted in the underlying *sotto voce* of food.

Firstly, my gratitude and thanks are due to my mother for showing me, at an early age, the beauty and magic of cooking. Now, every time I beat an egg to make a mayonnaise, I think of her.

My heartfelt thanks go to my two lovely aunts, Doreen and Eileen, for sharing with me their recollections and their valuable cooking tips.

A big thank you to my publisher and friend, the very creative Michael Leventhal, for choosing to publish my book. It wasn't an obvious choice, so I thank you, Michael, for your trust and confidence in my work.

I am profoundly grateful to my brilliant friend, Jennifer Joseph, for her guidance and for meticulously editing and proofreading my many manuscript drafts over the last five years – encouraging me throughout with her steadfast loyalty to the project.

I am especially grateful to my book designer Mike Blacker of Blacker Design for his unstinting patience, his professionalism, his editing and typographical skills. Working side by side with you Mike was a pleasure. Thank you for producing such a beautiful book.

A big thank you to my brother Eddie Dangoor, for lending me his camera and showing me how to maximise my photography; also for his wonderful photographs of London in the 1960s and 70s and for his iconic image of the Thames with the Battersea power station in the background. His technical advice and support has been invaluable, in making this book. A big thank you too to my friend, photographer Keith Hammond, for his interest in my book and for spending time advising and teaching me about studio lighting.

My warmest thanks to my friend and wonderful cook, Amanda Ellis, for her enthusiasm and for being the patient tester and taster of my many recipes. A big thank you to my occasional recipe tester and wonderful friend Tarryn Klotnick and to Silvia Nacamulli for her support and friendship.

Thank you Christine Vanderhurd for lending me your lovely textiles for my photo shoots; thanks to my food editor Anne Sheasby and my proofreader Sarah Prior for their attention to detail; to Jacky Ferneyhough for her thorough indexing and editing; to Peter Roden for his initial design ideas; to Hugh Allan for his professional advice; to my precious friends and family for their thoughtful input and contribution: Vanessa Rea Dangoor, Samira Balas, Sonia Shalam, Ruth Timman, Bethanie Alhadeff, Joey Bieber, Dympna Gergolin, Nadia Roden, Caroline Burnstein, Marlene Eleini; to my family and friends who listened patiently while I rambled on about the book and its cover design; and thank you to all those whom I might have, inadvertently and unintentionally, forgotten to mention.

And finally, my very special thanks to my husband, Frank for his characteristic patience, his constructive comments and for being my main recipe taster. You have been my rock, supporting me throughout.

Selected Bibliography

Adler, Tamar. *An Everlasting Meal* (Swift Press, 2011)
Andrews, Colman. *Catalan Cuisine* (Grub Street, 1997)
Barnes, Julian. *The Pedant in the Kitchen* (Atlantic Books, 2012)
Benjamin, Marina. *Last Days in Babylon* (Bloomsbury, 2008)
Dangoor, Linda. *Flavours of Babylon* (Waterpoint Press, 2014)
David, Elizabeth. *English Bread and Yeast Cookery* (Penguin, 2001)
Fisher, M.F.K. *Love in a Dish* (Penguin, 2011)
Gilbert, Martin. *In Ishmael's House* (Yale University Press, 2010)
Gill, A.A. *The Best of A. A. Gill* (Weidenfeld & Nicolson, 2018)
Hopkinson, Simon. *Roast Chicken and Other Stories* (Ebury Press, 1999)
Hyman, Clarissa. *Tomato* (Reaktion Books, 2019)
Iny, Daisy, *The Best of Baghdad Cooking* (E.P. Dutton, 1977)
Jones, Judith. *The Pleasures of Cooking for One: A Cookbook* (Alfred A. Knopf, 2009)
Kurlansky, Mark. *Cod* (Penguin, 1998)
Kurlansky, Mark. *Salt: A World History* (Penguin, 2003)
Lahiri, Jhumpa. *In Other Words* (Bloomsbury, 2017)
Laudon, Rachel. *Cuisine and Empire* (University of California Press, 2013)
Lawson, Nigella. *How to Eat* (Vintage, 2018)
Leventhal, Michael. *Babka, Boulou & Blintzes* (Green Bean Books, 2021)
McMorland Hunter, Jane and Dunster, Sue. *Quinces* (Prospect Books, 2015)
Montanari, Massimo. *A Short History of Spaghetti with Tomato Sauce* (Europa editions, 2020)
O'Connell, John, *The Book of Spice: From Anise to Zedoary* (Profile Books, 2015)
Okakura, Kakuzo. *The Book of Tea* (Penguin, 2016)
Roden, Claudia. *A Middle Eastern Feast* (Penguin, 2011)
Rodinson, Maxime, Arberry, Arthur J. and Perry, Charles. *Medieval Arab Cookery* (Prospect Books, 2001)
Rushdie, Salman. *Imaginary Homelands* (London Review of Books, Vol. 4 No. 8, 1982)
Safran Foer, Jonathan. *Eating Animal*s (Penguin, 2009)
Segnit, Niki. *The Flavour Thesaurus* (Bloomsbury, 2010)
Tannahill, Reay. *Food in History* (Three Rivers Press, 1989)
de Thample, Rachel. *Fermentation* (Bloomsbury, 2020)
Visser, Margaret. *The Rituals of Dinner* (Penguin, 1993)
Whittington, Richard. *Cutting Edge: A Cook's Californian Inspiration* (Conran Octopus, 1996)
Wilson, Bee. *The Secret of Cooking* (Fourth Estate, 2023)
Yahia, Mona. *When the Grey Beetles Took Over Baghdad* (Halban, 2000)
York, Miranda. *The Food Almanac* (Pavilion, 2020)

Glossary

UK	US
aubergine	eggplant
baking parchment	parchment paper
bicarbonate of soda	baking soda
biscuit	cookie
broad beans	fava beans
butter beans	lima beans
cake tin	cake pan
casserole, ovenproof	Dutch oven
caster sugar	superfine white sugar
chickpeas	garbanzo beans
chilli (fresh)	chile
chilli powder/paste/ oil/sauce	chili powder/paste/ oil/sauce
cling film	plastic wrap
cocktail stick	toothpick
coriander (fresh)	cilantro
cornflour	cornstarch
courgette	zucchini
dark chocolate	plain chocolate
desiccated coconut	dried shredded coconut
double cream	heavy cream
flaked almonds	slivered almonds
foil	aluminum foil
fridge	refrigerator
frying pan	skillet
grill	broiler/broil
hob	stove

UK	US
icing sugar	confectioners' sugar (or powdered sugar)
kitchen paper	paper towel
knob (of butter)	pat (of butter)
lengthways	lengthwise
minced (meat)	ground (meat)
muslin	cheesecloth
natural yogurt	plain yoghurt
okra	lady's fingers
oven tray	baking sheet/tray
pepper (sweet red/ yellow/green)	bell pepper
plain flour	all-purpose flour
prawn	shrimp
rapeseed oil	canola oil
rocket	arugula
self-raising flour	self-rising flour
sieve	fine-mesh strainer
single cream	light cream
stock	broth
sultanas	golden raisins
tin	can
tomato purée	tomato paste
wholemeal flour	whole wheat flour
widthways	widthwise
yeast (fast-action dried)	active dry yeast
yogurt	yoghurt

Cook's Notes

All eggs used in the recipes are medium, unless stated otherwise.

You can use your preferred type of butter in the recipes, but I recommend using unsalted butter where it is specified.

All olive oil used in the recipes is extra virgin olive oil, unless stated otherwise.

I recommend using full-fat milk in all recipes that call for milk.

All vegetables and fruit used in the recipes are medium, unless stated otherwise.

Sugar is granulated sugar unless otherwise specified.

Both UK metric/imperial and imperial US cup measurements are included in these recipes for your convenience. Conversions are approximate and may have been rounded up or down. Follow one set of measurements only and do not alternate between them within a recipe, as they are not interchangeable.

All spoon measurements are level unless stated otherwise. Use a set of measuring spoons for accurate measuring.
1 teaspoon = 5ml; 1 tablespoon = 15ml.

Ovens should be preheated to the specified temperature (check with an oven thermometer). Electric conventional (non-fan) and fan oven temperatures, as well as Fahrenheit and gas temperatures are included, but do check with your manufacturer's instructions when using a fan oven (generally the temperature of a fan oven is 20°C lower than the conventional one given). I used either a non-fan (conventional) electric oven or an electric fan oven for the recipes.

Index

Q

R

S

Useful Conversion Tables

OVEN TEMPERATURES

°C fan	°C	°F	Gas Mark
100	110	225	¼
110	130	250	1
130	150	300	2
140	160	325	3
160	180	350	4
170	190	375	5
180	200	400	6
200	220	425	7
210	230	450	8

WEIGHTS

metric	Imperial	US cups
25g	1oz	
50g	1¾oz	
100g	3½oz	
150g	5½oz	
200g	7oz	1 cup uncooked rice
200g	7oz	1½ cups flour
225g	8oz	1½ cups almonds
250g	9oz	
300g	10½oz	1⅓ cups sugar
380g	13oz	
400g	14oz	
450g	1lb	3¼ cups flour
500g	1lb 2oz	3½ cups flour
675g	1½lb	
800g	1¾lb	
900g	2lb	
1kg	2¼lb	

LIQUID MEASUREMENTS

metric	Imperial	US cups
50 ml	1¾ fluid oz	
60 ml	2 fluid oz	¼ cup
65 ml	2½ fluid oz	¼ cup
75 ml	2½ fluid oz	⅓ cup
85 ml	3 fluid oz	generous ⅓ cup
100 ml	3½ fluid oz	scant ½ cup
120 ml	4 fluid oz	½ cup
125 ml	4 fluid oz	½ cup
150 ml	5 fluid oz (¼ pint)	⅔ cup
175 ml	6 fluid oz	¾ cup
200 ml	7 fluid oz	scant 1 cup
250 ml	8 fluid oz	generous 1 cup
275 ml	9 fluid oz	
300 ml	10 fluid oz (½ pint)	1¼ cups
325 ml	11 fluid oz	
350 ml	12 fluid oz	1½ cups
375 ml	13 fluid oz	1½ cups
400 ml	14 fluid oz	1⅔ cups
450 ml	15 fluid oz	scant 2 cups
475 ml	16 fluid oz	2 cups
500 ml	18 fluid oz	generous 2 cups
550 ml	18 fluid oz	2⅓ cups
575 ml	19 fluid oz	2⅓ cups
600 ml	20 fluid oz (1 pint)	2½ cups
700 ml	24 fluid oz	scant 3 cups
750 ml	26 fluid oz	3 cups
900 ml	32 fluid oz	3¾ cups
950 ml	33½ fluid oz	4 cups
1 litre	35 fluid oz	4¼ cups

About the Author

Linda Dangoor is a designer, painter and ceramicist and now a food writer. She was born in Baghdad and came to the UK in the early 1960s. A graduate of the Central School of Art and Design, she has worked in the design field for many years, specialising in stationery, greeting cards and other products for the gift market in Paris and later in London.

Linda is the author of two cookbooks. The first one, *Flavours of Babylon*, is an exploration and a celebration of the dishes and flavours of her Baghdadi heritage. Her second book, *From the Tigris to the Thames*, published in 2025, is a tapestry, part memoir, part cookbook where she interweaves recipes with personal reflections on the idea of home and belonging.

You can follow her on Instagram at @lindadangoorcreativeliving or visit her website www.lindadangoor.com.

First published in the UK in 2025 by Green Bean Books
c/o Pen & Sword Books Ltd. 47 Church Street, Barnsley, South Yorkshire, S70 2AS
www.greenbeanbooks.com

Hardback edition: ISBN 978-1-80500-182-9
ePub: ISBN 978-1-80500-183-6
PDF: ISBN 978-1-80500-184-3

Every effort has been made to ensure that information published is accurate, should there be any errors of facts and figures, I take full responsibility, and apologise. Also, every effort has been made to identify and gain permission for the images used in this book, if any have been omitted please contact the publisher.

All photographs by Linda Dangoor, except for pages 13, 88, 90, 91, 95, 96, 109, 174 and 175 © Eddie Dangoor; pages 104, 199, 262, 317 © Keith Hammond; page 336 © Dr Bea Lewkowicz; page 136 © Catherine Reyer. Pages 92–95 photographed by Linda with the kind permission of the Museum of Brands, London.

Illustrations: Linda Dangoor; Cover artwork: Linda Dangoor.
Book design: Linda Dangoor and Mike Blacker @ Blacker Design
Typography: Mike Blacker @ Blacker Design and Peter Roden

Printed in China by 1010 Printing International Ltd

MIX
Paper | Supporting responsible forestry
FSC® C016973
FSC www.fsc.org